The
MOFFATT
NEW TESTAMENT COMMENTARY

Based on *The New Translation* by the
REV. PROFESSOR JAMES MOFFATT
D.D. (Oxon), LL.D., D.Litt.
and under his Editorship

THE EPISTLE OF PAUL
TO THE THESSALONIANS

The Moffatt
New Testament Commentary

MATTHEW
BY THEODORE H. ROBINSON, M.A., D.D.

MARK
BY B. HARVIE BRANSCOMB, M.A., PH.D.

LUKE
BY WILLIAM MANSON, D.D.

JOHN
BY G. H. C. MACGREGOR, D.D., D.LITT.

THE ACTS OF THE APOSTLES
BY F. J. FOAKES-JACKSON, D.D.

ROMANS
BY C. H. DODD, D.D., F.B.A.

I CORINTHIANS
BY JAMES MOFFATT, D.D., LL.D., D.LITT.

II CORINTHIANS
BY R. H. STRACHAN, D.D.

GALATIANS
BY GEORGE S. DUNCAN, D.D., LL.D.

COLOSSIANS, PHILEMON
AND EPHESIANS
BY E. F. SCOTT, D.D.

PHILIPPIANS
BY J. HUGH MICHAEL, D.D.

THESSALONIANS
BY WILLIAM NEIL, M.A., B.D., PH.D.

THE PASTORAL EPISTLES
BY E. F. SCOTT, D.D.

HEBREWS
BY THEODORE H. ROBINSON, M.A., D.D.

THE GENERAL EPISTLES
BY JAMES MOFFATT, D.D., LL.D., D.LITT.

THE JOHANNINE EPISTLES
BY C. H. DODD, D.D., F.B.A.

REVELATION
BY MARTIN KIDDLE, M.A.
ASSISTED BY M. K. ROSS.

THE EPISTLE OF PAUL
TO THE THESSALONIANS

BY
WILLIAM NEIL, M.A., B.D., Ph.D.
Lecturer in Biblical Studies,
King's College, Aberdeen

HARPER & BROTHERS · PUBLISHERS
NEW YORK

THE EPISTLE OF PAUL TO THE THESSALONIANS

PREFACE

A COMMENTATOR, more than any other writer, draws on the insight and scholarship of his predecessors. In writing this, the last of the Moffatt series, I have tried, not only to present in less erudite form the views of previous commentators and to reach a true interpretation with their help, but also to invoke their aid in achieving the chief aim of this series, which is to dig beneath the textual problems to the vital religious message of the New Testament for ourselves to-day.

On a first reading, the Thessalonian letters appear to be a mixture of rather ordinary sentiments and very obscure apocalypticism. For the reader who is prepared to take pains to find out what lies behind both, there is, on the contrary, a rich reward of spiritual nourishment and a real Word of God for our times.

Moffatt's translation is itself in a sense the best guide for this purpose, and the few points on which one differs from him throw more clearly into relief the genius of his work as a whole.

I have found particularly helpful the commentaries by Frame (in *International Critical Commentaries*), Milligan (*St. Paul's Epistles to the Thessalonians*), Dibelius (in *Handbuch zum N.T.*), Bicknell (in *Westminster Commentaries*), Denney (in *Expositor's Bible*), and Moffatt himself (in *Expositor's Greek Testament*). These are referred to in the notes simply under the names of their authors.

My warm thanks are due to Professor G. H. C. Macgregor, of Glasgow University, and Professor A. M. Hunter, of Aberdeen University, who read the book in typescript and made many helpful criticisms.

WILLIAM NEIL.

KING'S COLLEGE,
ABERDEEN.
September 1948.

CONTENTS

INTRODUCTION

COMMENTARY

The First Epistle to the Thessalonians

CONTENTS

INTRODUCTION

I. THE THESSALONIAN MISSION

IT was on his second missionary tour that Paul first came to Thessalonica. His intention to linger in Asia had been frustrated. Neither to Ephesus, his obvious goal as he made his way along the great Roman highway that stretched from the Persian Gulf to the Aegean, nor to Bithynia in the north was he allowed to go. ' The Spirit suffered them not ' and drove him down to Troas on the sea—an apparent blind alley if ever there was one. It proved to be, however, in the providence of God, a stepping-stone to the most historic moment of the mission—the crossing below the Hellespont and the landing of Christianity in Europe (Acts xvi. 6 ff.). Paul himself called it ' the beginning of the Gospel,' though he had by that time been a missionary for fifteen years.

Macedonia, the first European territory to be evangelized, was then a province of the Roman Empire. Some of its ancient greatness, however, still clung to it. It had not forgotten that Philip of Macedon had been its king and that his more famous son, Alexander the Great, had virtually founded the Empire. It still boasted its old highland independence, and for courage and integrity it most nearly approached Republican Rome. Paul's work in Macedonia radiated from three centres—Philippi, Thessalonica, and Beroea. Doubtless he chose them, less because each of them was the chief town of the three parts into which Macedonia naturally falls, than because each had a Jewish colony, and therefore also a number of Gentile adherents of the faith of the Synagogue. Of Beroea we know little, but, on the evidence of his letters, the warmth of the apostle's affection both for the Philippians and for the Thessalonians, his praise of their loyalty and generosity, suggest a people naturally receptive to the

Gospel ethic and responsive to the preaching in an unusual degree.

Thessalonica itself when Paul reached it was already an old city, the capital of Macedonia, and its largest town. The measure of its geographical importance is that it is still as Salonica a focal point in modern Greece, and a name with poignant associations for many dating from the First World War. Though later its population was to reach the 200,000 mark, it was, even in Paul's day, a large and prosperous seaport ' lying,' as Cicero said, ' in the lap of the Roman Empire.' Paul had reached it along the great Imperial Via Egnatia which continued the link of the East with Rome, and in crossing Greece ran through Philippi, Thessalonica, and so on to the Adriatic. The city was renowned for its hot springs —hence its older name of Therme—but the new town, founded about 300 B.C., was named after Thessalonica, the half-sister of Alexander the Great. It was not only a free city of the Roman Empire with the attendant privilege of remaining ungarrisoned, but was even later a rival to Constantinople as the possible capital of the Empire itself.

It was thus to no out-of-the way village that St. Paul came in the year A.D. 49, accompanied, so far as we can judge, by Silvanus and Timothy (see note on 1 i. 1). St. Luke, if we are to interpret the appearance and cessation of the first person plural in the narrative of Acts (cf. xvi. 6 with xvi. 10 and xvi. 12 with xvii. 1), had remained behind at Philippi, and relied therefore on second-hand information for his account of what happened at Thessalonica. The Philippian campaign had ended, after flogging and imprisonment, in a moral victory for the apostles, which must have given them doubtful satisfaction. Despite their ill-treatment, they appear to have proceeded directly to Thessalonica, where there was a larger Jewish population, evidenced by the presence of a synagogue. As was his custom, Paul preached the Gospel to the Jews first of all, both by proclamation and argument—and no doubt by invitation (cf. Acts xiii. 15). The mission was up to a point a success with the Jews, but was apparently more so with the devout Greeks who attended the synagogue services, including many of the leading ladies of the city. This type of pagan—repelled by the laxity of conventional morality, unsatisfied by idol-worship, and drawn by the high seriousness of the Jewish ethical code and the purity of its monotheism—proved to be the most fruitful ground for the activities of Christian missionaries. Christianity offered them on a religious and moral plane what had attracted them to the synagogue, without the nationalistic bias, legalistic restrictions, and ritual demands of Judaism.

The pattern of the mission thereafter is familiar. Resenting the success of the Christian missionaries—and particularly the loss of their Gentile proselytes, whom they had been sedulously enticing into the orbit of the synagogue—the Jews organized a riot, drawing for the purpose upon ' lewd fellows of the baser sort '—the ' corner boys ' who are always available on such occasions in the East. Paul and Silvanus were living with a certain Jason, apparently a Jewish convert, but fortunately were out of the way when the mob attacked the house. Jason and some of the other Christians were, however, haled before the magistrates and charged with harbouring and encouraging revolutionaries whose intention was to overthrow the Empire and set up a new kingdom with Jesus as head. Whether this was a wilful travesty of the preaching of the Kingdom or whether some of the crowd believed it, it is impossible to say. The magistrates, or, as inscriptions discovered since at Thessalonica confirm St. Luke's accurate local name for them, Politarchs, evinced some concern, but contented themselves with making Jason and the others responsible for keeping the peace.

This made Paul's departure inevitable. Any further outbreak of trouble would involve Jason and his friends. At the same time it was a signal to his sympathizers that for his own safety he had better leave. Accordingly, the same night he left with Silvanus, and possibly Timothy, for Beroea. So runs the narrative in the Book of Acts (xvii. 1–10). For the rest we must read between the lines and draw on the information given in the letters themselves. It seems unlikely, for example, that the whole campaign was over in a period covered by three sabbaths—at the most five weeks (ver. 2). It was long enough for Paul to need financial help from Philippi more than once, despite the fact that he was working hard himself at his own trade, which itself suggests more than a brief visit. It is probable that by ' three sabbaths ' St. Luke means the *Jewish* mission ; thereafter work among the Gentiles may have lasted some weeks longer. A point in favour of a longer stay at Thessalonica is that the readers of the letters appear to be mainly converts from idolatry. This implies neither Jews nor devout Greeks, and suggests therefore a subsequent post-synagogue period in the mission. On the other hand, the character of the mission was essentially evangelistic. Its modern counterpart would be the campaigns of Wesley or Moody and Sankey. It was therefore not a case of building up laboriously a strong congregational life, like a modern paro-chial ministry, but an intensive campaign with the contagious enthusiasm and sensational results that characterize a religious revival. The ground was in a sense prepared by the syna-gogue ; and its devout Greek adherents, profoundly dissatis-fied with superstition and questing for a new faith, provided a bridge to paganism.

According to St. Luke, the substance of Paul's preaching was that the Scriptures had been fulfilled, the Messiah had come, had been crucified and had risen again—in other words, the normal *kērygma* as it was preached everywhere by mission-aries. There is no reason to suppose, despite the prominence of eschatological issues in the Thessalonian letters, that the *kērygma* was in any respect different here from elsewhere. The response, however, must have been remarkable. Reading the letters, we are left with a profound impression of the real vital change which had taken place in the lives of the converts. The old paganism was sloughed off, and in its place appeared a buoyant faith and a consecrated witness which convinced the missionaries, if they needed convincing, that the Spirit was mightily at work in their midst. Seldom, except to the Philippians, does St. Paul express himself so warmly in praise of the total committal of a Church to God as he does to the Thessalonians. In all probability it was not a large group of men and women that renounced their pagan practices and turned to the ' One true God '—they were neither distinguished nor wealthy. (The admonitions in the letters suggest various temptations, but not the temptation of riches.) Rather is the picture one of a predominantly working-class congregation, who were later, however, prepared to stint themselves and give beyond their means for the help of the Mother Church at Jerusalem (2 Cor. viii. 2–4). Paul's connexion with Thessalonica did not end with his hasty departure. He not only visited it twice again himself (Acts xx. 2, 4), but also sent Timothy back on two occasions as his representative (1 iii. 2, Acts xix. 22), and on his subsequent journeys we read of three members of the Thessalonian Church who had become his companions : Aristarchus (Acts xix. 29, xxvii. 2), Secundus (Acts xx. 4), and Demas (Philemon 24, 2 Tim. iv. 10).

II. FIRST LETTER TO THESSALONICA

For our purpose, however, the most important of Paul's dealings with Thessalonica and the Thessalonians were in writing, and have come down to us under the titles of the First and Second Epistles to the Thessalonians. The situation that gave rise to them can be deduced partly from the narrative of Acts and partly from the letters themselves.

After leaving Thessalonica, Paul and the two other missionaries do not seem to have spent very long at Beroea. Trouble broke out there too, instigated by Jews from Thessalonica, the upshot of which was that Paul, the chief object of attack, went on to Athens alone, leaving Silvanus and Timothy— presumably to consolidate the mission, and join him later. Paul's movements are thereafter quite clear. He conducted an unsuccessful and dispiriting crusade in Athens—possibly as much due to the apostle's ill-health as to the scepticism of the philosophers—before proceeding to Corinth, where he remained for eighteen months. There is likewise no difficulty in accounting for Silvanus at this time. After being left behind in Beroea, he is stated to have rejoined Paul, not in Athens, but in Corinth (Acts xviii. 5). A complication arises, however, in the case of Timothy, who, according to Acts, arrived in Macedonia for the first time with Silvanus, but who, according to Paul's own statement in I iii. I, had already rejoined him in Athens. St. Paul's own account is obviously the one to follow, and there is no real problem of harmonizing it with Luke's version. Timothy came to Athens as arranged (Acts xvii. 15), but was immediately sent back by Paul to Thessalonica. There he was later presumably joined by Silvanus, and both then proceeded to join Paul at Corinth. (See note on I iii. I.)

The reason for Timothy's mission to Thessalonica is given in Paul's own words (I ii. 17 ff.). The campaign in Thessalonica had come to an abrupt end. The work had been left unfinished, and what results there were had been so promising that Paul's full intention had been to return. Apart from his own affection for the Thessalonians, there was the added reason that the persecution, which had broken out while he was still there, continued. It may be that other troubles had come to the ears of the apostle as well. At all events, having made various attempts to return himself, attempts which were invariably thwarted, he despatched Timothy as his representative from Athens, partly to encourage the Thessalonian Church and partly to bring back news of how exactly matters stood. In due course Timothy returned with Silvanus, as we have seen, while Paul was still in Corinth, and, as Paul tells us, it was on the return of Timothy with his report on the state of the Thessalonian Church that he wrote the first letter.

There is little difficulty in establishing the date of this epistle. From an inscription at Delphi it appears that Gallio (Acts xviii. 12) became pro-consul of Achaia in the summer of A.D. 51. By that time Paul had been already a year and a half in Corinth (Acts xviii. 11). He must therefore have arrived there at the beginning of A.D. 50, and as it appears that there was no great length of time between his visit to Thessalonica and the writing of the epistle—probably a few months only—the former might well be dated towards the end of A.D. 49 and the first letter some time in the spring of A.D. 50 (see Frame, *I.C.C.*, p. 9). Commentators who do not follow this chronology all place the letter at least somewhere within the early fifties.

Whether Timothy brought back with him a letter from Thessalonica is unimportant (see notes on i. 9, ii. 13). The significant facts in the Thessalonian situation can be deduced from Paul's reply, as can also the apostle's motive in writing. This was primarily one of thankfulness. It does appear as if Paul's confidence in the success of the mission had been shaken by his failure at Athens, and that his early days at Corinth were marked by unusual hesitancy and diffidence (1 Cor. ii. 3). The probable interpretation of Acts xviii. 5 is : ' When Silvanus and Timothy came down from Macedonia, Paul became engrossed in the preaching of the Word ' (*suneicheto tō logō*), i.e. it was the arrival of these two that gave him fresh heart and stimulated him to a new attack. This impetus to fresh efforts may well have been the good news they brought of the faithfulness and loyalty and increasingly Christian witness of the Macedonian Churches. That things were going so well in Thessalonica, despite heavy odds, was for Paul heaven-sent consolation. He thus launched into the Corinthian campaign with new enthusiasm, but before doing so took time to write to Thessalonica, expressing his joy at the news he had just received.

It is thus clear that Timothy's report had been almost wholly favourable. Nothing could be more unmistakable than the apostle's real pastoral pride in his flock and his thankfulness to God. He cannot say forcibly enough how deep an impression the success of the campaign at Thessalonica made upon himself, and how moved he is to think that nothing has been lost by his absence, but that their good work goes on from strength to strength. Besides this primary motive there were apparently one or two matters mentioned by Timothy which also needed attention : there was, for example, the continued machinations of the Jews in Thessalonica. Insinuating, slanderous, suggestive, they were doing their best to undermine the loyalty of the converts to Paul and to besmirch his character. This, in addition to the open persecution of their own pagan countrymen, was a heavy strain upon the young

Church's stability. There were also specific problems causing some concern, such as the fate of those who had died before the coming Second Advent ; a certain restlessness among some who wanted to know exactly when the Second Advent would take place ; the question of what value should be placed on ecstatic manifestations ; tension between the leading laymen and the congregation, and a tendency to live off their fellow-members on the part of a few religious cranks. There was also the permanent danger in a recently pagan Church of falling back into the sexual laxity of their environment. To provide answers to these problems, to encourage and strengthen their faith, and to offer a substitute for the visit he would much rather have paid himself, Paul writes what is his earliest undisputed letter, unless the letter to the Galatians comes before it, and the first New Testament document to reach us in its original form.

Paul begins his letter on a high note of thanksgiving—both for the success of the mission at Thessalonica as he recalls it and for the extraordinary impression it has made everywhere (chap. i.). He then launches into an apologia—not directed towards any party within the Church, there is no suggestion of disaffection—in which he is fairly obviously replying to Jewish insinuations of which Timothy had brought word. He asks them to remember his behaviour when he was with them : how he cherished and served them with the tenderness of a mother, how he refused to be a burden upon them but worked for his own keep, how his conduct among them was beyond reproach. Does this, he asks, look as if he were a religious charlatan, a money-making vagabond, mouthing pious insincerities ? Have no fear, he goes on, these wicked men who are trying to crush us and destroy the Church will reap their reward (chap. ii.). Do they say that I care so little for you that I leave you to face persecution alone ? Why, you know my love for you ; how I tried to come back to you ; and how, when this was impossible, I sent Timothy, whom I could ill spare, in my anxiety to know how you fared. But now all is well. Timothy has come back, and what good news he brings ! God be praised for all that he has told me ; and may it not be long before I am able to come and see you myself (chap. iii.). Meantime, remember all that I told you : keep your bodies pure, always be generous and hard-working. Don't worry about your loved ones who have passed away. Those who die in Christ remain in Christ for ever (chap. iv.). And don't be alarmed about all this talk of the end of the world. Doomsday is a terror to wrong-doers, not to Christ's people. For us it will be to experience life in all its fulness. Respect your leaders ; help those in trouble ; remember your prayers—and always be very chary of pouring cold water on other people's way of expressing their faith. Now God bless and keep you all (chap. v.).

Is this letter genuinely Pauline ? It was included as such in Marcion's Canon of the New Testament (*c.* A.D. 140), and from then onwards—until last century—its Pauline authorship was never questioned. True, there are no indisputable quotations from it in the Fathers before Irenaeus (*c.* A.D. 180), but this proves nothing one way or the other, as there is very little of a quotable nature in the letter compared with the other epistles. It is indeed largely this latter point which has given rise to the only serious attack on the authenticity of the epistle—that of F. C. Baur a hundred years ago. Like the other members of the Tübingen school, Baur was inclined to overturn established conclusions on principle. He suggested that the letter was written after A.D. 70 by a disciple of Paul who wished to stimulate interest in the Second Advent. The obvious comment is that the disciple went an exceedingly roundabout way to achieve his purpose, since the Second Advent occupies a definitely subsidiary place in the epistle. Baur's doubts as to the letter's genuineness—none of which is regarded as material to-day, and which are therefore not worth detailing at length—rest mainly on such grounds as : (*a*) the pedestrian nature of the letter and its lack of doctrinal teaching ; (*b*) its similarity to the account of the founding of the Thessalonian Church in Acts ; (*c*) its close verbal resemblance at many points to the Corinthian letters ; and (*d*) the unusual character of such passages as ii. 14 ff. and iv. 14 ff. All of this is pure subjectivism. (*a*) A Pauline epistle is not a theological treatise, but a pastoral letter, and as such the smallest problem of the congregation is as important to the writer as the cardinal doctrines of the faith. (*b*) Further, we have already seen that one of our problems is not the similarity but the discrepancy between St. Luke's narrative and the epistle's account of the travels of Timothy. A forger would have been more careful. (*c*) As for the resemblances to the Corinthian letters, they are no greater than those between other unquestionably Pauline epistles. Is it not perverse reasoning that the same writer must not use the same phrases in two letters without its being alleged that one of the letters is a forgery? (*d*) Finally, such a passage as ii. 14 ff.—the denunciation of the Jews—is, in the circumstances, more than natural. It is not an historical reference to the past destruction of Jerusalem in A.D. 70, but a prophecy of God's judgment upon Jewish unbelief. The apocalyptic language of iv. 14 ff. is perfectly explicable as an echo of the mission-preaching (see notes). It has been suggested that the reference to a forged letter in 2 ii. 2 must refer to this one. But a forgery during Paul's lifetime is incredible (see note on 2 ii. 2), and if this is a late forgery, it would have to be explained how a second letter, purporting to be by Paul, was also in existence and acknowledged by the Church at the same early date. Further, it should be added that the actual Greek vocabulary and phrasing are definitely Pauline (see Frame, *I.C.C.*, pp. 28–34). But surely the best argument in favour of Paul's authorship of the letter is the letter itself. What is its point if it is not a genuine message from the apostle to a Church he has founded and a people whom he loves? Every sentence rings true and reflects the affection or concern of the great missionary. A forger would have had to have the mind of Paul himself to produce so lifelike a letter, and it is difficult to see why anyone but Paul should have taken the trouble to write it. A later forger, for example, would certainly not have spent so much time dealing with the historical events of the Thessalonian mission. Further, if one of the striking features of the letter is the absence of the characteristic Pauline themes of the later epistles, would a disciple, trying to pass this off as a Pauline letter, not have made it his business to reproduce at least some of the great doctrines of Romans and Galatians ? Finally, it is inconceivable that after Paul's death he would have been made by one of his disciples to suggest that the Second Advent would happen in his lifetime (iv. 15). The letter is now accepted by all modern scholars as genuinely from the hand of Paul. Any suggestions of minor interpolations are dealt with in the notes. None of them is convincing.

III. SECOND LETTER TO THESSALONICA

Unlike that of the first epistle, the authenticity of the second still presents a problem. Let us for the moment assume that the judgment of the early Church was right and that this is also a message to Thessalonica from the hand of Paul. Why should he have written it ? We do not know how the first letter reached Thessalonica except that for private individuals there was no alternative but to send any message by hand. Someone unknown, therefore, carried the first letter from Paul to Thessalonica. Did he bring another letter back ? Again we cannot tell, or indeed whether the messenger came back at all. What we do know is that here we have a second letter addressed to the Thessalonians envisaging a situation not differing greatly from that in the first letter, but reasonably explicable on the assumption that it was written shortly after it. If this is so, then we may take it either that the messenger returned with news of such a kind that Paul felt called upon to write again, or that not long after the despatch of the first letter information from some Thessalonian source came to his ears and provoked a second pastoral message. It begins like the other on a note of thanksgiving to God for the continued steadfastness of the Church at Thessalonica in face of opposition and persecution which have apparently increased (chap. i.). Then—coming to the real point of the letter—the Apostle deals with rumours that are apparently upsetting some of the members. He is alleged to have said that the end of the world is to be expected at any moment, and as a result there is considerable excitement and anxiety in the community. He writes now to deny that he has said any such thing, and to remind them of the recognized indications of the coming climax of history, none of which has yet been given. Having done that, he reassures them that they have nothing to fear in any event. The lives of all who keep God's laws are in God's hands (chap. ii.). Then, having asked for their prayers in his own difficulties, Paul deals finally with the second issue which appears to have occasioned the letter. When he wrote last he had mentioned casually the danger of idleness (iv. 12)—presumably knowing the Thessalonians' temperament. Since then, the heightened tension of Second Advent expectation, induced by false ideas as to its immediacy, had intensified the problem. Some had become so unsettled that they had downed tools and were awaiting—not even with resignation but with irritating excitability and meddlesomeness—the end of everything. For them Paul prescribes tactful handling but, failing that, strong disciplinary measures. He concludes as before by invoking God's blessing upon the whole congregation (chap. iii.). There is no mention either of the calumnies of the Jews or of the sexual problems referred to in the first letter. Presumably the apostle's words had had a salutory effect in both cases. As for the date of writing, it cannot be more than a few weeks after the first. The place is therefore the same, namely, Corinth.

A cursory reading of the letter alone would appear to dispose adequately of the suggestion—made by some Continental scholars—that the second epistle antedates the first. In each of the topics dealt with—persecution, Second Advent, idleness—there is an obvious intensification of the difficulties, and development of the situation, as described in the first letter, which make any alteration of the sequence impossible. The personal reminiscences so characteristic of the first epistle are lacking here—they are no longer necessary in what is virtually an appendix. Further, if 2 Thessalonians precedes 1 Thessalonians, we have to account for a lost letter referred to in 2 ii. 15 and iii. 17; whereas, if 1 Thessalonians precedes 2 Thessalonians, the references are clearly to 1 Thessalonians. There is therefore no real reason to doubt the natural order which had been accepted by the Church since the second century, namely, that 2 Thessalonians is the sequel to 1 Thessalonians.

The difficulties raised by the nature and contents of the letter are not so easily disposed of. It is a fair summary of the general critical attitude to the epistle to say that the traditional view is only accepted *faute de mieux*. No solution is wholly satisfactory ; but to attribute the letter to Paul, and to date it shortly after the first letter, and to assign to it the same readers, is the solution which involves fewest difficulties. What is certain is that no one has yet given an adequate explanation of all the problems that are raised by the existence of this second letter to Thessalonica. The only question is whether, when we cannot solve such problems, we tend to denounce the document as spurious, or whether we rather content ourselves with the traditional view as a working hypothesis, admitting that if it does not clarify all the difficulties it covers most of them.

The problem of the letter is one of accounting for the similarity to and difference from a letter written by the same hand, to the same people, only a short while before. For an exhaustive discussion of the evidence one of the larger commentaries should be consulted, e.g. Frame (*I.C.C.*), pp. 39–54. Here only the salient points can be touched on. We have seen that so far as the general contents of the letter and the situation envisaged are concerned, there is no reason to doubt the authorship of Paul. Further, in respect of vocabulary, style, and fundamental theological assumptions, the second letter is as Pauline as the first. Its place in the early Church is, if anything, more firmly established. Not only is it included in Marcion's Canon and quoted by Irenaeus, like the first epistle, but, earlier than Irenaeus, it is quoted as a Pauline letter by Polycarp. Like the first epistle, its genuineness was not questioned until the radical German criticism of last century unseated it. Since then, although the grounds for scepticism have changed, it has remained very much a border-line document. The older school of Higher Criticism took offence mainly at the epistle's eschatological teaching, which they alleged was so different from that of the first letter that 2 Thessalonians could not possibly be by the same hand. In particular it was felt that there was a glaring contradiction between the imminence of the Second Advent in 1 Thessalonians and the historical prelude to it involved in 2 ii. 1–12. Further, the figure of Antichrist in this passage was held to be identifiable with the Nero Redivivus myth, which would put the date of the epistle well into the post-Pauline period. It is now recognized, however, that in the nature of eschatological thought the question of time-sequence does not arise. The passage on Antichrist could well be incorporated in the eschatological section of the first epistle without inconsistency or vice versa (see note on 1 i. 10 and p. xxxii). Likewise—largely thanks to Bousset in his *Antichrist Legend* —a truer appreciation of the mythological and Jewish background of the Man of Lawlessness disposes of any possible identification of the mysterious figure of 2 ii. 1–12 with Nero (see notes on 2 ii. 1–12). The present-day view would rather be that, far from the Antichrist passage being an interpolation—as was suggested by liberal criticism—it is, if anything, the part of the letter most likely to be genuine.

Accordingly, the emphasis has been directed away from the eschatological problem to the tone and contents of the epistle as a whole. (*a*) It is felt, for example, that there is a world of difference between the warmth and affection of the first letter and the rather chilly and official formality of the second. (*b*) It is pointed out that while 1 Thessalonians appears to be written to converted Gentiles (cf. 1 i. 9), 2 Thessalonians suggests an audience well acquainted with Jewish tradition and Old Testament phraseology (e.g. 2 i. 6–10, ii. 1–12). (*c*) It is asked whether readers who apparently know all about Antichrist (2 ii. 5) could be ignorant of such a fundamental part of Second Advent teaching as has to be explained in 1 iv. 13 ff. (*d*) Moreover, a writer of the mental stature of Paul would hardly repeat himself, in places verbatim, and, in general, surprisingly closely, in a second letter to the same people.

For all of these problems taken individually there is a more or less adequate answer. (*a*) The formality of 2 Thessalonians as opposed to 1 Thessalonians turns largely on the use of such phrases as ' We are bound to give thanks ' ; ' It is proper that we should ' (2 i. 3, ii. 13). It can be shown, however, by reference to the context, that the formality is largely apparent (see note on 2 i. 3). There is, further, no reason why the second letter should reproduce an emotional reaction which was particularly roused in the apostle by the arrival of Silvanus and Timothy when his spirits were at a low ebb. There is not this time the delighted response to what seemed to be a heaven-sent message (see p. xv). The fact also that Second Advent expectations and the problem of the work-shy had intensified must have caused the apostle a certain amount of annoyance with Thessalonica which damped the enthusiasm so characteristic of the first letter and made the tone of the second letter slightly less cordial. (*b*) Gentile readers who were familiar with the Old Testament imagery of the Parousia in 1 iv. 13 ff. would find little more of a Jewish flavour in 2 Thessalonians. (*c*) It is perfectly possible that the details of the appearance of Antichrist should be well known in a community which at the same time had never, through the death of some of its members, felt the need of having the problem of their share in the Parousia explained. (*d*) On the question of literary resemblance—which is indeed the biggest problem, suggesting more than anything else the hand of an imitator—it should be noted that, apart from the recognized greetings and farewells and general framework, which might be expected to reveal similarities in any case, the actual parallelism between the two epistles does not extend to more than one-third, and that not necessarily in the same sections. There is also the possibility that Paul read through the customary draft copy of his first letter before writing the second, and we must not forget the existence of more notable parallelism in Ephesians and Colossians.

But while these and similar questions may be answered more or less satisfactorily, there is no denying their cumulative effect. Consequently, there have been various types of solution, which fall into four main groups: (1) *The epistle is a forgery*. This would dispose of the difficult Man of Lawlessness (2 ii. 1–12) and would explain the existence of a letter, in outline, individual phrases, and subject-matter, so closely resembling 1 Thessalonians, other than supposing that it was written by the same man to the same people at almost the same time. But it would not explain why it was written at all ; why it should so closely follow the lines of 1 Thessalonians ; how a writer, necessarily after Paul's death (otherwise the forgery would have been patent), was so well able to convey to the reader the situation in Thessalonica as, for example, in 2 iii. 6–15. Further, the aim of 2 ii. 1–12 is to discourage excessive Advent expectations, whereas later writings, e.g. Revelation, had the opposite intention. The assumption behind attributing 2 Thessalonians to a forger is that it is a psychological impossibility for the same man to have written both letters to the same people. Apart from the fact that there is definite development in the situation in 2 Thessalonians compared with 1 Thessalonians which makes its writing intelligible, who is to judge what is psychologically impossible ? (2) *The epistle was written by Timothy or Silvanus.* This does not mean merely that Timothy or Silvanus acted as scribe to Paul's dictation, but that one or other of Paul's companions drafted the letter, read it over to the apostle, who then appended his signature in 2 iii. 17. (Burkitt, who sponsors the theory of Silvanus's authorship, would include 1 Thessalonians as well.) This would mean that while Paul gave general approval to the contents, it is not the kind of letter he would have written himself. We are not therefore obliged to harmonize all that is in it with the remaining Pauline epistles. The other alleged advantage of this theory is that authorship by Timothy or Silvanus would account for the stronger Jewish flavour (cf. their Jewish upbringing—Acts xvi. 1, xv. 22). But was Paul not a Hebrew of the Hebrews himself ? And is he likely to have signed a document containing anything of which he did not approve ? And if, according to Burkitt, both epistles are by Silvanus, does not this raise precisely the same problem of the relationship between 1 Thessalonians and 2 Thessalonians as if they are by Paul ? (3) *The second letter was written to Thessalonica by Paul soon after the first, but not to the same people.* This solution does justice to the Pauline features of both, and to the similarity of the situation described. Harnack, who first expounded the theory, suggested that there were two circles of readers in Thessalonica. The one was composed of Greek Christians, and to them the first letter was sent. The other was composed of Jewish Christians and the second letter was for them. In support of this, Harnack points to certain features of the second letter which become more easily explained on this theory. (*a*) Such conceptions as Antichrist and 'rules' (2 ii. 15, iii. 6) which do not occur in 1 Thessalonians would evoke response among Christian Jews. (*b*) Harnack suggests that the emphasis on 'all' in 2 iii. 16, 18; 1 v. 26, 27, indicates that there was this split in the Church, and, (*c*) reading *aparchēn* in 2 ii. 13, takes this to be a reference to the Jews who were the 'first-fruits' of the Thessalonian mission. On the face of it Harnack's is an attractive solution which appears to offer a working hypothesis. But (*a*) his side-tracking of the Man of Lawlessness does less than justice to the strong Old Testament texture of missionary preaching, which, after all, made its first approaches through the Synagogue and its pagan adherents. Likewise 'the traditions' or 'rules' which were received and handed on (see note on 2 ii. 15) were part of the technical vocabulary of the mission. (*b*) The apparent cleavage within the congregation is as readily explained by the absence of one or two loafers whom the apostle wishes to include in the fellowship (see note on 1 v. 27) and (*c*) *aparchēn* is much more probably *ap' archēs* and has nothing to do with the Jews at all (see note on 2 ii. 13). The greatest obstacle to Harnack's case is, however, the unlikelihood of Paul, the universalist, the destroyer of barriers between Jew and Gentile, perhaps fresh from writing to the Galatians on this very point, countenancing the existence of two factions within the Church of Thessalonica and condoning their continuance by praising their good works. The superscription 'To the Church of the Thessalonians' (i. 1) would also have to be discarded as a later addition or else have added to it such words as : 'who are of the circumcision.' (4) *The epistle was written to Thessalonica by Paul soon after the first, and was intended for the same people. But in the case of the second letter it was designed to be read in public as part of divine service, hence its formal style and cooler tone.* This view, put forward by Dibelius, brings the circle round again after a century of speculation almost to the traditional view. It is so near indeed that it seems hardly worth making any distinction at all. Since both letters came in fact to be read in public, it does not affect the issue whether one was specifically designed for this purpose and the other not. It seems unlikely that, having charged the readers of 1 Thessalonians to have it read aloud, which would normally happen at a meeting (1 v. 27), the apostle should alter his style in 2 Thessalonians to achieve the same result. Critical study of the text, therefore, points to the fact that though on many points concerning 2 Thessalonians we are still in need of enlightenment, there is no solution other than the orthodox view which does not raise more questions than it solves.

[*Note*.—For a discussion on the problem of the eschatological emphasis of the Thessalonian letters if they were written after Galatians see Bicknell (*West. Comm.*, xxxiv.–xxxviii.). His main points are : (1) that the advocates of an early date for Galatians have yet to prove their case, but, assuming that Galatians is early, (2) its eschatological basis can be shown to be as pronounced as that of Thessalonians. The fact that Galatians deals with a specific subject into which eschatological considerations do not enter is no more remarkable than that Thessalonians does not mention the Law. The strong eschatological element in Thessalonians is confirmed as Pauline by the proportion of eschatological teaching in the epistle next after Thessalonians, viz.—1 Cor., e.g. chap. xv. The nature of a Pauline letter is, generally, pastoral and specific, not theological and comprehensive. Paul does not attempt to deal with more than is actually occasioned by the circumstances, and we therefore may have in one letter an emphasis on one aspect of the Gospel rather than another without being entitled to draw conclusions as to date, authenticity, or development in the mind of the apostle.]

IV. Features of the Thessalonian Letters

Unlike the epistle to the Romans, which sets out to teach theology, or the epistle to the Galatians, which seeks to refute error, or the epistle to the Corinthians, which has as its aim the correction of malpractices, the Thessalonian epistles are simple letters of a great missionary to a young Church struggling to keep its feet—and its head—in difficult and trying times. There is here none of the doctrinal finesse of Romans, or the logical dexterity of Galatians, or the mystic sublimities of Ephesians, but plain, almost disappointingly straightforward, normal letter-writing, with little of the vehemence and passion, or, one might say, inspiration, of the later and greater epistles. It is almost as if we have caught Paul off his guard, but like most ' off the record ' comments, what he says here is none the less revealing. 1 and 2 Thessalonians are the Cinderellas of the recognized Pauline epistles ; partly for their unimpressive style, partly for the prominence of their obscure eschatological teaching. But if we are to understand the personality and methods of St. Paul aright, and learn something of the atmosphere and temper in which the primitive Church developed into the full flower of the Christian Faith, there is no better source-book than these two short epistles.

Among the characteristics of these letters, probably the most obvious is their intensely personal nature. Most of the time the apostle is not dealing with points of doctrine but with reminiscences of the mission, his own thoughts and prayers, and the small problems of congregational life. We are therefore given an insight into the nature of Paul the missionary such as we hardly get elsewhere in the epistles, except in Philippians and the autobiographical section of 2 Corinthians. But nowhere do we get a more human and lovable Paul—tender with his converts, generous with offenders (2 iii. 15), indignant with those who hinder the Lord's work (1 ii. 16), encouraging the timid (1 v. 4), comforting the mourner (1 iv. 13), and above all, masterly in the tactful handling of difficult situations (1 ii. 17 ff. ; iv. 1 ff. ; 2 iii. 6 ff., 16). Foremost of all is his intense delight in the souls he has won for Christ and his affection for them. In anyone else but Paul, the praise which he lavishes upon these ordinary working-folk of Thessalonica might be dubbed flattery or insincerity. But he is so obviously in deadly earnest. True, there is the tactful word of commendation, paving the way for stern reproof (e.g. 2 iii. 1–5), but by and large it is out of the fulness of heart of a great pastor that these tender thoughts are poured. He always thanks God for them ; he constantly remembers them in his prayers (1 i. 2 ; 2 i. 3, 11) ; he longs to see them again (1 ii. 17). If they stand firm in the faith, it is literally life itself for him (1 iii. 8). When they all come before the Judgment of Christ, his greatest boast will be their Christian witness (1 ii. 19). Likewise, in anyone else but one so obviously conscious that he was a servant of God, some of his words might suggest conceit or worse ; his preaching is no human message, but the word of God (1 ii. 13) ; he claims, as the right of an apostle, respect and deference (1 ii. 6)—though he mentions this claim only to waive it. He brackets his own name with Christ's (1 i. 6). His sensitiveness, too, to misrepresentation, and his hot resentment of the charges of being a religious quack (1 ii. 3 ff.) are similarly entirely dissociated from any personal vanity or concern for public opinion. They are to be interpreted as the anxiety of one whose only jealousy is for his Master, whose only fear and indignation are lest the Gospel should be hindered by the machinations of evil men (1 ii. 16). He is a man possessed by Christ. Nothing in these epistles— or in any other—is intelligible until we recognize that. He can talk of Christ and himself in the same breath (1 i. 6) because the union between them is almost physical. Real life for him begins and ends in Christ—life here or life beyond (1 v. 10). The whole purpose and meaning of his work everywhere is to bring others into the same vital new relationship, the same new dimension, in which he himself lived. It is this Christ-possessed man who can humbly ask for the prayers of these simple Macedonians (1 v. 25 ; 2 iii. 1) ; who is encouraged in his own difficulties by news of their progress in the faith (1 iii. 7). Here, then, is a living picture of Paul the pastor— proud of his converts' Christian attainments, yet with no illusions as to their perfection (1 iii. 10), equally eager to praise (1 i. 7), to encourage (1 iv. 1), and to comfort (1 iv. 13), as to exhort (1 iv. 3), to admonish (2 ii. 2), and to rebuke (2 iii. 14).

As illuminating as the impression these letters give of the apostle as missionary is the light they shed upon the primitive Christian community. Here we most nearly approach the glimpses of the early days of the Church as recorded in the Book of Acts. Paul, Silvanus, and Timothy reach this great pagan city. In its synagogue and among its pagan adherents they make their first contacts. Through them they reach a wider audience. They preach the Gospel of the one true and living God and the folly and evil of idolatry (1 i. 9). They tell of the Fatherhood of God (1 i. 3), and of His Son Jesus (1 i. 10, ii. 15), who came into the world to bring Light (1 v. 5) and Life (1 v. 10), who died for all (1 v. 10), and rose from the dead (1 iv. 14), to effect the salvation of those who accept Him as Lord (1 v. 9)—salvation which begins in the eternal purpose of God (2 ii. 13) is mediated as a call by the preaching of His Word (2 ii. 14), is realized as life with Christ on earth (1 v. 10), and has its end in the perfect fellowship with God in Christ of life in glory (2 ii. 14), together with all His faithful people (1 iv. 17). They preach the impending climax of history (1 i. 10). The Lord who died and rose again will soon return to gather His people to Himself (1 iv. 16), to banish the wicked (2 ii. 12), and to consummate in all its splendour the New Age which has already dawned (2 i. 10). For those who deny Him (2 i. 8), persecute His people, and oppose His Gospel (1 ii. 14–16), His coming will be a Day of Terror (1 ii. 16; 2 i. 9) ; for those who have turned to Him, it will be the fulfilment of all their hopes (1 v. 9 ; 2 i. 10), for it is this same Jesus who rescues them from the Wrath to Come (1 i. 10). Therefore, those who would be Christ's on His Day must be ever watchful (i. v. 6), keeping His commandments, and living lives worthy of Him (1 iv. 1). In faith, love, and hope (1 i. 2), in self-discipline (1 iv. 3), and honest work (2 iii. 12), and in obeying the precepts that the apostles had themselves received and now handed on (1 iv. 2 ; 2 iii. 6), the converts are to live soberly and peaceably together (1 v. 6, 13).

Here, then, is both the preaching (*kērygma*) and the teaching (*didachē*) as we find it throughout the early Church ; as outlined in the sermon-summaries in the Book of Acts, and in

Pauline references to what he had himself ' received ' (1 Cor. xv. 3, etc.). In these letters there is not the developed doctrine and theologizing of the later epistles. What theology there is is almost casually introduced and rather implicit than explicit. The value is, however, perhaps the greater in that what we find in Thessalonians may be taken to be echoes of the general pattern of Pauline missionary preaching, apart from his reflections on particular problems. Thus it would not be a correct judgment to regard doctrines which are not dealt with at length in Thessalonians, e.g. Justification by Faith, Atonement, Grace, and so on, as later developments in the apostle's thought. There is simply no occasion here to deal with them. It is much more true to say that what later was expressed is here suggested (e.g. 2 ii. 13; 1 v. 10; 1 i. 1). Similarly, belief in the Lordship of Jesus (1 i. 1 and *passim*), His equality with God (1 iii. 11 ; 2 ii. 16), the work of the Spirit (1 iv. 8), and, in effect, the Holy Trinity (1 i. 3, 6), is here as clearly accepted as the more detailed eschatological teaching.

More intriguing perhaps are the glimpses into the congregational life of the Thessalonian converts. Plain working-folk most of them (2 iii. 10), whether many or few it is impossible to say—most likely the latter. Probably of good Macedonian stock—independent and generous—they transferred both attributes into their Church life : the one perhaps with less happy consequences (see note on 1 v. 12), the other in a liberality that had to be restrained (2 iii. 10). Paul was later to speak with gratitude of the Macedonian Churches who gave ' according to their means, aye, beyond their means ' in support of their Jerusalem brethren (2 Cor. viii. 1 ff.). They know themselves to be part of the Ecclesia, the new Chosen People of God (1 i. 1 ; 2 ii. 13), which they represent in Thessalonica over against their late pagan associates (1 ii. 14), and their enemies the Jews—indignant that some of them should have forsaken the synagogue for Christianity (1 ii. 16). They are still afire with the message that was preached to them in what must have been a wonderful and moving campaign (1 i. 6). Paul's heart kindles as he recalls what was clearly, even in himself, an extraordinary evidence of the power of

God's Spirit (1 i. 5). With pardonable exaggeration he talks of its fame as world-wide (1 i. 8). Hyperbole of this kind must be seen against the background of what the lives of the Thessalonians had been like before their conversion. The enthusiasm of the missionaries had been met with equal zeal. Now their hearts are still warm towards the apostle who brought them to God (1 iii. 6). Some kind of elementary organization has arisen—with leaders and a rudimentary discipline (1 v. 12). It is suggested both that they meet regularly and that the apostle's letters would be read then (1 v. 27). There is also some kind of mutual instruction (1 v. 11) and a kiss of fellowship (1 v. 26). We glimpse their problems—how much value to put on ecstatic manifestations (1 v. 20) ; how to treat recalcitrant members (2 iii. 6) ; and through it all the atmosphere of expectancy of the final triumph of Christ, of an impending dénouement, in some giving rise to unhealthy unsettlement and idleness (2 ii. 2 ; iii. 11), in others to concern over their loved ones (1 iv. 13), but in most to a buoyant, exhilarating, joyous confidence in the future, coupled with a wholehearted obedience to the spirit and letter of the Lord's teaching. They are already living a new life which is only about to begin in earnest. No one who reads the Thessalonian letters, where more than anywhere else in the New Testament the eyes of the readers appear to be fixed on the coming Day of God, could ever suggest that the moral code of the early Church was in any sense an interim-ethics. Christian works are incumbent upon Christian people, not because they will thereby escape the Judgment, but because they are as much part of the Gospel as Christian faith (1 i. 3 ; 2 i. 11). It is God's will that they should be consecrated men and women (1 iv. 3), and Paul prays that body, soul, and spirit may be cleansed and purified in preparation for the Lord's Advent (1 v. 23). This new life, this sense of being plucked from a living death, is what gives them superhuman courage and resources. Persecution cannot harm them, opposition does not dismay them (1 ii. 14 ; 2 i. 4), for the power of the living Christ to whom they pray is with them (1 v. 28; 2 ii. 16, iii. 18).

V. The Eschatology of the Thessalonian Epistles

It is, however, traditionally in the eschatological sections of the Thessalonian letters that most interest has centred and most discussion has been aroused. They are by no means the only valuable feature of the epistles, nor, as is generally held, do they indicate that the *kērygma* at Thessalonica laid particular emphasis on the Second Advent. It so happened that in the case of the Thessalonian Church the practical problems that exercised their minds, and on which they sought the apostle's advice, were connected with the Parousia. But, on the other hand, it is difficult to explain the presence of such eschatological expressions in the later epistles as e.g. Col. i. 22 ; Phil. i. 10, iv. 5, if the Second Advent did not figure equally prominently in the later mission-preaching. Consequently, it is not Paul who is responsible for the large amount of space devoted in these letters to eschatology, but the queries of the converts. We are entitled, on the evidence of the New Testament generally, to assume (*a*) that the eschatological background of the *kērygma* was universally taught and believed in the early Church—probably indeed playing a considerably greater part than we imagine—and that, therefore, (*b*) the Thessalonian letters merely give us a clearer glimpse of a permanent feature of early Church belief, with its attendant perplexities, just as, say, Galatians crystallizes the then ever-present problem of Judaism. The general opinion also, that Paul's views on the Second Advent changed with time—the suggestion being that Thessalonians represents a primitive stage in his thinking—needs some qualification. It is, of course, possible for a missionary to change the presentation of his gospel, or a preacher to change his style of preaching, or a theologian to alter his dogmatic views. There is no reason, therefore, why Paul should not have ceased to hold his belief in the Second Coming of Christ so forcefully in his later years. But there is no real evidence that he did so. Argument from the absence of detailed mention in various epistles is no real argument. In Galatians, which may well be earlier than Thessalonians, little space is given to eschatology, yet the eschatological viewpoint is implicit throughout (see p. xxvi). In 1 Corinthians—the next to be written after Thessalonians—there is a large amount of eschatological teaching, again occasioned by circumstance (cf. xv. 12 ff.), but as well as this the eschatological viewpoint is determinative of the whole (i. 7, v. 5, x. 11, xvi. 22). It is said, however, that between the writing of 1 Corinthians and 2 Corinthians Paul's views changed, and that thereafter he ceased to believe in the imminence of the Parousia. Apart from the fact that in eschatological thinking the dénouement is always 'just round the corner,' and therefore such words as those already referred to in the later epistles (e.g. Phil. i. 10, iv. 5) indicate an eschatological hope as 'imminent' as the imagery of 1 and 2 Thessalonians, surely what happened between 1 and 2 Corinthians was rather that Paul's views on his own part in the Parousia changed. After that time he had reason to feel—probably through his harrowing experiences at Ephesus (2 Cor. i. 8)—that he might not survive until the Second Coming. This does not mean that the 'date' of the Parousia—if we can use the expression—was 'put forward' in his mind from what it had been as he wrote to Thessalonica. It simply means that a new and personal aspect of the problem affected his thought on the matter. His expectancy did not become any less intense; his belief in the imminence of the Parousia did not change; he merely had to reckon with the new possibility that he himself might be one of those about whom the Thessalonian Church was concerned who had 'fallen asleep' before the Lord came (1 iv. 13 ff.). There is therefore no question of Paul's having realized that he had been wrong at Thessalonica—as some writers suggest—and endeavouring to put it right by 'toning down' the imminence of the Second Advent in the later epistles. The prominence of eschatology in these two letters does not therefore presuppose either a passing phase in the mind of the apostle or a phenomenon peculiar to the Thessalonian Church. An eschatological background was an inevitable feature of the setting of the faith and the preaching of early Christianity.

As to the particular expression of this eschatological background in the letters to Thessalonica, three caveats are worth entering. The first concerns the nature of a Pauline letter in general. We cannot be too often reminded that these letters do not set out to construct a systematic theology. Paul writes, not as a systematic theologian—even to the Romans— nor as a preacher, but as a pastor. His letters were never intended to be scrutinized, set one against another, and used as material for constructing a Pauline *Summa Theologica* or *Institutes*. They are personal, occasional correspondence, designed to answer particular questions, and to meet particular situations. At times one aspect of the faith is stressed, at times another. The result is not a logical system free from all inconsistency, but a series of illuminations of specific facets of the *kērygma* by the profound and devout mind of the greatest of the Church's missionaries. We must not therefore expect to find in these Thessalonian letters an indexed *vade mecum* to the eschatology of the early Church.

The second caveat is related to the first. We must not misunderstand the nature of Paul's thought. Anderson Scott (*Christianity according to St. Paul*, p. 17) says of Paul's teaching that it is shaped by ' Art rather than science ; life rather than logic.' Paul's thought is not speculative or metaphysical, but imaginative, pictorial, and evangelical. He is concerned, above all, to bring men to the knowledge of God in Christ. The new relationship of life in Christ is the fundamental fact for him and therefore for all his thinking. All else is framework—ways of expressing the same vital fact, of leading men to it, of clarifying particular aspects of it. Now there are some occasions in expounding Christian truth when the best clarification is the language of poetry. To this Paul resorts in such passages as 1 Cor. 13 ; Rom. viii. 31 ff. Above all is this true in what concerns the Last Things. When, therefore, Paul thinks eschatologically, we should expect to find, not the clear-cut precision of the mathematician, but, as in the Hebrew prophets, in the direct succession to whom Paul stands, the language of the inspired preacher-poet, of the man of God who sees and experiences things inexpressible in words, and who seeks to convey truth by symbol, suggestion, image, and figure, rather than by detailed analysis ; by drawing a picture rather than by expounding a fact. A clear example of this is the eschatological teaching on the Resurrection-body in 1 Cor. xv.

The third caveat concerns the particular eschatological teaching of these letters. In both of them Paul presupposes previous knowledge on the part of his readers. ' You have no need of being written to,' he says in 1 v. 1, because ' you know perfectly well ' what you were taught about the Parousia during the mission. Similarly, in the second letter, in the midst of what to us is the obscurity of his teaching on Antichrist, he interjects almost impatiently : ' Do you not remember I used to tell you this when I was with you ? ' (2 ii. 5). What Paul writes here is, then, no new teaching. He is simply reminding the converts of something they know but have allowed themselves to forget. Just as a present-day pastor might remind one of his faithful flock, who was giving way to violent grief over the death of a loved one, of the ' Fourteenth Chapter of John,' presuming on his general knowledge of the Church's teaching on life after death. The only point which does appear to be new is the question dealt with in 1 iv. 13 ff. on the part to be played on the Last Day by Christians who had already died. We are therefore merely overhearing echoes of the missionary preaching, variations on a theme already played. It is like listening to one end of a telephone conversation, or trying to piece together a jigsaw puzzle without the master-picture to guide us. Particularly in the case of the figure of Antichrist, much that is now incomprehensible might become clear if we only knew what had been said before, which was well known to the Thessalonians, and which Paul assumes in writing.

On the other hand, there are certain facts that modern scholarship has illumined for us, in the light of which we can turn to the eschatological passages with greater understanding.

(1) The basis of our Lord's message, as of the preaching of the early missionaries, was the claim that the Scriptures had now been fulfilled. What the prophets and psalmists had foretold of the coming of the Messiah and a Golden Age had,

in fact, already begun to happen. The Messiah had appeared, the Age to Come had already dawned (see Dodd's *The Apostolic Preaching and Its Developments*).

(2) The chief part of that fulfilment was that the God whom the old Israel had worshipped, and whom the new Israel still worshipped, had been fully revealed in the person of Jesus of Nazareth, His Son. This Jesus of Nazareth, whom men had crucified, God had raised up and exalted as Lord of all (Acts ii. 36). The sacred name of God, Jehovah, which to all Greek-speaking Jews and Gentile adherents of the synagogue was *Kurios*, the Lord, now became the name by which the Church spoke of the risen Jesus. He was the *Kurios* they worshipped and to whom they prayed. When Paul throughout his letters speaks of Jesus as *Kurios*, he is giving Him the status and attributes of God. Consequently, by a fusion of the two factors—the belief that Scripture had been fulfilled and that Jesus Christ was Lord—prophecies made originally concerning the Lord of the Old Israel came to be applied to the Lord of the New. Believers searched the Scriptures: Testimonia—collections of Old Testament texts applicable to Christ—were compiled ; incidents in Jesus' life were seen to be fulfilments of what had been foretold by the prophets. The clearest indication of this is the use of the Old Testament made by the writer of St. Matthew's Gospel (see Rendel Harris, *Testimonies*). It is likely that much of the Old Testament atmosphere of the Thessalonian epistles comes, not directly from the Septuagint, but from these collections of Testimonia with which Christian missionaries, including Paul, were probably furnished.

(3) We should therefore expect that, as part of this process, beliefs connected with the Day of the Lord, which had been in Old Testament prophecy the event to which the whole of history pointed—Jehovah's final manifestation of Himself to the world and His Judgment on the nations—would come to be transferred to the person of Christ.

The traditional Day of the Lord, of Hebrew expectation, was to be the day on which the misfortunes of Israel were to be reversed and the oppressing Gentiles, struck down by the hand of Jehovah, Israel's Lord, were to become subject to the Chosen People in a New Age which would outshine the Golden Age of the great David. Under the withering scorn of the classical prophets, Israel had been taught that the Day would not be a day of national triumph for Israel, but a day of vindication of God's justice. The new Golden Age would come, it is true, but it would be a reign of righteousness. When the Great Day came, the Judgment of God would fall indiscriminately upon Jew and Gentile. The wicked would be punished, the good would be rewarded, and the Lord would reign supreme for ever. This was the hope which sustained the faithful in Israel's darkest hours, a hope which never left them comfortless. No matter how black the future might seem, how heavy the hand of their oppressors, their heart was light because they were Jehovah's people and the Lord's Day would come. Whether they looked, as in the time of the great prophets, for the New Age to be ushered in by political change, or whether they looked, with the apocalyptists, as the prospect grew more sombre and the world more evil, for a cataclysmic end of all things, the Day of the Lord remained the goal of all their expectations.

Beneath the symbolism and poetry which the Hebrew prophets used to clothe their hope of the future lay a very definite philosophy of history. The faith of Israel was not that history was a never-ending cycle, or that the world was the creation of impersonal forces and would eventually end in nothing, or that it was embarked on a process of perfectionism ending in some Utopia, but that the world was created by God, that man had been placed upon it to fulfil God's purpose, that, despite their sin and disobedience, God was overruling men and nations into conformity with that purpose, and that in His good time both His nature and purpose would be fully revealed and His will be done. Those who had responded to God's summons, so far as they had known it—in worship, service, and obedience—the faithful Remnant—would enter into the full privileges and status of the children of the Most High, for which men had been created. Those who had not so responded had damned themselves. They had made themselves unfit to realize the purpose of their creation, which would then be revealed as life together with God, savoured on earth, and lived to the full in the Age to Come.

This view of history was taken over by the Christian Church with this significant difference, that Jesus came proclaiming that the New Age was not ' round the corner,' but had, in fact, come. He Himself had inaugurated the new era. God had now revealed Himself to men, and His works were to be seen in their midst. The old age and the old order were passing, and in their place was a new relationship between God and man, sealed by a new Covenant, governed by a new Law, the law of love, and embodied in a new Israel, the Israel of God, the Church. This was the preaching of the early mission. The proof that God's rule had begun, that the ' Age to Come ' had in fact come, was to be seen in the Resurrection of Jesus, His presence within the Church, the manifestations of the Spirit, the evidences of God's miraculous powers of healing, the consciousness of new life, the rapid spread of the Gospel, the astounding conversion of pagans, their supernatural courage in face of opposition and persecution. All these things which had been foreshadowed in the Scriptures convinced the early Church that God's purpose was indeed being fulfilled, the new Golden Age had dawned.

But obviously there was a considerable element of prophecy unfulfilled. In our current theological jargon, eschatology was not fully ' realized ' : there remained a ' futurist ' element to be reckoned with. Evil had not been destroyed. The Lord had been exalted to the right hand of God, but the world did not acknowledge Him. Proof that He had not finally died on the Cross had been given to a few by the Resurrection appearances and was confirmed by the experience of believers. But mankind at large had yet to be convinced. The old and passing order must finally pass and something completely new take its place. Some much more fundamental transformation must take place, some more dramatic and supernatural intervention of God must bring to a close the present age of darkness and seal the advent of the Age of Light in which the faithful already lived. God's revelation of Himself was not complete. He must make Himself known in all His power and glory to vindicate His faithful servants and confound those who had rejected His Son and His Gospel. This final revelation, the consummation of all things, the full realization of all prophecy, and the real inauguration of God's Rule, must be close at hand. All the signs pointed to its speedy advent. The Day of the Lord was imminent—the triumph of the Gospel and the rout of the wicked, the visible end of the old world, and the enthronement of Christ as Lord of all. Only so could the Scriptures be fulfilled.

So it is that when the final revelation of God to men is spoken of, it is in the terms and spirit of Old Testament prophecy. In these Thessalonian letters, which most probably reflect more nearly the standard missionary preaching of the early Church than any other part of the New Testament except the Book of Acts, the language, the thought, and the inspiration of the eschatological passages are to be found in the Old Testament. Whether Paul is quoting from the Old Testament directly himself or from a collection of Testimonia cannot be said, nor is it materially important. As will be seen in detail, it was to the language of Old Testament prophecy of the coming manifestation of Jehovah or His Anointed (or of past revelations of Himself to men) that the Church turned when it tried to express its conviction that the full revelation and triumph of Christ was yet to come. The Day of the Lord became the Day of Christ. As Jehovah came down to Sinai, so He would return, said the prophet Joel, and thus will Christ return to earth also (cf. Exod. xix. 16 ff. with Joel ii. 1, 11, and 1 Thess. iv. 16–17). The Lord Jesus would come with angels and with fire (2 Thess. i. 7–8), as Zechariah (xiv. 5) and Isaiah (lxvi. 15) had foretold of the Lord Jehovah. When it is declared that the wicked will be destroyed (2 i. 9), it is in words used of Jehovah in Isa. ii. 10 that Paul describes their encounter with the returning Christ. When the Lawless One (2 ii. 4) who precedes the End comes, he will bear a marked resemblance to the wicked king of Dan. ii. 36. It is thus in a ' mosaic of reminiscences of the prophets,' as Kennedy puts it, that Paul describes the coming climax of history and the full revelation of Christ in these letters and indeed in his eschatological references generally throughout the epistles (see Kennedy, *St. Paul's Conceptions of the Last Things*, pp. 180 ff., for examples).

T. F. Glasson has shown us that there is much less reason than was thought to look for the antecedents of Second Advent hopes in the Messianic literature of Judaism (*The Second Advent*, chaps. II–V). He is less convincing when he seeks to show that it was merely from an interpretation of historical events by Old Testament prophecy that the doctrine arose in the first instance. It is impossible to escape the conclusion that the initial impetus to the Church's belief in the return of Christ was given by our Lord Himself. The Parousia strain is too deeply rooted in the gospels to be explained away, and the transition from the Old Testament Day of the Lord to the New Testament Day of Christ must be by way of the Day of the Son of Man. The evidence is too lengthy to be discussed here, and the reader may refer to Kennedy, op. cit., pp. 166 ff.; Gore, *Belief in Christ*, chap. V ; Manson, *The Teaching of Jesus*, pp. 260 ff., etc., etc., and the commentaries. It does seem that in several cases where our Lord appears to foretell His Parousia He is in fact indicating His future Resurrection and Exaltation and not a return. (Cf. Dodd, *Parables of the Kingdom*, chap. III.) Moreover, the Parousia passages of Matthew can be shown to be of dubious value, leaving comparatively few reliable sayings in M. and Q. (cf. Glasson, op. cit., p. 149). There is, further (as in Mk. xiii.), the complication of probable confusion with our Lord's prophecies of the Fall of Jerusalem. (Cf. Blunt in Clarendon *Mark*, p. 236 ; Gore, op. cit., p. 149.)

But when all this has been said, and despite the difficulties of the text, it seems almost impossible to account for the fact that the early Church was, from the beginning, agog with expectation of the end of the world and the return of Christ, without tracing the belief back in the last resort to Christ Himself. This, however, involves us in no small problem. Are we to say with Huxley that our Lord was guilty of a

' prodigious error,' or evade the issue by some convenient phrase such as the ' voluntary limitations of the Incarnation,' or beg the question by suggesting that our Lord ' talked down ' to His hearers and was misunderstood? None of these answers is satisfactory. Let us face the fact that our Lord prophesied His return, that the Church accepted it and believed it, and that it was the background of the mission-preaching. Does this mean that because He did not return as was expected, the validity of the driving force by which the Gospel spread is exploded ?

Surely the clue is in the nature of eschatological language and thinking as a whole. Not only is its Oriental imagery at the opposite pole from Western literalism, not only does it use pictorial, symbolical, imaginative description in place of logical exactitude, but in a real sense the question of time in terms of days, months, and years does not enter into it. Every Old Testament prophet who preached the Day of the Lord expected it to happen soon. The great prophets who looked for the Day to come through political events—Amos through the Assyrians, Isaiah of Babylon through Cyrus, Zechariah through Zerubbabel—or the apocalyptists, who expected nothing less than a new heaven and a new earth, all regarded the Day of the Lord as ' upon them.' But the date was irrelevant, the historical accidents of little account. They were, in fact, proclaiming the deeper truth that the Day of the Lord is a reality for each generation. It is God's timeless Judgment which is past, present, and future. In a sense it is always to come, in a sense it is always present, and in a sense it has already been passed. This is the essence of the Old Testament Day of the Lord, the trappings are incidental. When a prophet spoke of the Day, it meant for him primarily the vindication of God's Holy Will, the revelation of His Purpose, and the defeat of evil. So certain was this to come to pass that the prophet could speak of it as if it were almost there. Having recognized that the prophets were mainly forth-tellers and not foretellers, we must add the corollary that categories of factual accuracy and inaccuracy do not apply. Deutero-Isaiah was not ' wrong,' because Cyrus did not inaugurate the

Golden Age, any more than the author of Daniel was ' wrong ' in expecting the world to crash in pieces about the head of Antiochus. Both were right in their insight into the nature of history and its subjection at every moment to the Judgment of God. They saw that the great crises of history are but a magnification of the personal and social crisis which is perennial.

Our Lord, in speaking of the Day of the Son of Man, uses the language of the future. But the fact of the Son of Man is equally past and present. The Son of Man had come in the Incarnation ; for the New Testament writers He was even then the Head of His Body, the Church ; and His ' Coming ' was not an event to be marked on the calendar, but a fulfilment of the past and the present, part of the one redemptive Act of God. What Jesus foretold was His ultimate triumph over all the powers of darkness and the full revelation of Himself to men. He was and is and will be Judge. His ' Day ' was yesterday, to-day, and for ever. Thus the Parousia is, like Creation, in a real sense timeless ; not an historical event, but the underlying purpose of history and the summing up of all things in Christ.

When we confess our faith that Christ ' will come again to judge the quick and the dead,' we are not resting our hope upon the visible return of Jesus of Nazareth in flesh and blood to this earth. The words are symbolic and, as Dodd would say, ' the least inadequate ' to confess our faith that our life in this world is but a probationary prelude ; that history has an end which is governed by the purpose of God; that evil is not part of God's purpose and will be destroyed ; that obedience to God will have its reward in fuller fellowship with Him ; that in the full confrontation of human by divine men will see their lives in their true worth and in all the poverty of their failure and folly ; and that in the end of all things Christ will be recognized by all men as Lord. How are we to express something so indescribable, so remote from the thought-categories of everyday life, unless in the pictorial language of the gospels and epistles ? How could our Lord convey to His disciples the ultimacy of His rôle as Saviour and Judge more adequately than in the symbolism of the Parousia, and how could the early Church express more deeply their intense consciousness of living in the death-throes of the old un-redeemed world and on the threshold of a New Age than in the traditional language in which the prophets had expressed their conviction of God's nearness and judgment? There is no convincing indication in the gospels that Jesus spoke of the Parousia as an event which was about to happen immediately in time. Such prophecy would be strangely out of harmony with all His ethical teaching, His deliberate creation of a New Israel, His normal practice of spiritualizing traditional con-cepts, and would fail to account for such injunctions as that the Gospel must first be preached throughout the world (Mark xiii. 10 ; Matt. xxiv. 14, xxviii. 19–20). That the early Church believed in a speedy Parousia is simply a measure of the intensity of their sense of living already in the Age to Come.

When we look at the eschatology of the Thessalonian letters, it must be in the light of these considerations. For Paul, salvation is always seen in an eschatological context. God's purpose for men is to redeem them through Christ, so that they may enjoy eternal life—only fully possible when the frailty of the body and the sinfulness of the world have been left behind. The end of man is to reflect the glory of God in His presence—to be transformed into His likeness—having been delivered through Christ from the Wrath (1 i. 10) and the Judgment (2 i. 8) which are God's visitation upon sin and disobedience. When Paul writes to his converts that they had turned from idols to serve the living God and to wait for His Son from heaven (1 i. 9), he is saying what the writer of Hebrews says in xiii. 14, that ' Here we have no continuing city.' Their eyes have been turned from the shams and hol-lowness of paganism to the transcendent truth of God in Christ who guarantees its victory. When, in figurative language like the Hebrew prophets', he describes the final Triumph of Christ (1 iv. 15 ff.), what he intends his readers to take for their comfort—and what no doubt they did take—is not a factual description of what will happen, but the knowledge that the future holds no terror for those who are in Christ. He who is supreme in their hearts now will receive them unto Himself, so that they may be for ever with Him.

Similarly, the description of the Old Testament Day of the Lord, transposed into a Christian setting (2 i. 6 ff.), finds its real value and meaning in its insistence on the ultimate primacy of Christ, the joy of believers in His presence, and the separation from Him which sin inevitably brings upon the wicked. When Paul speaks of the Parousia as the 'revelation' of Christ (2 i. 7), it is in keeping with many other allusions to the same effect (1 Cor. i. 7 ; Rom. ii. 5)—and indeed our Lord's own words (Luke xvii. 30)—that he regards the Coming of Christ as much as anything as the removal of the veils which hide Him from us, the full perception of what we now see ' darkly.' That Paul—following our Lord—regarded the Second Advent as a religious truth rather than an historical prophecy is clear when he deals with the question of when all this will happen. Here is plainly preserved the tension between the present and future Judgment, between Christ the present Head of the Church and the future Lord of all the world. The Day comes ' as a thief in the night ' (1 v. 2), therefore not something that will ' happen to-morrow,' but something for which we must always be ready. What concerns us as Christians, says Paul, is not when it will please God to sum up all things in Christ, but that we should live to-day in such a way that even if the end came to-morrow we should not be caught unprepared. So it is in equally unprecise language that he describes the final overthrow of evil (2 ii. 1–12). This is not historical prognostication, but religious insight. The figure of the Lawless One is a supernatural amalgam of Evil. As part of the final triumph of Christ, all that he represents—pride, deceit, falsehood—will be destroyed.

It was thus immaterial for Paul, as for the early Church in general, whether the swan-song of the present world and the final victory of Christ came within their own lifetime or at the end of time, on earth or in heaven. That it will come they were certain, as certain as the Old Testament prophets and apocalyptists had been of the Day of the Lord, however they conceived of it ; and the intensity of their experience, their nearness to the historical Jesus, the striking manifestations of the Spirit, brought it within their grasp. The result, however, of this sense of the nearness of Victory and Judgment was to confirm them in their Christian obedience. It was precisely because they stood so directly before Christ as King and Judge that their own witness must be enhanced (2 ii. 15–17). As opposed to those whose heads were turned by thoughts of the impending climax, Paul's counsel to the Thessalonians— approving what they already practised—was to continue with their normal work, but with this difference, that they lived as citizens of this world who were prepared at any moment to enter the next.

Paul's views on his part in the Triumph of Christ changed, as we have seen, but his view of its imminence never changed. It is less true to say that Paul in his later letters approximated to the Johannine view of the Parousia—that the Lord had in fact come again at Pentecost and that Judgment was already being passed on men's attitude to the First Advent—than to say that both John and Paul preserve throughout their thinking the essential tension between the mystical and the eschatological—between the presence of Christ now with His people and His ultimate Triumph, between the Judgment which we daily pass on ourselves and the final revelation of ourselves as we are in the presence of God. (Cf. W. F. Howard, *Christianity According to St. John*, chap. V.) In both cases it is not reinterpretation of the Parousia of the Synoptists in the light of greater wisdom and experience, but a correct interpretation of what our Lord Himself said and which the Synoptists faithfully recorded. The primitive eschatological expectation is, in fact, the Johannine one. Linguistically and pictorially it differs in that it draws upon the imagery of Old Testament and Apocalyptic, but essentially it is the same. (See Duncan, *Jesus Son of Man*, pp. 253–4 ; Balmforth, Clarendon *Luke*, p. 283.)

In the Thessalonian letters many questions to which we should like to know Paul's reply remain unanswered : how he viewed the fate of those who never hear the Gospel, or how he related the intermediate state of the believer after death to his final entrance into the fulness of the Kingdom. Paul, as Kennedy says (op. cit., p. 21), 'has no eschatology,' that is, no formulated system of beliefs concerning the Last Things. The most impressive feature of his teaching on the subject is its restraint and reticence—the absence of the bizarre details beloved by the apocalyptist—and the real religious purpose underlying all. What he rather does is to illumine the traditional concepts with the intensity of his own conviction and to leave us with a twofold message, eternally true. (1) The believer who is in Christ here on earth remains by God's grace in Christ for ever. For him the new life begun here blossoms into the full glory of life with Christ hereafter, together with those whom he has loved and lost. (2) For the Christian, life has always an eschatological setting—he must watch and pray—the Lord is always at hand—every day is a Day of the Lord and the believer's cry must always be, Come, Lord Jesus. There is nothing here of the perverted eschatology of the Millennial Dawnists and other pious eccentrics of this and past generations, who construct out of Holy Scripture a time-table for Doomsday and a blue-print for the Kingdom of Heaven. In these Thessalonian epistles, which reflect so strongly the eschatological convictions of Paul and his converts, nothing is more marked than the apostle's discouragement of any feverish excitability or profitless speculation.

Were the apostle alive in our tottering European civilization to-day, where signs of the end are plenty and faith to meet it all too small, he would without a doubt brace us with the same robust counsel as he wrote to his Thessalonians. He would tell us that, for Christian men, death, however it comes, by universal cataclysm or quietly in sleep, has been robbed of its terrors—that they are already part of a fellowship which is hid with Christ in God and that the end is not a dark unknown but to ' be with the Lord for ever ' (1 iv. 17). He would remind us that Antichrist is with us until the end of time and never lacks a following, and that if we expect a carefree untroubled life, we have not begun to understand our Christian vocation (1 iii. 4). He would urge us to stand firm and hold to our rule of life, and in a critical time to keep quiet, to do our work, and—a pointed thrust !—to earn our own living (2 ii. 15, iii. 12).   He would remind us of the wonder of God's love (2 iii. 5), of His purpose from the beginning that we should gain the glory of our Lord Jesus Christ (2 ii. 14), of our knowledge of the power of the Spirit in our own lives (1 i. 5). And what better prayer for a war-torn and war-scared world is there than his prayer for the perplexed and anxious church-folk of Thessalonica : ' May the Lord of Peace Himself grant you peace continually, whatever comes ' (2 iii. 16).

I. GREETING

(i. 1)

**Paul and Silvanus and Timotheus, to the church of the Thessa- 1
lonians in God the Father and the Lord Jesus Christ :
grace and peace to you.**

These opening words remind us, as we need constantly to
be reminded, that Thessalonians is, like the other Pauline
epistles, neither a theological treatise nor a sermon, but a real
letter, written at a specific time to meet a specific situation.
For this is precisely the way in which any private letter of the
times would begin, with the name of the writer, followed by
the name of the addressee, and a polite greeting. Paul
adopted the conventional literary practices of the day much
as he accepted the structure of society, as something to be
infused with a new spirit and given a new content. A pagan
letter, as has been established by the discoveries of papyri at
Oxyrhynchus and elsewhere in Egypt, provided the pattern
that we find more or less closely followed in all the Pauline
letters : Greeting, Thanksgiving, Special Contents, Personal
Messages, Salutation, and Farewell. As Deissmann has put it:
Paul's letters ' differ from the messages of the homely papyrus
leaves from Egypt, not as letters, but only as the letters of
Paul.' It appears, from 2 iii. 17 (as well as Rom. xvi. 22 ;
1 Cor. xvi. 21 ; Col. iv. 18), that Paul's practice was to dictate
his letters and only to add the closing lines in his own hand.
This, too, was the normal practice of the times, though in Paul's
case it was not a professional scribe who was employed, but a
friend like Silvanus or Timothy or Tertius.

If we picture Paul, as has been suggested, holding in his
hand some letter to which he is replying, and dictating answers
to points raised in it as his eye catches them, it not only gives

us a point of view from which to regard the epistles as a whole, but also explains much of the abruptness with which sometimes one subject switches on to another. Incidentally, of course, if we knew whether Paul dictated *verbatim*, or how much he left to the scribe's expansion of his notes, we might be able to solve many a difficult problem of authenticity and many an obscure turn of phrase. The Greeting, then, follows the normal pattern of a pagan letter. It was written at the top, if the letter was a long one—consisting of several sheets of papyrus gummed together—or on the cover or the outside if the letter consisted of only one folded sheet. The epistle to Philemon is about the size of a single sheet of papyrus, so that the first Thessalonian letter would appear in the form of a small roll with this greeting at the beginning.

It is interesting to note how the apostle rings the changes on his introduction of himself to his readers. Mostly he begins his letters officially by calling himself Paul, an apostle of Jesus Christ (1 Cor. i. 1 ; 2 Cor. i. 1 ; Eph. i. 1 ; Col. i. 1, etc.). Here he is simply *Paul*, partly no doubt because he is writing to a Church with which he is on particularly friendly terms, partly because he had no need to insist on his apostolic authority. When he writes to his beloved Philippians, the other Macedonian congregation, he is equally intimate (Phil. i. 1), as in the very personal letter to Philemon. Whereas in the Galatian letter, where he is nettled at their challenge of his authority, he emphasizes his apostolic status at length (Gal. i. 1).

In his greeting he associates with himself **Silvanus and Timothy,** who were with him in Corinth when this letter was written in A.D. 50. They had been Paul's companions on the second missionary journey during which the Church at Thessalonica had been founded, as Barnabas and Mark had been on the first journey into Asia Minor. Their relative positions were also similar, Silvanus and Barnabas being older men of some standing in the Church, while Mark and Timothy were junior colleagues under instruction. **Silvanus,** whom Paul always calls by the commoner Gentile form of his name, is the Silas of Acts xv. 22, who is described as a prominent member of the brotherhood at Jerusalem, a prophet (xv. 32), and a Roman citizen (xvi. 37-8). We first hear of him as one of the deputies, appointed by the leaders of the Mother Church there, to convey to Antioch the official decision of the Council on the relative position of Jews and Gentiles in the Christian Church. When Paul and Barnabas at the outset of the second journey quarrelled over John Mark (Acts xv. 37) and separated, Silvanus was selected by Paul to take Barnabas's place (xv. 40). They journeyed together through Asia Minor over ground already covered by Paul, and then broke new ground by crossing into Europe. Both at Philippi (xvi. 19 ff.) and Thessalonica (xvii. 4, 10) Silvanus's name is coupled with Paul's as joint-founder of the new Churches there. Burkitt (*Christian Beginnings*, pp. 128 ff.) even suggests that Silvanus was the author of the Thessalonian epistles (see Introduction).

Timothy, on the other hand, was a much younger man (Phil. ii. 22) whom Paul had attached to himself on his second journey as an assistant (Acts xvi. 1-3). He was presumably at Thessalonica when the Church was founded, though he is not specifically mentioned in Acts. But his chief right to be associated with Paul and Silvanus in this triple greeting is that it was he who was sent by Paul from Athens to strengthen the young Thessalonian Church in a difficult time (1 iii. 2), and who, on his return to Paul, by this time settled in Corinth, brought back such a good report that this letter was written (1 iii. 6-7).

The greeting is addressed **to the church of the Thessalonians in God the Father and the Lord Jesus Christ**, a phrase which is obviously meant to be taken as a whole. In this form it is unique among the Pauline greetings, but it is none the less a clear expression of his view of the nature of the Church. The word *Ecclesia*, Greek for our English *Church*, was in common use in pagan society. It meant any ordinary secular collection of people. But it meant much more to the Dispersion Jews and the devout pagans who frequented the synagogue, for their Greek Bible had taught them to think of the Ecclesia as a very special kind of assembly, namely, the congregation of Israel, the Chosen People, the People of God. To them the

3

message of the early Christian missionaries was that the old Ecclesia, Israel, had failed ; the Chosen People had been rejected ; they had crucified the Messiah instead of acclaiming Him ; and now their inheritance had been taken from them and given to the New Israel, the New Ecclesia, the Christian Church. In this they were clearly following the intention of Jesus, whose actions in such matters as choosing twelve disciples, and instituting a New Covenant at the Last Supper, as well as His words in a parable like that of the Vineyard, or a saying like ' I am come not to destroy, but to fulfil,' can only thus be understood (see J. W. Bowman, *The Intention of Jesus*).

Paul sees this new Ecclesia, this new People of God, as inheriting all the best of the old dispensation without its racial and legalistic limitations, and universalized and infused by the living Spirit of the risen Lord. The new Ecclesia is the Body of Christ, indissolubly joined in spiritual union with its Head, who alone gives it life. Wherever Paul founds a little congregation of believers, he never sees them in isolation, but always as part of this great new Ecclesia, whether they are at Corinth, or Philippi, or Rome. Perhaps in the early letters to the Thessalonians and Galatians this idea is not so fully formed in Paul's mind as later on. In this case he writes to the Ecclesia **of the Thessalonians** (cf. Gal. i. 2) as if he were thinking of the local gathering as a detached unit, rather than as local representatives of the universal Church, as for example when he writes to the Ecclesia of God in Corinth (1 Cor. i. 2 ; 2 Cor. i. 1). The Thessalonian Church was at this time most likely very small indeed, and probably not very distinguished ; perhaps a kitchen-meeting of working-class folk in Jason's house (Acts xvii. 5 ff.). But for Paul it was part of the New Humanity, for its life was hid **in God the Father and the Lord Jesus Christ.**

This unusual phrase, only found here and in 2 Thess. i. 1, might simply be a round-about way of saying ' Christian,' and mean that Paul wants to distinguish the Ecclesia to which he refers from any merely secular ecclesia by adding ' in God the Father,' and from any confusion with the synagogue by adding ' and (in) the Lord Jesus Christ.' But it would probably

4

be truer to Paul's mind to see the phrase with its characteristic use of ' In '—a phrase never found in the Synoptics and seldom in the New Testament outside of Paul's letters—as yet another way of expressing his conviction that each local Church is part of the great Fellowship, bound up in God through Christ. The members of the little Ecclesia at Thessalonica were in Paul's eyes and their own really living **in God** as truly as they lived in the air they breathed. They were part of His New Creation, Redeemed Humanity, enjoying a new life—in a sense sharing God's own life—through their membership of the Body of Christ. It was through this corporate experience and not just as individuals that they knew Him as **the Father** in a deeper relationship and understanding than was possible to Jews and pagans who also recognized the Fatherhood of God. Paul's highest title for the Creator of the universe is the Father of our Lord Jesus Christ (Rom. xv. 6 ; 2 Cor. i. 3, etc.).

But it is when he adds **and [in] the Lord Jesus Christ** that his own distinctive experience comes to light. Paul was above all a man ' in Christ.' From his conversion to his death he lived in a new dimension, a new atmosphere. Whether he clearly distinguished between life ' in Christ ' and life ' in the Spirit ' is difficult to say. What he would certainly have said was that life for him had no meaning unless it was lived in the presence of Jesus. A. D. Nock, like Deissmann, describes Paul's conception of life ' in Christ ' as being as vital a relationship as that of a fish to water ; it is the spiritual counterpart of the physical union of man and woman (1 Cor. vi. 15–17). We are either ' in Christ ' or ' in Adam '—who for Paul symbolized all that is involved in being purely human, in experiencing death, sin, decay. To be ' in Adam ' is to live in animated death. The Christian, however, has been called out of life ' in Adam ' to life ' in Christ.' Thereby he becomes one, not only with Christ, but with all his fellow-Christians who are part of Christ's Body (*St. Paul*, pp. 150–1). He is ' in Christ ' in being part of the Fellowship of which Christ is the Head ; but in a phrase such as this, where it would seem almost as if ' in the Lord Jesus Christ ' meant simply membership of the new Ecclesia, the Body of Christ, we must not overlook the fact that for Paul this meant no mechanical or paper membership, but the real vital living relationship of each Thessalonian man or woman with Jesus.

When he calls Jesus **Lord,** he is giving Him the title *Kurios* which the Christian community from the earliest days applied to Him (cf. Acts ii. 36, vii. 59). It has therefore nothing to do with the *Kurios* of the mystery-religions, any more than with the *Kurios* which was the official title of the Roman Emperors. As Burkitt says, Paul's knowledge of the mystery-religions was probably no more profound than the average cleric's acquaintance with the theory of Evolution (*Christian Beginnings,* p. 107). The clue is, as in the case of Ecclesia, to be sought in the Septuagint, where the word is used as the Greek version of Jehovah. What the Old Testament therefore said of God, His status and authority, the early Christians said of the risen and exalted **Jesus** of Nazareth. It was also their conviction, however, that Jesus was the **Christ,** the long-promised Messiah of Jewish expectation, to whose coming the whole of the Old Testament pointed. The whole name, therefore, **Lord Jesus Christ,** and the significance of each of its component parts and of all of them in conjunction, was essentially pre-Pauline, the faith of the Church from the beginning. Paul's contribution was to deepen its meaning through his own experience and reflection (see Anderson Scott, *Christianity According to St. Paul,* chap. VI).

At the end of the address comes the greeting itself : **grace and peace to you.** This is Paul's usual formula at the beginning of his letters—generally with the addition ' from God our Father and the Lord Jesus Christ ' (cf. 2 i. 1). The A.V. has this ending, but the best MSS. omit it. When Claudius Lysias writes to Felix (Acts xxiii. 26), he prefaces his letter with the word *chairein,* which is very like this word translated ' grace '—*charis.* It was the ordinary pagan word of greeting. Similarly, ' peace be unto you ' in its various forms (O.T. *Shalom*) was like the universal ' Salaam ' to-day, the ordinary greeting of the Middle East, e.g. Judges xix. 20. It would almost seem as if Paul, in devising his formula, was

making a play on the Greek word *chairein*, and combining with
it the Jewish salutation—a combination which an older commentator calls ' that union of Asiatic repose and European
alacrity ' !—to form a distinctively Christian partnership that
went very much farther than either. So he greets them, not
just with good wishes, but with a prayer that **grace** may be
granted them—that unmerited gift of God's love to men
through Christ, forgiving, strengthening, uplifting them ;
making them at one with Him, and thereby giving them the
peace that passes all understanding, the inward tranquillity,
health, and soundness of life in harmony with God. The
grace and **peace,** of course, derive the only meaning they have
from the nine words which precede them. It is also possible
that the phrase **grace and peace to you** is older than Paul. Its
occurrence—with the addition of ' from God the Father and
the Lord Jesus Christ '—so frequently in his letters (see note
on 2 i. 1) suggests that it may be either a liturgical formula of
the early Church, part of a confession of faith, or a recognized
form of blessing.

II. THANKSGIVING FOR THE GOOD PROGRESS OF THE THESSALONIAN CHURCH

(i. 2–10)

We always thank God for you all when we mention you con- 2
stantly in our prayers, as we recall your active faith and 3
labour of love and patient hope in our Lord Jesus Christ,
before our God and Father. O brothers beloved by God, 4
we know he has chosen you ; for our gospel came to you 5
not with mere words but with power and with the holy
Spirit, with ample conviction on our part (you know what
we were to you, for your own good), and you started to 6
copy us and the Lord, welcoming the word, though it
brought you heavy trouble, with a joy inspired by the holy
Spirit. Thus you became a pattern to all the believers in 7
Macedonia and in Achaia ; for the word of the Lord has 8

7

9

10

resounded from you not only through Macedonia and Achaia—no, your faith in God has reached every place. We never need to speak about it. People tell us of their own accord about the visit we paid to you, and how you turned to God from idols, to serve a living and a real God and to wait for the coming of his Son from heaven—the Son whom he raised from the dead, Jesus who rescues us from the Wrath to come.

After the greeting comes a prayer of thankfulness to God in the usual sequence of the Pauline letters—all except the letter to the Galatians, where he gives them the sharp edge of his tongue instead. The reason for his thanksgiving here is the outstanding witness of the Thessalonian Church. It is therefore no conventional formality, but a real outpouring of gratitude to God. Despite persecution, they have remained constant in the faith which was preached to them ; the success of the mission has become a byword throughout the whole Church as a result of the lives and works of the Thessalonian members and the obvious presence of the Spirit in their midst.

When Paul uses the plural here—**we** thank God, **our** Gospel, etc.—does he mean Silvanus, Timothy, and himself, or is he merely using the ' literary plural ' ? There is no hard-and-fast answer to this question. ' I ' and ' we ' seem to be interchangeable both in Paul's other epistles (e.g. 1 Cor. ix. 11 ; cf. 1 Cor. ix. 15) and in the general style of letter-writing of the times. In the two Thessalonian letters, however, the plural is used throughout—which is not the case elsewhere. In the others (e.g. 1 Corinthians, Galatians, Philippians, Philemon), after an introductory greeting in which Paul associates with himself Sosthenes, or Timothy, or the ' brethren ' generally, he immediately switches to the first person singular. It seems, therefore, that in the two Thessalonian letters, owing to the fact that Silvanus and Timothy had played some considerable part in the mission and were with him at the time of writing, we ought to associate them with Paul whenever he speaks in the plural, where it is at all possible, though, of course, in the last resort Paul is himself the primary author (see Milligan, op. cit., pp. 131–2).

We always thank God for you all when we mention you con- 2
stantly in our prayers.

When Paul, after his great apologia to the Corinthians
(2 Cor. xi.), adds that not the least of his burdens is the care
of all the Churches (ver. 28), he is using no empty words. Here
is part of the burden, a constant intercession for the little
Christian communities he had founded. Paul gave his life to
this task—' This one thing I do '—and it was not a matter of
establishing a Church and leaving it to its own devices, or even
of keeping an ever-watchful eye and a ready ear open for its
trials and misfortunes, but a never-ceasing holding up of each
Church and its members to God for His blessing. Here, then,
is a glimpse of the daily prayer life of the three missionaries,
joining together wherever they happen to be, or alone if need
be, in laying the needs of the different Churches before God,
and in the case of Thessalonica thanking Him for His goodness towards it. **Always** and **constantly** are the operative
words, and both of them ring true. An older commentator
remarks ' there are some prayers in Homer's poems but how
few thanksgivings,' and he goes on to quote the Puritan who
said ' Grace (i.e. gratitude) is like a ring without end : and the
diamond of this ring is constancy.' It is worth noting that
this thanksgiving is all the more from the heart, in that the
apostles can thank God for **all** the Thessalonians. There are
no waverers, no disaffected members, no trouble-makers.
Next to the Philippian Church, the Thessalonian congregation
would seem to have filled Paul with greatest joy.

Then comes the reason for the constant thanksgiving—**as we** 3
recall your active faith and labour of love and patient hope in
our Lord Jesus Christ, before our God and Father. This is
what they thank God for, not vaguely for unspecified well-
doing, but for the concrete evidence of the virtues of faith,
love, and hope, in action. Here, indeed, as Calvin says, is ' a
short definition of true Christianity,' and the great Christian
triad of Graces, so classically rounding off the wonderful hymn
in praise of Charity (1 Cor. xiii.), now makes its first appearance in Paul's writings. It occurs so frequently in the New
Testament, both in Paul and elsewhere, that it would seem to

9

have been part of the pre-Pauline tradition of the Church and to have been regarded as the hall-mark of the Christian life. (Cf. 1 v. 8 ; Col. i. 4–5 ; Gal. v. 5–6 ; Rom. v. 2–5 ; Heb. vi. 10–12 ; 1 Pet. i. 21–2, etc.) In the Corinthian hymn the triad is progressive from the faith that is child-like, through the hope that is saint-like, to the love that is God-like, as Eadie puts it (*Commentary on Thessalonians*, p. 38). But the present order is faith, love, hope, and in a way it is a better order. For as Lightfoot says, ' Faith rests on the past ; love works in the present ; hope looks to the future.' (See on Col. i. 4–5.) St. James would heartily endorse the combination of the words **active** and **faith**. The Greek reads literally, ' Recalling your work of faith,' and ' faith ' is clearly what produces the ' work.' The problem of Paul's Roman and Galatian letters to distinguish between Christian ' faith ' and the merit-earning ' works ' of the Jewish law is obviously not here in his mind. Here, as indeed in a real sense everywhere, he sees faith and action as inseparable. He believed, like St. James, that faith that does not issue in works is dead (Jas. ii. 17). And, however he uses the word **faith**—and there is a variety of uses in his letters—it is true to say that it is for him fundamentally a personal relationship of trust and loyalty to Christ. It is the same attitude to the risen and ever-present Lord as Jesus on earth demanded of His followers—the self-surrender and affection of little children. It is man's response to God's love ; the converse of grace. That for Paul was the characteristic of a Christian—not intellectual assent to a system of beliefs. As such it could not do other than issue in action. As Christ's disciples, Christians must do His will and, however falteringly and imperfectly, continue His work of helping, healing, serving, praying. There is no Christian faith without Christian works. This, Paul rejoices to see, the Thessalonians have grasped.

Such a faith is inseparable from **love**—the second of the triad—for as Paul says elsewhere : faith works through love (Gal. v. 6). Love is at once the greatest of the Christian virtues and the most original. At the moment there is much to be said for a return to the fine A.V. rendering ' charity. ' Unlike nineteenth-century Christianity, our danger lies not so much in a confusion of Christian charity with almsgiving, as in the debasing of the whole concept of love by twentieth-century films and dance-bands. It was the claim of the Church—largely justified—that by substituting Christian *Agapë* for pagan *Eros* it had created a new and distinctive attitude to life. For Christian love is briefly the reproduction in our everyday affairs of Jesus' attitude to the men and women of His time. Here Paul speaks of the Thessalonians' **labour of love.** This is obviously the result of their faith. Their trust and loyalty towards Jesus must not only express themselves in action, but inspire them to the more toilsome and costly service of love ; that *gemina caritas*, as the old Latin hymnologists called it, the twin-love that is towards our Lord for Himself and our neighbours for His sake. This is therefore not merely an action that is done willingly, without hope of reward, as we understand a ' labour of love ' to-day.

Parallel with the triad of Christian Graces, Paul constructs a triad of these virtues expressed in workaday life. ' Faith ' produces ' work,' ' love ' produces ' labour,' ' hope ' produces ' endurance '—an ascending scale of the fruits of the Christian believer. Perhaps, when Paul speaks of their **active faith,** he is thinking of their ordinary everyday witness as Christians, while their **labour of love** is more the tiresome, exhausting, often discouraging work of missionary service. When he speaks of his own evangelistic efforts, labour (*kopos*) is the word he uses (iii. 5 ; 2 Cor. x. 15), as likewise when he speaks of his own toiling to support himself so as not to be a burden upon anyone (ii. 9 ; 2 iii. 8). There may indeed be some reference here to the difficulty of raising money for missionary work in Thessalonica.

The third feature of life in the Thessalonian Church which the apostle recalls with thankfulness is their **patient hope. Hope,** though clearly bound up with faith and love, was perhaps more than either of them the differentiating mark between the Christian and the pagan attitude to life. The pagan had little to look forward to : for himself a speculative immortality of the soul; for the world, who knows ?—perhaps at best an eternally recurring cycle of history. The Christian, however, like the Jew, did not regard hope for the future as a pleasant piece of self-deception, but as a fundamental basis for living. The Jew had his hope of the coming of the Messiah, the Christian, in those early days especially, transferred this hope to the speedy return of Christ. It is in this primitive sense that the phrase is used here. It was their hope in the Parousia that made them **patient.** This had obviously played a leading part in the apostle's first preaching to the Thessalonians, as it did everywhere in the early mission, and, as it happens, it is problems connected with it that form the distinctive feature of these letters. Perhaps **patient** is not the best translation here. The Greek word *hypomené* means rather ' endurance ' and ' perseverance .' Paul's meaning is, then, that it is their hope of Christ's coming which has nerved them to endure the trials and opposition, and, no doubt, persecution, which have beset them. There is thus a climax to the triad of Work, Toil, and Endurance as the expression of the Christian virtues of Faith, Love, and Hope.

This part of the sentence would be expected to end at the word ' Hope.' The clauses **in our Lord Jesus Christ, before our God and Father** are characteristic Pauline expansions. Paul's sentences, as Jowett said, ' grow under his hand.' Both clauses may refer to Hope, when the meaning would be ' your patient hope (in the Coming) of our Lord Jesus Christ, a hope to which you hold fast as men who live in the very presence of God the Father Himself.' (On the other hand, of course, ' before our God and Father ' may refer back to the verb ' recall ' ; viz. we recall before our God and Father your faith, love, and hope.) But it seems a pity—and grammatically unnecessary—to limit these expansive phrases to a comment on Hope. Rather would it be in keeping with Pauline thought in general to see them both as referring back to the whole Christian life of the Thessalonians as being ' in Christ.' Their works of faith and love and hope were no achievements of their own. They were possible only because the Thessalonians were part of the mystical Body of Christ—they manifested the Christian Graces because they were ' in the Lord Jesus Christ.'

Paul then, as it were, leads his thought up to its climax : ' And these, faith, love, and hope, are Christian graces which can only flower in the Christian community through the power of Christ, nay more, which can only be truly manifested by men who are consciously living in the presence of God our Father.'

Moffatt (like the A.V.) breaks up into shorter sentences a 4 typically Pauline period which begins at verse 2 and ends with verse 5. This has advantages and disadvantages. One disadvantage is that it destroys the climactic effect of the next clause. The apostles *make mention of* the Thessalonians in their prayers ; as they *recall* their faith, love, and hope ; because they *are convinced* from what has happened that God has chosen them. This is the ultimate ground of their thanksgiving in verse 2. And not only did their good works and labours and endurance (ver. 3) prove this, but also the nature of the apostles' campaign among them (ver. 5) and their reactions to it (vers. 6–7). So, says Paul, with a full heart, **O brothers beloved by God, we know he has chosen you. Brothers** has lost most of its significance as a mode of address between Christians, yet what a grand word it is ! It was in common enough use among the pagans and the Jews (Acts ii. 29, 37, iii. 17, etc.), but in early Christian use—and Paul uses it affectionately twenty-one times in the Thessalonian epistles alone—it implied the new relationship of brothers in Christ under God the Father. Here it comes to his mind immediately after using these very words. No doubt its Christian currency goes back to our Lord's own teaching (Matt. xii. 49, xxiii. 8). Because of Him the ' Hebrew of the Hebrews ' can say ' brother ' to the once-despised Gentiles. Now they are one in Christ. Not only are they loved as brothers by Paul, Silvanus, and Timothy, but they have always been **beloved by God** as His children. ' Having been loved ' (Greek perfect tense) does not imply a new relationship so much as an old relationship now made real. God loved them before they became Christian **brothers,** but only now do they fully know it. The phrase is unique in the New Testament, the nearest approach being 2 ii. 13. **We know He has chosen you** (literally ' knowing your election '—*eklogé*). Moffatt's translation makes plain what the Authorized Version obscures—the vital content of the word ' election.' It is above all a personal act of God. It is God's love in action—the Thessalonians are **beloved by God**, therefore **he has chosen** them. As Denney says (ad loc.), 'The doctrine of election has often been taught as if the one thing that could never be known about anybody was whether he was or was not elect'; and adds, ' the assumed impossibility does not square with New Testament ways of speaking.' Although Paul's idea of election is fundamentally supra-historical (cf. note on 2 ii. 13), and by his casual use of the word he implies that his readers knew what election meant, here it is quite clear that it is the practical issue that is in his mind. He concludes that the Thessalonians have been chosen by God, not because it is a necessary stage in some theological system he has devised, but because of what he has seen among them and heard about them (vers. 5 ff.). Obviously they had not chosen God. Their Christian witness was only possible because God had first selected them, a tiny handful in a pagan city, to be among the first to embody His Kingdom in Europe. They had responded finely; but the initiative was with the grace of God. Election for Paul is inseparably connected with love. God calls because God loves.

The use of the word **chosen** indicates here, as so often elsewhere in the New Testament, the predominant consciousness of the early Church that they were in an historic succession. The story of old Israel had been the story of a nation whom God had chosen out of the world to be His people, to spread His word, to do His will, to bring the Gentiles to the knowledge and service of the Most High. But that nation failed in its task ; and through the death and resurrection of Jesus Christ, who alone in Israel had offered to God the perfect obedience, a new day had dawned ; a new possibility for mankind had been created ; a new people had been constituted, the Christian Ecclesia, into which were being incorporated those who, whether Jew or Gentile, by God's grace were chosen to fulfil His purposes and who responded. This was the new chosen priesthood, the new holy nation, the new peculiar people (1 Pet. ii. 9) who inherited the hopes, privileges, and promises of the old (Deut. vii. 6–8)—and also their responsibilities. The election, or selection, or choice, is now spiritual and not national, into a new unit, the Israel of God (Gal. vi. 16). It is individual, not corporate—an ' election of grace ' (Rom. xi. 5). Why God had chosen old Israel—How odd, Of God, To choose The Jews—remains the classic posing of a problem that affects every man. Why God should choose one continent, one nation, one town, one man rather than another is the unsolved mystery of the doctrine of election. All we·know is that in fact He does. Sometimes we think we see part, at any rate, of the answer—in the case of the Jews what we are pleased to call their ' religious genius,' that in some at any rate of the rarer spirits among them answered God's call. As far as the ' election ' of the Thessalonians was concerned, it must have seemed afterwards to Paul that the events leading up to his visit there were singularly under the guidance of God. The failure to reach Bithynia as he intended, and the vision of the man from Macedonia (Acts xvi. 6, 9), all prepared his mind to see in the beginning of the European campaign a clear leading of the Holy Spirit.

When, therefore, in addition to these glimpses of the divine 5 purpose at work, Paul and his companions saw the remarkable results of the mission, their conviction that this was all in God's eternal plan was confirmed. Verse 5 deals with the subjective side of the proof, verse 6 with the objective. The Thessalonians had clearly been singled out by God (1) because of the unusual sense of mission that the writers themselves felt at the time (ver. 5), and (2) because of the eager response of the Thessalonians (ver. 6). **For our gospel came to you not with mere words** but with unmistakable signs of the working of the Spirit. **Our gospel,** that is, the common denominator of the Gospel or Good News (*Euangelion*) which formed the preaching of all the early missionaries, which Paul himself had received and in turn passed on (1 Cor. xv. 3 ff.). It is now generally recognized (see C. H. Dodd, *The Apostolic Preaching and its Developments*), firstly, that there was a common proclamation (*kērygma*) of the Good News in the early Church, and secondly, of what it consisted. This common *kērygma* is assumed in all of Paul's letters—as indeed in the whole of the New Testament (see A. M. Hunter, *The Unity of the New Testament*). The earliest indications of its contents in the sermons in Acts (e.g. x. 36–43), and Pauline allusions to what he himself did not originate but merely handed on (e.g. Rom. x. 9 ; 1 Cor. xi. 23), show that from the beginning it was a full-blooded offer of salvation through Jesus Christ. Old Testament prophecy has been fulfilled ; the Messiah has come ; Jesus of Nazareth, who did mighty works, died for our sins and rose again, has been exalted to the right hand of God and will soon come again in judgment. Therefore repent, believe, and be saved while there is yet time. This common background must be understood behind all the various facets which Paul stresses in his letters, now emphasizing one point, now another. In our present epistles, we must not imagine because they deal at length with the return of Christ, that therefore that had been the main theme of Paul's missionary preaching at Thessalonica. His **gospel** to them there was the same as to the other Churches he founded, but part of the need for these letters arose because this question of the Parousia was the feature of the *kērygma* which the Thessalonians found most perplexing.

It need hardly be added, therefore, that when Paul says **our gospel** he means no more than ' the gospel which we preach.' It was not his gospel, but God's gospel (ii. 8, 9) or Christ's gospel (iii. 2 ; 2 i. 8), the apostles' job was to proclaim it (ii. 4, 9). On the other hand, he can call it in a real sense **our gospel** because it was as much Good News for the apostles as for their hearers. They were offering something which now for them was Life itself. The word Paul uses for **came** conveys the idea, not simply of the gospel's coming through the visit of the apostles, but that their coming with the gospel was under an impulse beyond themselves. He rather thinks of the gospel itself, not as a dead letter, but as a living force— ' God's saving power ' (Rom. i. 16) that ' came upon them ' (cf. 2 iii. 1).

Therefore, harking back in his mind to the circumstances in which he first proclaimed it to them, he recalled that it had not

been **with mere words but with power and with the holy Spirit,
with ample conviction on our part.** He and his companions
had had no sense that the issue was at all in doubt, or fear that
their message might fall on deaf ears, or lack of confidence in
themselves. Paul knew what it was to be prevented from
preaching at all (Acts xvi. 6 ff.), as well as to engage in many
a bout of barren controversy with the Jews, when his words
must have seemed empty rhetoric. There was too, no doubt,
vividly in his mind the contrast between his reception at
Thessalonica and the opening of his campaign in Corinth, the
very place from which he was writing this letter, where he
came before them ' in weakness and fear and great trembling '
(1 Cor. ii. 3) and had to be assured by God that, despite appearances, He had ' many people in this city ' (Acts xviii. 10).
How different things had been in Macedonia. There they felt
themselves mightily moved and inspired, and that it was no
mere human-eloquence—or in Calvin's phrase, ' the idle and
dead eloquence of men '—that they uttered. They were in a
real sense ' beyond themselves.' Paul says the same thing in
his letter to the Corinthians : ' What I preached did not rest
on the plausible arguments of wisdom, but on the proof sup-
plied by the Spirit and its power ' (1 ii. 4).

With power (*dynamis*) here does not mean, as it sometimes
does in the epistles (usually in the plural), outward signs of
the presence of the Holy Spirit during a campaign, such as
speaking with tongues, healing, and other miracles, but simply
the sense the preachers had themselves that their message
was striking home, and that they were possessed of more than
ordinary fervour as they spoke. They knew how little they
were able to do of themselves and what they were up against.
Only power given to them from beyond themselves could
accomplish the task, and this power they were sure was none
other than the **holy Spirit.** For this they had our Lord's
own word : ' You will receive power when the holy Spirit
comes upon you ' (Acts i. 8), and ' The Spirit of truth who
issues from the Father, he will bear witness to me ; and you
too are witnesses ' (John xv. 26–7). The apostle, as Denney
says, came to Thessalonica ' aglow with Christian passion.'

Paul did not rule out other possible sources of power, unholy spirits (cf. 2 ii. 9), but at Thessalonica he had been unusually conscious that they were speaking for God. Their message was delivered with full inward **conviction** and assurance, or as the Geneva Bible said, ' In muche certaintie of persuasion.' As confirmation, the apostles then ask their readers to recall the impression they made upon them themselves—**you know what we were to you, for your own good.** The manner in which the apostles had conducted the mission, the obvious fact that they were men inspired, and that they were prepared to spend themselves utterly to bring the Thessalonians to the knowledge of God's love in Christ ; not least, their daily labours to support themselves ; and all this obviously for the sake of the Thessalonians themselves, showed what kind of men God had enabled them to be. In the next chapter, verses 1-12, Paul returns to this point and elaborates it.

6   After this argument from the apostles' own experience during the mission comes (ver. 6) the objective ground for their conviction that the Thessalonians had been specially chosen by God (ver. 4), viz. their response to the preaching of the gospel. **And you started to copy us and the Lord.** Here ' you ' is emphatic—literally ' you on your part came to be imitators of us and of the Lord ' : not merely ' followers ' as in the A.V. This rather startling sentence, in which on the surface the Lord takes second place to the apostles, is, of course, not an example of Pauline megalomania. In one sense it is the only possible way in which the idea could have been expressed, in that for the early converts the most real instruction in the Christian way had to come through seeing it lived out in the practice of the missionaries themselves. In copying them they were copying Christ. The same is true of Africa, China, and India to-day. But in a deeper sense it gives us a real insight into the apostle's mind. The addition of **and the Lord** is almost like an instantaneous self-correction. No sooner does Paul speak of his own good example than (as in 1 Cor. xv. 10) he hastens to add in effect : ' Yet not I, but the grace of God which was with me ' (cf. Gal. ii. 20 ; Phil. iv. 13). It is once more an expression of the profound sense the apostle

had that they were men ' in Christ.' They did not live among the Thessalonians as good men setting a fine pattern of Christian life, but as men possessed by Christ. They were able to speak of Christ and themselves in the same breath without self-consciousness, because they were Christ-men. What they did He was doing in them and for them. The Thessalonians, then, were enabled to become imitators of the apostles because they now shared the same power—this was the real proof of their election (ver. 4).

It was not so much an Imitatio Christi of the Thomas à Kempis variety, covering the whole range of Christian conduct, that the apostle referred to, as a distinctive temper and tone that the new converts evinced in **welcoming the word, though it brought you heavy trouble, with a joy inspired by the holy Spirit.** Joy—despite heavy trouble, despite affliction, this is the real mark of God's people ; it is the perennial Christian paradox. The Thessalonians, in their response to the apostles' mission, displayed the characteristic tokens of the Christian life and proved thereby that they had been chosen by God. They became imitators of Christ, obviously not by **welcoming the word,** that is, the Good News of Christ which the apostles preached to them, but by displaying the same victorious mastery over outward circumstances as He did. It is thus clear that in these pre-Marcan days the Thessalonians knew something of the events of Jesus' life. **Heavy trouble** was, of course, the inevitable meed of an early Christian community. St. Paul had experienced it in bodily hurt and mental anguish. Opposition, hatred, and violence had pursued him from the day of his conversion, principally from his kinsmen the Jews, and in this he shared the experience of his Lord. Paul would, however, have said with Luther : ' If Christ wore a crown of thorns, why should His followers expect only a crown of roses ? ' The Thessalonians had found their path no easier. Hostility beset them from the very beginning, while the apostle was with them, and after he had left (Acts xvii. 6 ; I ii. 14 ; iii. 2, 3 ; 2 i. 4). To accept the Gospel openly in a pagan city was to court, not only derision, but opprobrium. We simply cannot appreciate to-day what it must have cost

in terms of family, friends, society, to become a follower of the
Way. The nearest parallel is perhaps the Hindu Christian to-
day.

But what singled out the Thessalonian Christians, what
gave rise to the apostle's strong affection for them, and put
the coping-stone on his conviction that they were indeed under
a special dispensation of God, was that despite all their
afflictions they had received the gospel **with a joy inspired by
the holy Spirit.** This paradoxical Christian experience and
witness was one which was very real to the apostle himself.
It had been the epitome of his own life since conversion—the
sense of Christ's victory over his own weakness ; of a power
within him stronger than any evil that befell him ; that enabled him to glory in his own frailty that was nevertheless
strong through Christ ; dying but alive ; grieved but always
glad ; without a penny but possessed of all (2 Cor. vi. 9–10).
This is no stoical resignation in face of fortune's arrows. It is
a consequence of a vital, buoyant Christian faith which among
other things makes possible the acceptance of life's *viae
dolorosae* as evil that God can transmute into good. The
Christian gospel says much more than just ' Grin and bear it.'
' I never knew,' said Rutherford, ' by my nine years' preaching,
so much of Christ's love as He hath taught me in Aberdeen
by six months' imprisonment.' All of us in lesser degrees
know that the same is true in our own experience, if in less
dramatic ways. In sharing this characteristically new experience—a mark indeed of a new order of being—the Thessalonians were in a true sense imitators of the apostle as he was
of Christ Jesus ' who for the joy that was set before Him en-
dured the cross, despising the shame ' (Heb. xii. 2). The
Macedonian Churches generally are specially commended by
Paul for exhibiting this new combination of outward suffering
and inward gladness (2 Cor. viii. 1–2)—the deepest grounds
for which are to be found in Paul's profound conception of the
Christian man's part in making up the full sum of all that
Christ has to suffer on behalf of His Body, the Church (Col.
i. 24). It is worth noting that in verses 5 and 6 Paul introduces the Holy Spirit in a way that indicates that his readers

were well acquainted with His active presence in the Fellowship, and that in the first few verses of this very early Christian letter the doctrine of the Holy Trinity is clearly implied.

St. Paul then goes on to show a further proof that Christianity is caught not taught. The supreme example of Christ, imitated in turn by the apostles and the Thessalonians, is communicated through them to others : **Thus you became a pattern to all the believers in Macedonia and in Achaia.** The Thessalonians, from being followers, became themselves leaders—an invariable rule of the Christian life—and St. Paul thinks of their leadership, not as individual, but collective. It is the new Church as a whole that is the **pattern.** The Greek word *typos* used here meant, among other things, the stamp made by a die. The idea in the apostle's mind is probably that the Thessalonians, having been stamped with the likeness of Christ, became themselves a die for stamping others. It is clear that the witness of the Thessalonian Church was outstanding. Paul calls no other ' a model Church.' They became, not merely a shining example to their pagan contemporaries, but **to all the believers**—to their Christian brethren—which is a much more difficult thing. **Macedonia** and **Achaia** were the northern and southern provinces into which the Romans divided territory more or less equivalent to modern Greece. No doubt Paul is thinking here, in the first instance at any rate, of the towns in which he had founded Churches—Philippi, Beroea, Athens, and Corinth. Philippi and Beroea, like Thessalonica, were in Macedonia. Corinth—from which he was writing this letter—was the capital of Achaia. Athens, though strictly not part of Achaia, was situated in it. While Paul was at Corinth, not only did Timothy's report (Acts xviii. 5 ; 1 iii. 6), dealing with the spread of the faith in Macedonia, give credit to the Thessalonians, but the apostle must have had some opportunity of assessing the value of the Thessalonian Church's example in Achaia. Paul had a penchant for talking in terms of provinces. He says Cilicia when he probably means Tarsus, and Syria when he means Antioch (Gal. i. 21). It is a corrective to our tendency to think of the early Church as an affair of the

7

cities, because this preference for speaking of provinces suggests rather what was in fact true, that the faith generally spread from the town missions into the highways and byways (cf. iv. 10 ; 2 Cor. i. 1).

8   In amplification of his last statement, the apostle becomes more explicit—**for the word of the Lord has resounded from you not only through Macedonia and Achaia—no, your faith in God has reached every place. We never need to speak about it.**   Paul uses this phrase **the word of the Lord** only here and in the second Thessalonian letter (2 iii. 1).   Clearly he means the same as the other expressions of the same kind which he uses elsewhere ; the Word, the Word of God, the Word of Christ, the Gospel of God, the Gospel of Christ, the Gospel of our Lord Jesus, and our Gospel (ver. 5).   All of them are technical terms for the common content of the missionaries' message, the Good News of salvation, which is ' a word having the Lord for its origin, its centre, and its end ' (Eadie, op. cit., p. 47).   In their reading of the Old Testament, Christian converts knew the ' Word of the Lord ' as signifying what God had to say to men.   But for Christians now the Gospel was *par excellence* the Word of God to man in Jesus Christ, the Lord of all.   This Good News from God, says Paul, **has resounded from you** like the clarion call of a trumpet —perhaps the silver trumpets of the Temple—or the crash of thunder—and not as a nine days' wonder, but continuously **has** resounded and still does.   The meaning is not only that the Thessalonians themselves had become a great new centre for the propagation of the Gospel, but that the news of events in Thessalonica, the remarkable conversions, the zeal and fervour of the little community in the midst of persecution, made a profound impression wherever it was recounted.   The very telling of it won new converts.

In this sense also the Thessalonians acted as a summons to believe the Word of the Lord which echoed, **not only through Macedonia and Achaia,** but everywhere.   In a similar vein Paul speaks later of the Word of the Lord ' speeding on ' (2 iii. 1 ; cf. note on ii. 13).   Macedonia and Achaia are here intended to be taken together as meaning Greece in contradistinction to the rest of the world, not as two separate provinces as in the previous verse. This sentence, which looks from the Greek as if it should stop at ' in every place,' is an example of Pauline impetuosity which Moffatt disguises by changing the order. Literally it reads : ' From you there has sounded forth the Word of the Lord, not only in Macedonia and Achaia, but in every place.' . . . Then it is as if the apostle, thinking rightly that this is going a bit too far—after all, there were limits to the influence of the Thessalonian Church and the world was a big place—decides to tone it down somewhat, which he does by adding a fresh idea in the characteristic Pauline manner, this time in less flamboyant vein—prose for poetry. So, after ' in every place,' he tacks on ' your faith towards God has gone forth so that there is no need for us to say anything.' Moffatt, however, though he covers up this interesting train of thought, produces more or less the same result : **no, your faith in God has reached every place** (literally : your faith which is towards God ; A.V. to God-ward). Their faith **in God** is stressed in contrast to the faith in idols which they had renounced and which is mentioned in the following verse. The good report of their faith had **reached every place** (literally, ' has gone out '). It seems as if Paul, still thinking in terms of ' resounding,' may have had Ps. xix. 4 in mind, which he quotes in a similar sense in Rom. x. 18.

There in the LXX (xviii. 4) this word is used of the glory of God in nature which is proclaimed to the ends of the earth. So the fame of the Thessalonians has been noised abroad in **every place.** This may be Pauline enthusiasm (cf. Rom. i. 8), or colloquial hyperbole like ' every schoolboy knows ' or ' *tout le monde sait*,' or it may have a basis in fact. Aquila and Priscilla had arrived at Corinth from Rome shortly before this epistle was written (Acts xviii. 2). If they had heard of the Thessalonian Church in the capital of the Empire and informed Paul, it is not so far off the mark to say that what Rome knew the world knew. It is quite likely, for example, that the charge of treason levelled against the Thessalonian Christians (Acts xvii. 6–7) would be reported in Rome. At all events it

23

is clear that the Thessalonian mission had been an outstanding success and a subject for general comment—and on the part of Christians for deep thanksgiving. The town was so placed and such a commercial centre that travellers and merchants probably became the Church's best advertising agents, more so if some of them were Christians. The success of the mission was apparently the most impressive thing that had so far happened in the history of the Church. It might be mentioned that it was not only then that Thessalonica was renowned as a pre-eminently Christian community. 'No city has had so distinguished a Christian history, with the single exception of the Syrian Antioch. . . . The heroic age of Thessalonica was the third century. It was the bulwark of Constantinople in the shock of the barbarians ; and it held up the torch of the truth to the successive tribes who overspread the country between the Danube and the Aegean. . . . Thus, in the mediaeval chroniclers it has deserved the name of the Orthodox City' (Conybeare and Howson, *The Life and Epistles of St. Paul*, p. 249). So great, then, was the fame of the gospel and the fame of the Thessalonians' new faith, and so quickly had it spread, that the apostles could add : **We never need to speak about it.** Everyone was talking about it. The apostles found when they began to extol the Thessalonian Church its merits were already known and their own reputation correspondingly enhanced.

9   Why the apostles never need to speak about the exciting story of the Thessalonian Church is now related. It is because **people tell us of their own accord about the visit we paid to you.** Before the apostles, during their travels in the two provinces, have a chance to talk about their successful mission, they find that not only are the facts known, but strangers from all parts keep bringing up the subject themselves. By a slight alteration in the Greek, the sentence could read : ' You ' tell us of ' your ' own accord, etc. Rendel Harris has therefore suggested that the whole epistle is in reply to a letter sent by the hand of Timothy from the Thessalonians to Paul. But as any such letter is conjectural, it seems a trifle gratuitous to establish its existence by another conjecture (cf. note on ii. 13).

Not only is it common knowledge that the apostolic mission has been an outstanding success, but equally well known is the reaction of the Thessalonians. Here Paul sheds some interesting light on what at this point in the history of the Church seems to have been the approach to paganism from Christianity, and on what were accepted as the tokens of conversion : **and how you turned to God from idols, to serve a living and a real God and to wait for the coming of his Son from heaven—the Son whom he raised from the dead, Jesus who rescues us from the Wrath to come.** There are thus two aspects of accomplished conversion from paganism to Christianity : one, the renunciation of idolatry in favour of monotheism, and two, the establishment of the centrality of the Person of Christ, with a sense of the urgency of decision. This passage would appear to be in Paul's mind a summary of the presentation of the Christian gospel to the Thessalonians. The fact that the mission had gone according to this programme is taken by him to be part of the proof that they were specially chosen by God.

The chief difficulty about the passage is that when we compare it with Pauline thought generally, the characteristic features appear to be lacking, and some which are generally not found in the other epistles are included. Here the marks of a Christian community are not that they are justified by faith, and members of Christ's body ; that they have been redeemed and reconciled to God ; or any other categories of what we should call the Gospel according to St. Paul. The Thessalonians are described as a notably Christian community because they have turned to God from idol-worship, and are waiting for the Advent of the Risen Son of God from heaven, who saves them from the Wrath to come. On the surface this is so different from what we should expect that it is not surprising that this passage should, together with others, have been taken by some as clear proof that Paul did not write the letter at all. Another solution has been to explain it as an early stage in the development of the apostle's thought. But as is always pointed out in reply to suggestions of this kind, affecting not only this but other alleged developments in the apostle's thought, Paul had been a missionary for approximately fifteen years before he wrote anything at all.   It is odd, therefore, that these fundamental changes of outlook should have taken all these years to materialize and, when they did, that they should then have taken place within a period of approximately ten years and sometimes within a period of months.   This is not to deny for a moment that Paul's ideas did sometimes change—for example, in the matter of his own survival until the coming end of the world (see Introduction, p. xxxii f.).   But a passage like this compared with the later epistles calls for more explanation than a rapid change in the apostle's mind.

The suggestion of Dibelius (ad loc.) is therefore plausible, that Paul is here using intentionally, with a view to striking a responsive chord in Thessalonian memories, the terms in which the Gospel had been preached to them—namely, to turn from worshipping idols to worshipping the only true God, because of what He had done in sending Jesus Christ and raising Him from the dead, and because that same Jesus was now about to return in Judgment.   This, as we have seen (note on ver. 5), was the common basis of the missionaries' message which Paul in another connexion acknowledges that he himself received and handed on (1 Cor. xi. 23, xv. 3).   Dibelius would say that Paul is merely using common mission terminology—strongly Jewish and strongly eschatological—as he probably did in his actual campaigns.   Only when he came to write his principal letters did the real Pauline thought come to the surface.   We are therefore to distinguish his missionary phraseology, of which this is an echo, from the more individualized thought of the important epistles, and are to understand such phraseology where it is used in the light of the apostle's own mind as we have learned to know it elsewhere.   Here, for example, as much as in the later epistles, the ' real God ' is for Paul the God who ' justifies ' ; the Resurrection involves for him the ' New Age ' ; Jesus is the ' Rescuer' because God's ' Grace ' has been revealed in Him.   Characteristic Pauline thought is therefore there, but implied rather than expressed.   Paul's personal transmutation of the common missionary tradition can be seen in such a passage as 2 Cor. v. 20*b*–21.

Common reports of the Thessalonian mission emphasized in the first place the change from idol worship to the worship of God—**how you turned to God from idols, to serve a living and a real God.** This is, as it were, the first stage in their conversion, and makes it clear that it was a question of the conversion of a pagan rather than a Jewish community—otherwise presumably they would have ' turned to the Lord ' or ' Christ.' **How** refers back to verses 3 and 6, ' With what enthusiasm and what results.' **Turned to God** is not Paul's usual phrase for conversion. Generally he uses a word that goes a stage farther, like ' believe,' or ' respond ' ; but the rest of the sentence makes it clear that the Thessalonians did both. In a sense it is a ' return ' to God, since idolatry is regarded as apostasy from the natural knowledge of God that, according to Paul, even the pagans have.

They turned to God **from idols.** Properly an *eidolon* is a phantom, a figment of the imagination. From that it came to mean a false god. The mention of idols at all suggests that most of the Thessalonians (despite Acts xvii. 4, 5) had not even been God-fearing Gentiles, that is, adherents of the synagogue ; which would, of course, make the story of their conversion the more dramatic. Here Paul aligns himself with prophet and psalmist in denouncing idolatry (e.g. Ps. cxv. 4–7 ; Isa. xliv. 9–20 ; Jer. x. 1–10). When we are inclined to stress the beauty and symbolism of paganism, and shed a tear over the shattered statues of the Acropolis or the Forum, we should remember that Paul condemned the whole system, root and branch—and he was there, and we were not. He saw, not only that the best minds of the time had long outgrown any sense of reality in pagan religion, but he saw also the moral degradation that it had brought with it. The idols that moulded life were not the austere images of Pallas Athene and Apollo, but the obscene figures that desecrated public and private altars. There was also the fact that, although the idols themselves might be regarded as unreal, the evil spirits and demons they represented were very real to those who worshipped them—and to Paul himself (1 Cor. x. 19–20).

For a keen conscience like that of Paul the greatest condemnation of idolatry must have been that it made morality impossible. A multiplicity of gods reduced religion to belief in none of them, but in some kind of blind fate behind life—amoral and impersonal. The idea of serving the gods by obedience to their will was therefore fantastic. But as his birthright every Hebrew knew that gods were created by man, but that man was created by God—a living, personal, moral being, at work in life and history, and this was the God Paul had preached at Thessalonica. So the people had turned from idols **to serve a living and a real God** (literally, to serve God living and true). Their service was the service of bondmen—the word means the absolute obedience of the slave. For Paul, of course, who calls himself Christ's bondman (e.g. Rom. i. 1), to be a Christian ' bondman ' means the service that is perfect freedom. This is what the Thessalonians now have in exchange for their slavery to superstition. They serve a living God—**living,** not only in the sense of not being lifeless like idols, but, in accordance with all the thought of the Old Testament, active in the world and human affairs—who speaks to men (Deut. v. 26), delivers His people (Jos. iii. 10 ; Dan. vi. 20, 26), sustains His creation (Acts xiv. 15), and breathes His Spirit into His children (2 Cor. iii. 3) ; and **real,** or genuine, as distinct from shams, ' very ' (*verus*) God, as the Nicene Creed says, the ' only true ' as St. John says (John xvii. 3). Anderson Scott (*Christianity According to St. Paul*, pp. 6–7) points out very properly what he calls the intense ' God-consciousness ' of the apostle—and this despite his passionate loyalty and intimate fellowship with Christ. Paul was a monotheist to the uttermost depths of his Jewish being and rabbinical training. Nowhere is that more clearly expressed than in these epistles, where the whole of the new Life in Christ is shown to begin and end with God. God has destined us from eternity (2 ii. 13) to enter through Christ into His own realm and glory (1 ii. 12). Even though the figure of Christ as present Lord and coming Judge holds the centre of the apostle's thoughts, the end of all things is the subordination of the Son to the Father (1 Cor. xv. 28)

So far the conversion of the Thessalonians to Christianity 10 has only been described as far as the half-way house of Hebrew monotheism. Now comes the second and distinctively Christian part of their new creed. They began to serve a living and a real God **and to wait for the coming of his Son from heaven** (literally, to await His Son from the heavens). It is not clear whether Paul, when he says **from the heavens**, is thinking in rabbinical terms of a plurality of heavens, i.e. the seven stages of the celestial sphere (cf. 2 Cor. xii. 2), or whether this is merely used casually, as we would say indifferently either ' heaven ' or ' the heavens.' The phrase communicates the tenseness of the atmosphere of the early Church. They had turned to serve the true God in a mood of expectancy. At any time the world as they knew it might come to an end, and in a miraculous and shattering new revelation the Son of God would come again in power and glory. They lived in days of miracle indeed, but this would be something beyond anything they had experienced, either of the strange workings of the Spirit in themselves or the healing ministries of the apostles. It is abundantly clear, from the earliest sermon-summaries in the Book of Acts to the last epistle in the New Testament— and beyond that into the Fathers—that the primitive Church was intensely, acutely conscious of the fact that they were living in the End of the Times.

One of the latest studies of the Second Advent (T. F. Glasson, op. cit.) has sought to show that this expectation of the end of the world and the return of the Messiah was something that did not exist in A.D. 30, but did exist in A.D. 50, and that it was created by reflection on the action of Caligula in desecrating the Temple in A.D. 40, and thereby, according to Old Testament prophecy, showing himself to be Antichrist, the herald of the End. To say this is to do less than justice to the nature of eschatological expectation. The sense that they were living in the last times needed no historical confirmation. It was present in the Church from the start. It is true that if we count the number of times that the Second Advent is referred to in early sermons in the Book of Acts, the total is surprisingly small—namely, once (iii. 20–21). But it is permissible, surely, to include also the angelic promise in i. 11, the reference in x. 42, and the significant use of the Aramaic *Marana tha* (Our Lord, come) in 1 Cor. xvi. 22. The proof, however, that the expectation of the End of the World existed from the beginning, and was not something which supervened through a combination of historical events and Old Testament study, lies in the eschatological setting of the whole Gospel.

We need not enter into the vexed question of how far Jesus spoke of His imminent return to earth, for the question is wrongly put. Only the curse of literalism could ever have made a problem of it. The answer is not to take sides either with those who say that our Lord was wrong in this and therefore unreliable in other respects, or with those who say that all His eschatological pronouncements have been attributed to Him by the evangelists. The Church believed that Christ would return, not only because of what He said—or what they thought He said (see Introduction, pp. xl, ff.)—but because of what had happened. Paul's teaching here is crystal clear. The old age is passing away and the new age has begun. The Resurrection was proof that what the prophets had foretold was coming true before men's eyes. The Messianic age had begun—the age of miracles, of the outpouring of the Spirit of God. These things were going on in ways that brooked no denial. The power of God was mightily at work ; men spoke with tongues and saw visions ; many were healed of their diseases, others displayed superhuman endurance ; and for those with deeper perception, above all, a new quality of life had become real. There had been a new Act of Creation with Christ as the first-born, and those who were in Him were to share it. In a real sense the old world had come to an end already. All that remained was the consummation, the full realization of the Kingdom which Christ had inaugurated. The Messiah had come, had died, and been exalted to the right hand of God. This Act of God must reach its climax in Judgment, in the vindication of the just, and in the supreme, and final, and visible Victory of the Lord.

That this conviction was couched in the traditional language and imagery is inevitable. How far the attempt is possible or valuable to separate the elements that made it up—whether from Jewish apocalyptic, Old Testament prophecy, or our Lord's own words, is an open question. What is essential is to grasp that when the New Testament throughout speaks of the Lord's return as imminent, it does so, not so much in the sense of time, but as a religious conviction. The task of the missionaries—as in these letters Paul's task with his Thessalonians—was to try to dissociate the time-concept from the religious message. What the converts must feel is that the Lord is always at hand : they stand under the Judgment of God which is here and now ; the old order is passing away and the final victory is with Christ. If by ' prophetic foreshortening ' the missionaries saw the solution of the perennial tension of good and evil as about to take place, and if those who heard their message were apt too often to take their words in a literal sense which was never intended, it should not lead us into the error either of discounting the former or imitating the latter.

The true assessment of the primitive expectation of the Second Coming is not to dismiss it as a hope that was never realized but that may be some day, but to recognize that it is not an event in time at all. St. John, in affirming both a Last Judgment and a present Judgment, an ultimate Triumph and a living Presence, was not revising earlier views which had been proved untrue, but interpreting correctly the real sense of the early Church's hope which had been held from the beginning. The Christian life is essentially eschatological— whether the end be personal death or universal cataclysm. The Lord is always at hand and comes to every generation, and we pass the Judgment of Doomsday upon ourselves every living moment. Christians are in the world, but must not be of the world : ' For we have no lasting city here below, we seek the city to come.' When the unknown writer to the Hebrews (xiii. 14) uses these words, he defines the Christian attitude to the world in the same sense as Paul in the present passage (see Introduction, pp. xxxvii, ff.).

They waited, then, for the coming of God's Son—**the Son whom he raised from the dead,** that is, who is now their exalted Lord. The fact that God raised Jesus from the dead is not, as elsewhere in Paul (e.g. Rom. i. 4), the chief argument proving that He is the Son. It seems to be introduced as a necessary link in the chain : Historical Jesus—Ascended Lord —Coming Son, for at once the Risen Lord is identified with the historical **Jesus who rescues us from the Wrath to come,** when the pride of man shall be brought low and all his idols avail him nothing, and the terror and glory of God will be supreme. Here **the Wrath** is clearly used in the traditional sense of the impending Day of Judgment, as in Old Testament prophecy (e.g. Isa. ii. 10–22 ; Zeph. iii. 8 ff.). This is not the present retribution for sin as elsewhere in Paul (e.g. Rom. i. 18 ; Eph. v. 6 ; Col. iii. 6), but it is its complement and is equally impersonal. Just as there is no real distinction between the Lord who is present with His people and the Lord who is yet to come in triumph, so there is no real distinction in the mind of Paul between the Wrath which is the working out of the moral order of the universe and the Wrath pictured as the Last Judgment. The one is the fulfilment of the other —its full revelation—a prophetic pictorialization of truth. The word (*orgé*) means ' anger,' but C. H. Dodd has shown clearly (Moffatt, *Romans*, pp. 20 ff.) that Paul never uses it as referring to an emotion or attitude of God towards man, but always as meaning ' an inevitable process of cause and effect in a moral universe.' An angry God—i.e. an irrational God— is no part of Christian teaching, but a just God, whose laws must be obeyed otherwise disaster ensues, most certainly is. It is the teaching of the prophets that failure to run God's world in God's way, or failure to live our lives according to His Will, ends in tragedy—personal, national, or international.

This is the substance of Paul's teaching too. Not that God gets angry with us, but that God has created a moral universe in which retribution follows sin as surely as night follows day. ' The wrath of God is, as it were, the instinct of self-preservation in the Divine Nature : it is the eternal re-

pulsion by the Holy One of all evil' (Denney, ad loc.). But the
prophets also taught that it is not the Will of God that His
people should so suffer. Rather would He in His love save
them from the sin that involves them in disaster. Paul, in
line with this, therefore, holds up to the Thessalonians the only
escape from the Wrath to come, namely, Jesus, the Deliverer
sent by God to save His people from the consequences of their
sins. There is, therefore, implicit in this word **rescues**, Paul's
whole teaching of redemption and reconciliation through
Christ. Only the man in Christ is safe from the Wrath to
come. Clearly a compelling factor behind the remarkable
conversion of the Thessalonian Church was the preaching of
the coming Judgment upon idolatry and dissolute living. It
is difficult to see how the preaching would have been successful without it.

III. JEWISH OPPOSITION
(ii. 1-16)

(1) PAUL ON THE DEFENSIVE (ii. 1-12).

But you remember yourselves, brothers, that our visit to you 1
was no failure. At Philippi, as you know, we had been 2
ill-treated and insulted, but we took courage and confidence in our God to tell you the gospel of God in spite of all
the strain. For the appeal we make does not spring from 3
any delusion or from impure motives—it does not work by
cunning ; no, God has attested our fitness to be entrusted 4
with the gospel, and so we tell the gospel not to satisfy
men but to satisfy the God who tests our hearts. We 5
never resorted to flattery (you know that), nor to any
pretext for self-seeking (God is witness to that) ; we never 6
sought honour from men, from you or from anybody else,
though as apostles of Christ we had the power of claiming
to be men of weight ; no, we behaved gently when we 7
were among you, like a nursing mother cherishing her own
children, fain, in our yearning affection for you, to impart 8
not only the gospel of God to you but our very souls as well

33

9   —you had so won our love. Brothers, you recollect our
       hard labour and toil, how we worked at our trade night
       and day, when we preached the gospel to you, so as not to
10   be a burden to any of you. You are witnesses, and so is
       God, to our behaviour among you believers, how pious
11   and upright and blameless it was, how (as you know) we
       treated each of you as a father treats his children,
12   beseeching you, encouraging you, and charging you to lead
       a life worthy of the God who called you to his own realm
       and glory.

1   Paul now returns to the visit of the apostles to Thessalonica
(i. 9) and expands what he has already said in i. 5. **But you
remember yourselves, brothers, that our visit to you was no
failure.** That is, ' apart from the fact that people go out of
their way to tell us of the success of the Thessalonian mission,
nobody knows that better than **you yourselves.**' Paul is
obviously uneasy and worried. But it is not on account of
the opinion of the Thessalonian Christians themselves about
him, but on account of the insidious effect of scandalmonger-
ing outside the Church on the part of his old enemies the Jews.
The next verses (2–12), as we can see by reading between the
lines, are a reply to calumnies of which Paul has no doubt
heard from Timothy—or even from the hypothetical letter
(see note on i. 9)—suggesting that he was no better than a
religious charlatan whose chief concern was to feather his own
nest. The fact that there were plenty of pagan specimens of
this kind roaming the country lent colour to the charge. What
was easier, or more suggestive, than to insinuate that this
man who had thrown up the faith of his fathers had done it
for his own ends ? Paul's reply is to ask the Thessalonians if
his behaviour and that of his associates fitted in with such a
character.

   When he says their visit was **no failure** he is thinking back
to what he had said earlier (ver. 5) of the accompanying signs,
power and the **holy Spirit,** proving that it was no ordinary visit
of itinerant religious quacks. The fact that, having been so
violently man-handled at Philippi, they had nevertheless proceeded with their mission, was proof positive that they were

true servants of Him who said, ' When they persecute you in one town, flee to the next ' (Matt. x. 23).

At Philippi, as you know, we had been ill-treated and in- 2 **sulted.** The story of that visit as related in Acts xvi. 12 ff. must have been notorious. Not only the exorcism practised on the girl ventriloquist with its riotous consequences, but the apparently miraculous intervention by which the apostles were delivered from the town prison, must have been deeply impressed upon all minds. But the aspect of the Philippian visit of which Paul now reminds the Thessalonians was the subsequent illegal public beating and the affront to his Roman citizenship. This outrage—a crime in Roman law—was atoned for by the magistrates, but the injustice of it still rankled. It is also probable, judging from the epistles as a whole—especially the autobiographical passage in 2 Cor. xi. 23 ff.—that Paul was particularly sensitive to bodily pain, fearing it and remembering it, as here, with horror. If this was so, it makes the man more astounding than ever for sheer moral courage. To leave one scene of torture and face the immediate possibility of the same treatment in an adjoining town demands no ordinary resolution. Yet he would at once have said it was in no spirit of self-discipline or stoical endurance, but in the power of God, as indeed he goes on to say now. **But we took courage and confidence in our God**—that is, **our God** and not the idols of the pagan Philippians—**to tell you the gospel of God in spite of all the strain** (R.V. ' In much conflict '—*en pollō agōni*). The Greek does not make it clear what the ' strain ' was—whether it was the active opposition of the anti-Christian majority in Thessalonica, or the effects of the apostles' misfortunes at Philippi—perhaps Paul meant a combination of both. At all events, the Jewish opposition at Thessalonica seems to be in his mind, not only as it was displayed on the occasion of his first visit, but as it had continued in his absence. For the next verses, without mentioning the Jews specifically, obviously proceed to rebut their allegations against the apostles' integrity.

Apparently the insinuations levelled against them—and no 3 doubt Paul in particular—were that they were mentally un-

35

balanced, morally corrupt, and spiritually dishonest. The fact that charges like these against Paul of all people seem to us absurd does not alter the fact that the apostle himself takes them very seriously. To share his view we have to picture an age when religious teachers of every sort were rife. There has probably never been such a variety of religious cults and philosophic systems as in Paul's day. East and West had united and intermingled to produce an amalgam of real piety, high moral principles, crude superstition and gross licence. Oriental mysteries, Greek philosophy, and local godlings competed for favour under the tolerant aegis of Roman indifference. ' Holy Men ' of all creeds and countries, popular philosophers, magicians, astrologers, crack-pots, and cranks ; the sincere and the spurious, the righteous and the rogue, swindlers and saints, jostled and clamoured for the attention of the credulous and the sceptical.

No city lacked its pantheon of deities indigenous or imported ; no market-place was without its quota of rival exponents of strange faiths and practices. Here was the happy hunting-ground of the ancient variety of twentieth-century ' spivs ' and ' drones,' Hyde Park orators, and revivalist faith-healers. In such an atmosphere, as open to trickery as a modern spiritualistic seance, the honest exponents of a new philosophy or faith had to run the risk of being identified as quacks and crooks and of being treated accordingly. Suspicion was easily aroused, and events, innocent in themselves, often lent colour to the charges of opponents.

The Jewish whispering-campaign in Thessalonica was therefore a formidable adversary, and Paul treats it with the respect which is its due. He calls the Thessalonian Church to witness that **the appeal we make**—i.e. the Gospel we preach— **does not spring from any delusion** (*plané*), that is, ' we are obviously not impostors.' To paraphrase Lincoln's historic words : we could fool some Churches all the time, and all the Churches some of the time, but not all the Churches all the time. The best proof of the genuineness of the apostles' mission was its growing and continuing success everywhere. In particular the Thessalonians' own inward conviction was the best refutation of the charge. Nor does their appeal spring from impure motives (*akatharsia*).

This charge is not one of having generally unworthy intentions, such as Paul answers later (vers. 6 ff.), but is a direct accusation of sexual immorality. Religious prostitution was very common in pagan temples, where it was justified on the grounds that union with a servant of the god was tantamount to union with the deity. Sacramental fornication was one of the foulest blots on pagan worship—as it was in Amos' day in Palestine and as it is in some places in India now—and in one temple in Corinth alone there were a thousand girls used in this monstrous traffic in perverted religious emotion. It was a favourite accusation of their opponents that the early Christians practised sexual promiscuity. Some of their activities certainly gave colour to this libel—such as the risky custom of encouraging unmarried men and women to live together as brother and sister (1 Cor. vii. 36 ff.), the ambiguous early name of the Lord's Supper which was the ' love-feast,' the exchange of the kiss of peace, and the fact that in Rome at any rate the Christians met in the catacombs—a suitable place for nameless orgies ! The pagans were, of course, in no position to make accusations of sexual depravity against the Christians, though, in fact, they did ; but the Jews did not include the indulgence of the flesh among their public lapses. However they might be accused of bigotry, legalism, exclusiveness, and divers sins of the spirit, their worst enemies could not but acknowledge that, at least as a community, they were, as far as sex morality was concerned, relatively irreproachable. They lost no opportunity, however, of suggesting that it was quite otherwise with the Christians ; and here Paul has to refute their insinuation that this was one of the apostolic vices.

The third charge which seems to have been made against them would appear to connect them with the strolling jugglers, gamblers, and tricksters, frequenting the market-place, who then as now could make a comfortable living by parting fools from their money. But our appeal, says Paul, **does not work by cunning** (*dolos*). It is not black magic. Paul does not go

into details in countering these three accusations. He relies
on the mere mention of them to show how preposterous they
are. He is adducing, not only his visit to Thessalonica, but
his practice everywhere as the best proof that his message was
true, his motives pure, and his approach sincere. There is no
fifth column inside the Thessalonian Church which necessitates
a detailed defence.

4 So in the next few words he gives what is for the purpose an
adequate reply to the three accusations. **No, he says, God
has attested our fitness to be entrusted with the gospel, and so
we tell the gospel not to satisfy men but to satisfy the God who
tests our hearts.** It is not hard to see in this a threefold
answer. We cannot be ' deluded ' because our message is
concerned with and springs from the true **God.** We cannot
be guilty of ' vicious practices,' because God Himself has
attested our fitness. We cannot work by ' cunning,' because
we are responsible to **God** and not to **men.** In attesting their
work, God had proved them before approving them. Having
passed them as fit—and that not in their own strength but in
His—He trusted them to be His messengers. Paul implies
that no man bearing this great responsibility through God's
grace, could possibly be guilty of the charges brought by the
Jews. The kind of gospel that would **satisfy** men would not
be one that showed up their utter helplessness and total dependence upon God, that gloried in the ' offence ' of the Cross,
and affirmed the ' idle tale ' of the Resurrection. All this is
unpalatable truth. But Paul is not concerned about accommodating the Gospel to men, but about accommodating men to
the Gospel—he is not a ' popular preacher.' **God who tests our
hearts** is a frequent Old Testament expression, e.g. Ps. xvii. 3,
where **heart** is used, not of the emotions, but of the centre of
personality, the real self. Moffatt's use of **tests** and **attests** in
the same sentence reproduces in English a characteristic play
upon the word (*dedokimasmetha—dokimazonti*).

5 Having restated his credentials in general terms, Paul now
comes down to the particular, and defends his behaviour while
at Thessalonica, calling the Church there as his witness. This
occupies verses 5–12. Once again the apostle suggests three

accusations which he proceeds to deny. These charges are of behaving like any pagan itinerant teacher in using flattery, seeking his own gain, and his own glory. He begins, as in verse 3, by answering these accusations negatively (vers. 5-6), then (as in ver. 4) with specific contradictions (vers. 7-12). **We never resorted to flattery (you know that).** Flattery here has the sense of cajolery, and means more the smooth-tongued ' cunning ' of the vagrant rhetoricians already referred to than ' insincere praise.' **Nor to any pretext for self-seeking (God is witness to that).** The A.V. translates picturesquely ' a cloke of covetousness,' but the word (*pleonexia*) means more than greed for money. It includes crass selfishness of any kind, and Paul never used his missionary campaign as a means to cover up some private purpose of self-aggrandisement. **God,** who knows every motive, is a witness.

We never sought honour from men, from you or from any- 6 **body else.** The emphasis is, of course, on the fact that he did not ' seek ' honour. He, in fact, received it in plenty from the Churches he founded everywhere, but his own glory was never his aim in the mission field. **Though,** he adds, **as apostles of Christ we had the power of claiming to be men of weight.** The word translated ' weight ' here (*baros*) may mean either ' burden ' or ' importance.' The A.V. takes the former, and translates ' we might have been burdensome, as the apostles of Christ,' i.e. we might have claimed the right to be supported by you as the apostles of Christ. But it seems to fit the sense better to refer the word back to ' honour ' and translate as Moffatt does. Weymouth paraphrases : ' We might have stood on our dignity.' Paul here as elsewhere does not confine the word ' apostle ' to the ' Twelve,' but includes other mission-aries as well as himself (cf. Rom. xvi. 7). Any messenger or emissary could be an *apostolos* in those days. Jews and pagans both used the word. But an ' *apostolos* of Christ ' bore a message from heaven. Paul himself always regarded his apostleship as of equal status with the Twelve by virtue of our Lord's appearance to him on the Damascus road (1 Cor. xv. 7-9) (see note on *Apostles of Christ*, Bicknell, ad loc.).

Next, the apostle having answered negatively the three 7

charges of deceitfulness, self-seeking, and self-importance, proceeds to answer them positively. **No, he says, we behaved gently when we were among you, like a nursing mother cherishing her own children.** There is a variant reading here (see R.V.), the choice being between ' We behaved as babes ' and ' We behaved gently ' (*nēpioi*—' babes ' and *ēpioi*—' gentle '). The former has better MSS. authority, but the latter makes better sense, though Paul is quite capable of comparing himself to an infant and a nursing mother in the same sentence— he calls himself a father a few lines farther down (ver. 11) and an orphan in the same chapter (ver. 17)! The Greek MSS. leave no spaces between words, and the final ' n ' of the previous word has probably been tacked on to *ēpioi*. Bicknell defends ' babes ' as an application of the principle of the Incarnation : ' the condescension of the true Christian pastor who is willing to put himself on the level of others.' But this idea is surely conveyed sufficiently by the word ' gently ' (cf. 2 Tim. ii. 24). The apostles did not stand on their authority, but were as tender and affectionate as a mother clasping her

8 child to her breast—**fain, in our yearning affection for you, to impart not only the gospel of God to you but our very souls as well—you had so won our love.** The Gospel cost the apostles nothing. It was a free gift to them which they were bound to pass on. But with the Gospel they were prepared to give themselves, to spend themselves utterly in the service of their little flock. It is a sobering picture of what a real pastor should be to his people. The old Italian proverb says : ' The teacher is like the candle which gives light to others by consuming itself.' Paul's simile of the right relationship between minister and people is more profound—it is the utter self-giving of a mother to her child.

9 The next remark, though clearly emphasizing and illustrating the last one, possibly also refers back to the charge of trying to make money out of the mission (ver. 5) which apparently rankles (cf. Acts xx. 33–5). **Brothers, you recollect our hard labour and toil, how we worked at our trade night and day, when we preached the gospel to you, so as not to be a burden to any of you.** ' Toil and moil ' would bring out the

similarity of sound in the Greek (*kopos kai mochthos*) better than **hard labour and toil**. Paul—and it seems from this Silvanus and Timothy as well—was as far as possible independent. **Night and day** probably means ' incessantly,' ' from dawn till nightfall '—not necessarily a routine division of the day into evangelism and manual work, as at Ephesus (Acts xix. 9). The picture is of a strenuous and full life, preaching the Gospel and supporting themselves by their own hands. It may be, however, that Paul, as he says elsewhere (Acts xx. 34), supported his companions as well as himself. Whatever the occupation of the other two missionaries was, Paul's is described in Acts xviii. 4 as a *skēnopoios*. This is translated variously as a tent-maker, a leather-worker, or a saddler.

Generally, every Jewish boy had to learn a trade, whether he was going to be a scholar or a craftsman. According to the Talmud, what is required of a Jewish father in regard to his son is : to circumcise him, to teach him the law, and to teach him a trade. One of the rabbis said : ' He that teacheth not his son a trade doth the same as if he taught him to be a thief.' Perhaps the rule sprang more from necessity than from a desire for an integrated life. There was no class of salaried teachers in Palestine, and a rabbi needed to have a more reliable source of income than casual contributions and hospitality. To this rule Paul was no exception ; moreover, it is quite consonant with the impression we get that his father as a Roman citizen was well-to-do. It is possible that Paul was apprenticed to his father's own business, and possibly disappointed his hopes of a successor, as St. Francis was later to do also. In any case, Paul would not work in Thessalonica as a labourer, but as a skilled craftsman. Despite this, he does not seem to have earned enough to enable him to exist without subsidies from his friends at Philippi (Phil. iv. 16). His main contention here is, however, that wherever he got money to live on, it was not from the profits of the Thessalonian campaign. For although the Thessalonian Church consisted probably, like that at Corinth, of ' waifs and workers ' (1 Cor. iv. 12 ; 1 Thess. iv. 11), there were apparently some members who could well have afforded the missionaries financial support (Acts xvii. 5). There were then two motives behind his labours, one expressed in the text, that he should not be a burden to any of them, the other by implication, in answer to Jewish charges that he was simply a strolling evangelist out to make money. Later he uses his self-support as an example of Christian responsibility (iv. 11 ; 2 iii. 6–12).

10 **You are witnesses, and so is God, to our behaviour among you believers, how pious and upright and blameless it was.** Paul has previously called God and the Thessalonians to witness to his conduct (ver. 5). Then there was a distinction between outward behaviour and inward motive. Here there is no such distinction, as both are involved together. **Believers** (literally, you who believe) is a common Pauline expression for Christians. But here it means more than that. The point is that whatever others (e.g. the Jews) might think and say of the apostles, at any rate the readers among whom they had laboured knew what type of men they were. ' Piously,' ' uprightly,' and ' blamelessly ' are better than the A.V. ' holily,' ' justly,' and ' unblameably.' The older commentators tried to separate the three adverbs into three separate relationships—firstly, the apostles' behaviour to God; secondly, to the people ; and thirdly, among themselves. It is very doubtful whether Paul had any such clear division in mind. The three words, like the ' soberly,' ' righteously,' and ' godly ' of Titus ii. 12, are cumulative, and are rather designed to describe their conduct generally as irreproachable before God and man. It is a general summary of the Thessalonian ministry on the lines of Paul's claim before Felix to strive after ' a clear conscience before God and men all the time ' (Acts xxiv. 16).

11 Now comes a statement with a more remote context point-
& ing back to verse 5. Paul has defended himself generally
12 against imputations of cajolery, self-aggrandisement, and ambition (vers. 5–6). He then specifically answers these charges in reverse order. ' Ambition ' is dealt with in verses 7 and 8, ' self-aggrandisement ' in verses 9 and 10, and now ' cajolery ' in verses 11 and 12. He reminds them that he did not use any guile in his approach to them, no fair words, but rather **how (as you know) we treated each of you as a father treats his**

children, beseeching you, encouraging you, and charging you
to lead a life worthy of the God who called you to his own realm
and glory. Here is no smooth-tongued orator seeking to pro-
pagate pernicious doctrines, but a real pastor and teacher, a
father in God, dealing with his people according to each one's
needs (cf. Acts xx. 31), **beseeching,** or urging, the hesitant,
encouraging the faint-hearted, and **charging,** or adjuring, the
wavering. The apostle covers here (' beseeching ' and ' encouraging ' on the one hand ; ' charging ' on the other) the
two aspects of the particular problem which the Thessalonian
mission had presented—the danger of discouragement due to
persecution, and the danger of defection due to the converts'
own weakness. He reminds them how he comforted and ad-
monished them then, as he does throughout these epistles now.
The emphasis on **each of you** implies, not only public teaching,
but house-to-house visitation (cf. Acts xx. 20). The three
words tumble after each other in quick succession as Paul
relives the experience. All his effort—beseeching, encouraging, and solemnly charging them—was concerned with one
thing, that they should live a life worthy of God—the highest
vocation of the Christian. The A.V. literal translation, ' that
ye would walk worthy of God,' reproduces a metaphor common in Paul and taken from the Old Testament, where ' walking ' is used of moral behaviour and inward attitude. Hence,
perhaps, the reason that the earliest name for Christianity was
' the Way.'

So high a vocation is that of the Christian that it must be
ruled out as an impossibility but for the fact that God had
called them **to his own realm and glory.** A more probable
reading of the Greek makes the call a present fact rather than
a past event (*kalountos* instead of *kalesantos*). This is surely
more truly the apostle's view here. God's call to His service
is timeless, because of the empowering fact of the Holy Spirit.
His grace is not merely ' prevenient ' but ever-present.
Obviously, of course, the supreme moment of the ' call ' in
the case of the Thessalonians was the time of decision when
they were faced with the challenge during the apostolic mission. Just as in Paul's own life the dramatic suddenness of his

conversion would always be for him the clearest proof that he had been called, tending to make him speak of God's call generally as a moment in time, so the obvious success of the Thessalonian mission, as evidenced by their changed lives, was equally indicative of the Divine call to them. But Paul would go on to say that God has to continue to call men into His own realm and glory even while they are within the Fellowship. It is not merely a past summons that can be remembered, but a present fellowship to be enjoyed, with a future consummation. They are already in His **realm** or under His rule, but it is only a foretaste of what the future **glory** will be.

The **realm** of God (*basileia*—A.V. kingdom—more correctly 'kingly rule') is for Paul, as for the gospels, the new order that God has given to men, and that Jesus Himself has brought into being. What the prophets prayed for has come to pass. The rule of God has begun ; Jesus inaugurated it ; the Church embodies it. The old order—the rule of darkness or of Satan (Acts xxvi. 18)—though still dominating the world—has been in principle destroyed by the Death and Resurrection of Jesus. Those who by God's grace are called, and who by self-surrender answer His call, live henceforth in the new order, under God's rule, in the Kingdom, in the Holy Spirit, in Christ. They have stepped out of darkness into light, they have died and risen again with Christ, they have put off the old man and put on the new. By such metaphors Paul expresses the same conviction. But while believers live in this new order, its fulfilment is yet to come (Rom. viii. 23). Its **glory** has yet to be revealed—the full manifestation of the power and majesty of God in the climax of history and the final triumph of Christ.

Glory (*doxa*) is one of the words in the Christian vocabulary which we generally use without much thought—especially when we are singing hymns. Paul's conception of glory is not as precise as might be expected from the number of times he uses the word, but it is probably as precise as in the nature of things it can be. In the Old Testament, **glory** is generally used of the self-revelation of God—as in Isaiah's vision in the Temple (vi. 7). It is associated with Light and Radiance—the ineffable brightness of the Divine power before which mortal man must bow his head. In Paul's own experience it is notable that at his conversion a recurring motif in all the accounts is a bright light which throws him to the ground (Acts ix. 3, xxii. 6, xxvi. 13). The glory of God is something that was revealed to him as nowhere else on the Damascus road, and which is inextricably bound up with the Lord Jesus. Thus Paul's conception of the future state of believers, which is eternal life with Christ, is coloured by this thought of sharing His Light and Radiance. It is, however, not merely the material manifestation of the power and majesty of God which Paul carries over into his thought of the glory that is to be.

At the end of all things, when the Lord comes to judge the world, His glory, which will be shared by His people, is more than the effulgence of His self-revelation : it is the Power and Energy of which the Light is the outward symbol. But this is no blind Energy or arbitrary Power. When God's glory was seen in the flesh, men saw that it was ' full of grace and truth ' (John i. 14), and in its ultimate sense, the glory of God for Paul is His goodness—the Power of His Radiant Love. This is the glory of which we come short here on earth through sin (Rom. iii. 23), but which we not only see but share at the end of the day. Paul thinks of the glory of God as something which is reflected in the Christian life. God's Spirit, transforming the believer into His own likeness, communicates something of Himself, so that the Christian mirrors His glory, inwardly now, outwardly in the spiritual body hereafter (2 Cor. iii. and iv.). In the fulness of the consummation, God is revealed in all the majesty of His goodness and Love ; and His people, having grown into the measure of the stature of the fulness of Christ, are able to live in His Presence for ever. This is the true end of man, the fulfilment of his destiny. Man has missed his mark, but now the way has been opened up for him again through the work of Christ. It is to be noted here how closely in the early Church ethics and eschatology are bound together. It is because they are called to be citizens of God's realm and because that realm is shortly to be consummated in the glorious Advent that they must lead a life worthy of their calling (cf. i. 9, 10). Teaching about the

' Kingdom ' would seem to have taken a larger place in the original mission than is reflected in the letters, if we are to judge from the narrative in Acts, where the charge brought against the missionaries was of teaching that there was another king than Caesar, namely, one Jesus (xvii. 7).

This whole passage (ii. 1–12) raises the very pertinent question why it should be necessary for the apostle to defend himself so vigorously. He is not apparently concerned, as he is in the Corinthian epistles, to refute charges being made against him from within the Church. What he says in these twelve verses lacks the heat and passion and irony with which he deals with the Corinthian situation. In addition to which, the passage in the following chapter (iii. 6 ff.), in which he tells the Thessalonians of Timothy's tribute to their loyalty to himself, and to their Christian witness, is an obvious indication that the apostle is deeply moved by the zeal and devotion of all of them. The general view of commentators, which we have adopted here, is that he is in this second chapter replying to slanderous charges from opponents outside the Church— principally his old enemies the Jews, but possibly pagans as well. The difficulty about this is that if he were as sure of the Thessalonians' loyalty as he claims to be in the following chapter (iii. 6 ff.), it would seem to be unnecessary to make such a sustained apologia for his behaviour when among them. It may be that the general view is the correct one, and that on Timothy's advice Paul thinks it prudent to deliver his blow before the insidious suggestions of the opposition begin to take effect within the congregation, and thus to forestall any criticism from within. But it is not quite satisfactory.

Dibelius makes an interesting guess at the answer, which may be the right one. He suggests that there was no real occasion—either within the Church or outside it—for such an apology. When Christian missionaries, or genuine pagan teachers, undertook a campaign in a new area, their greatest handicap was that they were at once suspect of being the all too common wandering addle-pates, who foisted upon the public scatterbrain philosophical theories or bizarre religious beliefs like present-day soap-box orators. The more devoted and self-sacrificing they appeared to be, the more suspicious people became that they were in some way making a good thing out of it for themselves. It was therefore an essential part of any evangelizing effort that this suspicion should be at once allayed and any suggestion that there were ulterior motives stoutly denied. Dibelius suggests that missionaries had set rhetorical phrases, which they used in pagan surroundings ; protesting their honesty, denying the impurity of their motives, almost, in fact, like the parrot-talk of the conjurer at the fairground, who announces to the crowd that there is no deception and that he has nothing up his sleeve ! Here, then, through reliving the mission at Thessalonica, the apostle almost insensibly, and without real occasion, finds himself using the language he used then. Whether Dibelius's form-critical passion for formulas ' is admitted here or not, it is at least arguable that something of this kind lies behind the passage, rather than a somewhat unimpassioned defence against current denigration.

(2) PAULINE EXASPERATION (ii. 13-16)

We thank God constantly for this too, that when you received 13
   the word of the divine message from us, you took it not
   as a human word but for what it really is, the word of God.
   It proves effective in you believers, for you have started, 14
   my brothers, to copy the churches of God in Christ Jesus
   throughout Judæa ; you have suffered from your compatriots just as they have suffered from the Jews, who 15
   killed the Lord Jesus and the prophets, who harassed ourselves, who offend God and oppose all men by hindering us 16
   from speaking words of salvation to the Gentiles. So they
   would fill up the measure of their sins to the last drop !
   But the Wrath is on them to the bitter end !

This is a most interesting little paragraph. It begins on a renewed note of gratitude to God for the way in which the Gospel had been received at Thessalonica. This leads into a move for better understanding between the Gentile and the Jewish branches of the Christian Church, and ends with a violent denunciation of the Jews unique in the epistles.

47

13   As he has done at the beginning of the letter (i. 2), Paul
once more, perhaps to round off this first section (i. 2–ii. 16),
breaks out into the gratitude to God which fills him whenever
he thinks of the campaign in Thessalonica. **We thank God
constantly for this too.**   Rendel Harris would translate : We
too thank God constantly for this, etc., and thinks that this is
another allusion to a letter from the Thessalonians, in which
they had thanked God as Paul now proceeds to do (see note
on i. 9).   Other passages where he finds possible references to
a letter brought from Thessalonica by Timothy, to which Paul
is replying, are iv. 9, 13, v. 1. **That when you received the
word of the divine message from us, you took it not as a human
word but for what it really is, the word of God.** This may be
in reply to Jewish insinuations that Paul's was a man-made
gospel.   If so, Paul's reply is that when he preached to them
his words were his own, but it was God speaking through him
(cf. 2 Cor. i. 19).   He makes a distinction here between ' re-
ceiving ' the Word and ' welcoming ' it.   The word used here
meaning ' received ' (*paralambanō*) is the technical word used
in the transmission of the contents of the Christian *kērygma*.
What the missionaries ' received ' they then ' handed on '
(*paradidōmi*) to the converts, who in their turn ' received ' it
(cf. iv. 1 ; 1 Cor. xv., 3 xi. 23).   (Moffatt translates ' welcomed ' (*dechomai*) as ' took.')   They not only heard the apostles' message, they took it to their hearts (cf. i. 6) as a Word
straight from God, which indeed it was (cf. Rom. x. 13–17).
The result of this dynamic Word of God, here almost synonymous with the Holy Spirit (cf. i. 8 ; 2 iii. 1), working in them,
influencing them, and empowering them, has been their subsequent valiant resistance to their enemies.   That is a sign
that the seed has borne fruit.

14   **It proves effective in you believers**—conversely, it would
cease to prove effective the moment they ceased to believe.
Paul's teaching is that when faith begins, life begins—life as
God meant us to live, new life as Paul himself had experienced
it since his conversion.   When we lose our faith we are to all
intents and purposes dead men. **For you have started, my
brothers, to copy the churches of God in Christ Jesus through-**

out Judæa. 'The Church of God' (*ecclēsia*: A.V. 'congregation') in the Greek Old Testament (e.g. Deut. xxiii. 1-3; Neh. xiii. 1) consisted of those who had been called out of the world by God—the assembly of the Chosen People. It was practically synonymous with *synagōge*. Churches of God in Judæa therefore would, or could, be synagogues. The difference between them and the Christian Churches was the Christian acceptance of Jesus as Messiah—hence they are churches of God in Christ Jesus. Later, *Ecclēsia* was reserved by Christians for the Christian Church, and *Synagōge* for the Jewish. Paul had already noted that the Thessalonians had begun by imitating the missionaries (i. 6). Now the whole Church is described as an imitator of the Palestinian Christian communities (Judæa is here used in this wider sense, e.g. Acts x. 37). In both cases the bearing of the Thessalonians under persecution is in his mind. We may assume that the riot in the early days of the mission (Acts xvii. 5) was not an isolated affair, and that interference and attack from their compatriots continued to harass the little community's development (cf. iii. 3). This attack from their own folk was proof that they were worthily serving Him who said: 'A man's own household will be his enemies' (Matt. x. 36). But what they suffered the Palestinian Churches had had to endure from their countrymen the Jews before them. Their constancy is held up as an example to all the rest.

There is here the suggestion that even at this early stage the Gentile Churches were conscious of their difference from the Jewish Christian communities. If the Galatian letter was written before Thessalonians, Paul was certainly not at this time *persona grata* with the Jerusalem Church, and this verse may well be an effort on his part to bridge the gap between them by drawing attention to their similar plight. Silvanus in particular had a special interest in the Church at Jerusalem (Acts xv. 22, 32). Later the split developed, and the Churches of Judæa came to be regarded as a conservative backwater, with overmuch attachment to their Jewish upbringing, and in time were dubbed ' Ebionite ' and ' Nazarene ' heretics by the Gentile Churches, who saw in them the dead hand of Jewish legalism such as Christ had condemned. Being the first Churches to be founded, they had been the first to face the inevitable opposition of the Jews, though we have no information about any such persecution except at Jerusalem. **You have suffered from your compatriots**—the word seems to be used locally as much as racially. It could therefore include the Jews who were stirring up trouble behind the scenes in Thessalonica. The Thessalonians were passing through what Melanchthon called the best of the three schools of Christian training—prayer, meditation, and suffering. For Paul that was a reason for congratulating them, not for condoling with them. The more they suffered persecution from the world, the more is it proof that they are faithful to their Master—as the Churches of the Continent discovered during the Second World War. The next words—**just as they have suffered from** the **Jews**—lead Paul to indulge in a polemic which is so vitriolic, and so unlike his general attitude to his countrymen, that some commentators have regarded it as an interpolation. If, however, we take it in conjunction with what precedes it and what follows, it comes perfectly naturally as an exasperated missionary's outburst against the people who are bent on destroying or undermining whatever he achieves.

It was the Gentile rabble at Thessalonica in the early days of the campaign who broke into riot—but it was the Jews who instigated it (Acts xvii. 5). They were behind Paul's troubles in Beroea (Acts xvii. 13), and now in Corinth (Acts xviii. 5 ff.) he was still their victim. The most reasonable explanation of his apologia in ii. 1–12 is that Timothy had reported Jewish trouble-makers at work trying to besmirch Paul's motives, and the apostle's subsequent anxiety to explain his delay in returning to Thessalonica (ii. 17 ff.) suggests that the Jews were using this fact, too, to insinuate that he had no real interest in his converts. This whispering campaign, conducted by the Thessalonian Jews who were determined to stultify every effort of the man they regarded as a black-hearted traitor and an emissary of the Devil, coming as the culmination of a series of direct attacks, gives adequate grounds for the outburst—not of wounded vanity or a sense of personal

injury, but of hot resentment against those who from the beginning of the Lord's public ministry had bent all their
energies on compassing His death and strangling the Gospel.

It was the Jews **who killed the Lord Jesus and the prophets**— 15
first the prophets, the ' servants ' in Jesus's parable of the
Wicked Husbandmen (Mark xii. 4–5), the preachers and reformers of Israel, who sought to bring their people back to the
service of the true God and their appointed vocation of gathering the whole world to His feet ; then finally the Son Himself,
Jesus of Nazareth, their countryman, but also the Lord of
Glory. This was the crime above all crimes which their
present actions showed they condoned. This was presumably also the common charge of the early Church against the
Jews (cf. Stephen—Acts vii. 52). Some have thought it odd
that **the prophets** should come as an afterthought. The
obvious order would be ' who killed the prophets,'—and, as a
climax—' the Lord Jesus.' By altering the punctuation, ' the
prophets ' and ' ourselves ' can easily be taken together with
' harassed.' The text would then read ' who killed the Lord
Jesus, who harassed (or persecuted) the prophets and ourselves.' This is probably the better reading. The Greek
separates ' the Lord ' and ' Jesus ' : ' who killed the Lord ;
yes, Jesus.'

It was the Jews **who harassed ourselves**—not only the three
missionaries in Thessalonica, but from the very start of Paul's
life's work as a Christian in Damascus (Acts ix. 24). And if
' ourselves ' means the apostles in general, it was equally true
of Peter and James. **Who offend God and oppose all men**— 16
this reads like Tacitus's sweeping condemnation of the Jews,
that they are like no other race, a nation of misanthropes,
rather than the comment of a Jew himself. Paul's patience
is momentarily exhausted, and he borrows the Gentiles' catch-
phrases as he joins them in their general abuse of his countrymen—a view which, of course, was not normally his (cf. Rom.
x. and xi.). But unlike the pagans, he sees the ground for their
' *adversus omnes alios hostile odium* ' (*Hist.* v. 5), not in their
natural make-up, but in their rejection of the Gospel, and their
determination to thwart its progress. He speaks here, there-

fore, not like a pagan philosopher, but like an Old Testament prophet. The Jews have made themselves enemies of humanity by hindering us from speaking words of salvation to the Gentiles. The pagans, says Paul, are wrong in so far as they accuse the Jews—partly through ignorance and misunderstanding of their background—of being by nature at loggerheads with the rest of mankind, but at this point in history the Jews are, in fact, showing their disobedience to God and their enmity to man, by opposing God's Good News of salvation which is for the whole world. It was above all the universalism of Christianity which the Jews could not stomach. That the God of the Jews should be also God of the Gentiles was to them insufferable. Their reaction to Paul's speech on the Temple steps (Acts xxii. 21-3) on this very point is a sample of their fanaticism. The best example is, of course, Paul's pre-Christian behaviour.

Salvation (*sōtēria*) is a surprisingly uncommon word in Paul's letters. Even here it is part of the verb to ' save ' (*sōzō*) that is used (literally, preventing us from speaking to the Gentiles that they might be saved). Yet salvation is for Paul the most comprehensive way of describing what Christianity offered to Jew and pagan alike. In a sense it is what all religions offer—the difference between them is what they profess to deliver their worshippers from and how they claim to do it. But in Paul's case the antecedents of his thought came straight from the prophets and the psalmists of the Old Testament. Salvation was for Israel God's work of personal and national deliverance in its widest sense—His merciful intervention in their history in choosing them to be His people, in setting them free from all their enemies, in providing for them, in forgiving their sins, and in giving them the hope and promise of better things to come. This salvation—now clarified, actualized, verified, sealed, by the coming of Christ—is what Paul and his fellow-missionaries offered to the world in the name of God. Within it is comprised all his theology—election, justification, sanctification, and the rest—it means deliverance from all past bondage, strength and freedom in the present, and hope for the future—it involves the work of

Christ, the power of the Spirit, and the growth of the Church—
and all is summed up in the restoration of the broken relationship between God and man through Christ.

In the last resort, salvation means in Paul's mind to be
saved from destruction (Phil. i. 28), death (2 Cor. vii. 10), and
judgment (v. 9). That is, it is part of the eschatological
picture. Ideally, the Christian believer is already saved, in
that he possesses the converse of destruction and death,
namely, eternal life. But his salvation is not complete in this
world. Its consummation lies beyond. His sins are for-
given, he is a citizen of the Kingdom ; but his full citizenship,
his full salvation—which is life in perfect fellowship with God
—can only be attained when he has passed beyond the lusts
of the flesh and the corruption of the world. Thus Paul, with
prophetic pictorialization of the issues at stake, sees salvation
in association with the Wrath to Come and the Return of
Christ. Men must be saved from the impending Doom, from
the consequences of their sins. So the Gentiles are given their
opportunity—and so, if not in the same eschatological framework, is twentieth-century man.

**So they would fill up the measure of their sins to the last
drop!** The Jews as a nation had been steadily through the
ages adding to their record of crimes : disobeying God's law,
rejecting the prophets, crucifying the Messiah ; now they are
bent on completing the toll of their sins, capping all the rest
by rejecting the Gospel. Peter, in his sermon at Solomon's
Portico, voices the view that the Jews had still a chance—a
breathing-space in which to repent for all their crimes, and
especially that of crucifying the Messiah. At the end of that
time Jesus would come again in Judgment (Acts iii. 19–21).
This was Paul's hope too—judging by his practice—though
here he is too angry to qualify his statement. The metaphor
is of a cup being filled to the brim. Originally the idea was
of a host passing the cup of wine to his guest. In the Old
Testament God was thought of as filling man's cup with good
things (Ps. xxiii. 5)—but also, conversely, He makes the
wicked drink the cup which contains their punishment (Ps.
xi. 6). The same metaphor is used in the Old Testament of

53

the Amorites in Abraham's day (Gen. xv. 16) and of the Pharisees by our Lord in Matthew's Gospel (Matt. xxiii. 32). In both cases the filling up of the cup is the prelude to impending judgment. Having filled their cup with their evil deeds, they must now drink it. This is clearly in Paul's mind too, for his next words are: **But the Wrath is on them to the bitter end!**

This is a difficult sentence. Two ideas seem to be involved —one, that God's Judgment—the Wrath of God (cf. i. 10), the inevitable retribution for sin—is already at work upon the Jews, their doom is sealed ; and, two, that the climax of that retribution—the Day of Judgment—is at hand. Perhaps Moffatt's translation might be improved if 'end' were spelt with a capital letter. The words are clearly eschatological and prophetic. They are living ' in the closing hours of the world ' (1 Cor. x. 11), and the Jews' rejection and hindering of the Gospel are part of the signs that the End is at hand. Kennedy points out the parallel between Paul's conviction that the anti-Christian activities of the Jews were a sign of imminent Judgment upon them, and the prophecy in Dan. viii. 23–5, where the hostile acts of the nations against the old Israel were similarly regarded as a prelude to the End. ' When their sins are fulfilled ' comes the crisis—in their case heralded by the ' king of fierce countenance,' in 2 Thessalonians by the Man of Sin (*St. Paul's Conceptions of the Last Things*, pp. 49–50). Later Paul makes it clear that finally Jew as well as Gentile will be redeemed (Rom. xi. 25–6) ; but here, so far as their existence as the People of God on this earth is concerned, he sees the sword of judgment poised over their heads.

It is not possible to be any more precise as to what the apostle meant. He is speaking in terms of ethical values, not of historical events. The Jews have forfeited their right to any mercy, and they must pay the price. That price will be paid very soon, and whether Paul prophetically identified the Fall of Jerusalem, A.D. 70— which must by A.D. 50 have seemed more than probable—with the Day of Judgment for them is immaterial. Certainly the Wrath cannot be identified with any past event, such as a famine (Acts xi. 27–30), or Claudius's persecution (Acts xviii. 2). Equally certainly there is no reason to regard it as referring to the Fall of Jerusalem as a past event. That would involve treating the sentence as a post-Pauline interpolation. In the Jewish ' Testament of the Twelve Patriarchs '—*c.* 100 B.C.—(Levi vi. 11) these words— with the addition of (the Wrath) ' of God '—appear with reference to the fate which befell Shechem. There it is an allusion to past history. ' The Wrath of God came upon them to the uttermost.' What connexion, if any, there may be between these two it is impossible to say. Paul may be consciously quoting and adapting the words to suit the changed circumstances, or the phrase may even be proverbial.

IV. NARRATIVE OF POST-CAMPAIGN EVENTS
(ii. 17–iii. 10)

What follows now is a more or less continuous narrative lasting till almost the end of chapter iii, in which Paul recalls what had happened since he visited Thessalonica, including his reasons for not visiting them again, then Timothy's visit in his stead, and subsequent report. It is, however, characteristically interrupted in ii. 19 f. and iii. 3*b* f. by short digressions. For convenience, however, we can divide the passage into three : (1) Paul explains his absence (ii. 17–20) ; (2) Timothy is sent instead (iii. 1–5), and (3) Timothy's report and Paul's reaction (iii. 6–10).

(1) PAUL EXPLAINS HIS ABSENCE (ii. 17–20)

Brothers, when we were bereft of you for a little while (out of 17
sight, not out of mind), we were the more eager to see you ;
we had a keen longing for you. (We did want to reach 18
you—I did, I Paul, more than once—but Satan stopped
us.) For who is our hope, our joy, our crown of pride 19
(who but you ?) in the presence of our Lord Jesus on his
arrival ? Why, you, you are our glory and joy! 20

Paul, after his onslaught on the Jews, appears to make a complete change of subject, and proceeds to discuss why he had been unable to visit Thessalonica again. It is very probable, however, that the change is not so abrupt as it seems, and that indeed behind this further piece of self-defence lies the same mischief-making which made his earlier apologia (ii. 1–12) necessary, and provoked the outburst in ii. 15–16. The local Jews would find in Paul's prolonged absence from Thessalonica one of their most useful rods for beating him. Here was a fine friend, a fine Christian missionary, professing his unbounded affection for his converts while he was with them, and then promptly putting them out of his mind and turning to some new crowd of dupes who would listen to his blandishments, bolster up his vanity, and keep him in comfort on their hard-earned money. This is the subtle propaganda that Paul has now to cope with. He does it by stating the facts with such obvious sincerity that any lingering doubts in the minds of the Thessalonians must have been at once dispelled.

17 **Brothers, when we were bereft of you for a little while (out of sight, not out of mind), we were the more eager to see you ; we had a keen longing for you.** Paul has already (vers. 7 and 11) compared himself to a mother and a father in his affection for them. Now he changes the metaphor and pictures himself without them as an orphan. (The word translated here ' bereft ' (*aporphanisthentes*) means, literally, ' orphaned.') He uses this strong word to express a sense of the deepest anguish. Like Jacob, Paul would say : ' If I be bereaved of my children, I am bereaved ' (Gen. xliii. 14). It was only, as he had then hoped, to be a separation of short duration. Yet no sooner was he parted from them—a parting that was only apparent because they were ever in his thoughts—than he was longing to see them again. They themselves had sent the apostles away from Thessalonica to Beroea for safety (Acts xvii. 10). The apostles had gone so unwillingly that they were the more eager to get back to them. Thinking about them was not enough, they wanted to see them face to face. As Denney says, nobody more than Paul more fully proved the truth of our Lord's words, that no one leaves house, wife, brothers, parents, children, for the Kingdom of God's sake, who does not

receive ever so much more (Luke xviii. 29). Paul had 'no home, no wife, no child . . . yet no father ever loved his children more tenderly . . . and no father was ever rewarded with affection more genuine ' (ad loc.).

(**We did want to reach you—I did, I Paul, more than once—** 18 **but Satan stopped us.**) Paul here breaks away from his habit in this letter of including the other missionaries with himself. As already noted (i. 2), the most likely explanation of this is not stylistic but practical—the fact that Timothy and Silvanus were very much involved in the Thessalonian Church and its fortunes. Generally the ' we ' passages, then, should be taken wherever possible as, out of courtesy, including the three apostles, though, of course, Paul's is the mind behind the thoughts expressed. Here, however, he specifically singles out himself. The reason is not simply that during a large part of the time since leaving Thessalonica Paul was alone—at Athens (cf. Acts xvii. 14 ff. ; I iii. 1), or Corinth (Acts xviii. 5). It is surely rather that the attacks of the Thessalonian Jews were directed against Paul personally as the leader, and the apostle uses ' I ' instead of ' we ' to emphasize his personal concern to return. **More than once** is better than A.V. and R.V. ' once and again,' which involves conjecturing definite occasions for his desire to revisit Thessalonica. It is much more likely that Paul means ' repeatedly.'

But what does he mean by **Satan stopped us** ? First of all, by reintroducing ' us ' he makes it plain that not only he himself but all three wanted to return, but were prevented in some way which he attributes to the agency of Satan. Satan is rarely mentioned in the Old Testament. In Israel's early days, evil as well as good is due to the inscrutable will of Jehovah. As time went on the difficulty of accounting for evil, as the conception of Jehovah became more ethical, was met by introducing ' Satan,' the Adversary, first as subordinate to Jehovah, almost a paid leader of H.M. Opposition (Zech. iii. 1—c. 500 B.C.), later, as a dignitary in the heavenly council with limited powers (Job. i. 6—c. 400 B.C.), and, finally, as an independent being, able to act contrary to God's will (I Chron. xxi. 1—c. 250 B.C.). Between the Old Testament and New Testament this conviction of a power of evil in the universe, independent of God, was strengthened. A hierarchy of evil spirits and demons—originally fallen angels—was constructed with Satan as their ruler.

In New Testament times, therefore, there are two kingdoms—the heavenly and the earthly—ruled over by God and Satan. Satan is now the personification of evil, the originator of temptation, disease, and all human wickedness (e.g. Mark i. 13, viii. 33 ; Luke xiii. 16), but whose power has begun to totter through the coming of Christ (Luke x. 18). Paul shares this view. Satan is the Tempter (iii. 5), the Evil One (2 iii. 3), the god of this world (2 Cor. iv. 4), the Prince of the air (Eph. ii. 2), still fighting valiantly for victory, and bent on thwarting the growth of the Kingdom and the spread of the Gospel. It is perhaps, however, truer to Paul's mind to say that while he regards Satan as the ruler of this passing age, it is chiefly with the thought of the whole army of demonic forces on a cosmic level that he is concerned. These are the Principalities, the Powers, the Forces of Darkness, the Spirits of Evil (Eph. vi. 12), antagonistic to God, perverting men, but conquered now potentially by Christ and soon to be finally destroyed. The salvation which Christ brought was in the first instance in pagan communities—as in the mission-field to-day—emancipation from the terror of evil spirits in men's minds.

Paul does not attribute all the obstacles that were put in his way to the Evil One. It was the Holy Spirit, or the Spirit of Jesus, that prevented the missionaries from evangelizing Asia and Bithynia as they had wished (Acts xvi. 6–7). It was God who allowed that messenger of Satan—Paul's ' thorn in the flesh'—to torment him (2 Cor. xii. 7–9). Possibly on reflection these were hindrances that appeared to have a purpose, and therefore were to be attributed to Divine agency. But the obstacles that prevented him from returning to Thessalonica had no Divine purpose behind them. Of that he was sure. They were the work of none other than Satan. This would therefore lead us to connect the hindrances, whatever they were, with the Jews. That would be in keeping with the whole tone of his protestations up till now. What particular obstacle it was, however, that prevented him from going back to Thessalonica he does not say.   Some commentators, not satisfied that Paul is referring to machinations of the Jews behind which he detects the hand of the Arch-Enemy himself, suggest that he is referring to illness—but that would not have prevented Silvanus from going to Thessalonica from Beroea.   Likewise the suggestions either that Satan = the Politarchs, and that the apostles were unwilling to compromise by their public return the position of Jason and their friends in Thessalonica, who had been bound over to keep the peace, or that the Jews in Thessalonica were on the look-out for an attempted secret return, are open to the objection that the Thessalonians would have been the first to know of these difficulties and would have understood their absence.   Nor would Paul have called the pressure of mission work in Athens or Corinth the work of Satan.   We must assume some obstacle put in the way of their return, of which the Thessalonians, through Timothy's visit, are now partly aware, and which therefore needs no further description.

Then in a burst of emotion he asks : **For who is our hope,** 19 **our joy, our crown of pride (who but you ?)**—how could they suspect that he was more interested in his more recent converts than in them ?   They were his chief boast.   The **crown of pride** has nothing to do with ' royal diadems.'   It is the victor's laurel wreath awarded at athletic games or a garland worn at some festive occasion.   The Thessalonians are ' something to be proud of.'   The same expression is used in the Old Testament of virtuous old age (Prov. xvi. 31).   They will be the apostle's crowning glory **in the presence of our Lord Jesus on his arrival.**   Elsewhere he speaks of his chief ambition as a missionary being to bring every man into God's presence, made perfect through Christ (Col. i. 28).   Now, he says, when Christ appears, his greatest boast and triumph will be his Thessalonian converts.   From which it appears that the apostle expected the Second Advent in his own lifetime. Yet when we have said this we have really said nothing.   The apostle's thought is in a realm beyond space and time.   The essence of his message is that when they meet in the presence of Christ—whenever or wherever that may be is a matter of no moment—his greatest pride will be this little handful of idol-worshipping Macedonians, now so unmistakably changed into devoted followers of the Lord Christ and part of His Body. Like the Philippians—the other of his favourite Churches—the Thessalonians will be his joy and crown (Phil. iv. 1).

> *' Thou shalt look round about and see*
> *Thousands of crown'd souls thronged to be*
> *Themselves thy crown.'*
> (Crashaw's lines to St. Teresa in heaven :
> quoted by Moffatt, *E.G.T.* ad loc.)

This is the first of many occasions in these epistles and in Christian theology where the word Parousia is used of the expected **arrival** of Christ, and it is apparently assumed that the readers are familiar with the word and the idea (cf. note on i. 9). Later Paul expands the bare statement by detailed description, and makes it clear that the word Parousia throughout these letters is used in a technical sense of the return of the glorified Christ to earth. It is sometimes used elsewhere in the epistles (e.g. 1 Cor. xvi. 17 ; 2 Cor. vii. 6 ; Phil. i. 26, ii. 12) with reference to himself and other missionaries in its original sense of ' presence' ; but in the Thessalonian epistles (iii. 13, iv. 15, v. 23 ; 2 ii. 1, 8) and in 1 Cor. xv. 23, where it is used with reference to Christ, it has the same significance of His impending Advent in Messianic power as it appears to have in the other letters of the early Church (e.g. James v. 7, 8 ; 2 Pet. i. 16, iii. 4, 12 ; 1 John ii. 28) and in Matthew's Gospel (xxiv. 3, 27, 37, 39). It is worth noting that the primary sense of ' presence ' is not excluded by the technical sense of ' coming.' Only at His Coming would the Lord be fully manifested to His people ; but He was even now ' present ' with them though absent from sight—the sense of His Coming was so acute that the early Christians were already in His presence, just as conversely the knowledge of the presence of His Spirit in their midst was so overwhelming that the hope of His Coming in person was the obvious sequel. The fundamental fact was Christ's nearness to them. This no doubt gave rise to the later use, after New Testament times, of the word Parousia to signify the Incarnation, which then became the First Advent, and the Parousia in the New Testament sense became the Second Advent.

The word is not used in the Old Testament of the Coming of the Messiah, nor, contrary to opinion, can it be definitely shown to have been common in Jewish apocalyptic writings (cf. Milligan, op. cit., p. 146). In Hellenistic times, however, the word Parousia was used both for the manifestation of a god and for a royal visit. These would appear to be the nearest clues to its use in the New Testament. The early Church thought of a future Parousia because the work of Redemption still awaited its climax—the historical fact of Jesus and the presence of the Spirit in their midst were a pledge to them of greater things to come, but what was known to them must still be revealed to the world at large. As time went on they came to recognize the appearance of Jesus in history, and all that it involved, as sufficiently a Messianic Advent to talk of a Parousia also in the past.

When the Lord Jesus comes, Paul replies to his own ques- 20 tion, need you ask who will be my chief boast ? **Why, you, you are our glory and joy ! Glory** is presumably here praise from other people ; **joy** is one's own happiness.

(2) Timothy is Sent Instead (iii. 1–5)

So, unable to bear it any longer, I made up my mind to be left 1
behind at Athens all alone ; I sent Timotheus our brother, 2
a minister of God in the gospel of Christ, for your strengthening and encouragement in the faith, to prevent anyone 3
from being disturbed by these troubles. (Troubles are our 4
lot, you know that well ; for we told you beforehand,
when we were with you, that ' we Christians are to have
trouble '—and, as you know, it has been so.) Well, then, 5
unable to bear it any longer, I sent to find out about your
faith, in case the Tempter had tempted you and our labour
had been thrown away.

The chapter division is awkward here, for these verses 1

clearly connect up with the last verses of chapter ii. Paul picks up the thread from ii. 17–18. ' I was dying to see you again, but a visit from me proved impossible. To send Timothy in my place was the next best thing,' so, **unable to bear it any longer, I made up my mind to be left behind at Athens all alone.** Moffatt makes it quite plain in verses 1–3 that Paul is referring to himself only, though the Greek (cf. A.V.) uses the plural. The movements of the missionaries after they departed in haste from Thessalonica are a little difficult to follow. The story in Acts suggests that Paul, Silvanus, and presumably Timothy, went together to Beroea (xvii. 10) where, after more Jewish trouble-making, it was thought best for Paul, the chief target, to leave by himself—Silvanus and Timothy remaining behind (xvii. 14). Paul went to Athens, sent back word with the Beroeans who had accompanied him, that Silvanus and Timothy should join him immediately (xvii. 15). According to Acts, however, they did not arrive until the Athenian visit was over and Paul was established in Corinth (xviii. 5). Yet we are told in this epistle that Timothy was with him in Athens and was sent back from there to Thessalonica (iii. 2).

There is no real contradiction if we explain the situation thus : Paul arrived in Athens alone ; Timothy joined him there, and was sent back to Thessalonica when Paul found it impossible to go himself. Paul then went on alone to Corinth, and was joined there by Silvanus and Timothy, both from Macedonia—Silvanus presumably from Beroea, and Timothy from Thessalonica. Luke has simply omitted Timothy's extra journey. This is much more likely than explaining the use of the plural by the fact that Silvanus and Timothy joined Paul at Athens. In that case Paul's loneliness at Athens (after Timothy was sent back to Thessalonica), which he strongly emphasizes, was largely a figure of speech.

Apart from other considerations, this *cri du coeur* rings true—he had to face Athens and its philosophers alone—and, having failed miserably, as he felt, arrived at Corinth in deep dejection (1 Cor. ii. 3)—which was probably as much physical as mental. The fact that he had to be accompanied by friends to Athens, apparently only to assist him on the voyage, is significant (Acts xvii. 15). His low spirits were only dispelled by the arrival of Silvanus and Timothy with the glad news from Macedonia which occasioned this letter. Athens was the least successful chapter of Paul's missionary career. His valiant attempt to meet the Athenians on their own ground missed fire—the sermon-summary itself sounds flat still (Acts xvii. 22 ff.). How much the companionship of Timothy would have meant to him in this unfriendly city, ' wholly given to idolatry ' (xvii. 16), and how much he thought of the Thessalonians to part with him to them !

I sent Timotheus our brother, a minister of God in the gospel 2. **of Christ**—the reading is doubtful here. Some MSS. give ' servant or minister of God ' (*diakonon*)—an unusual title for Timothy (except 1 Tim. iv. 6), who is generally only ' our brother.' Other MSS. read ' fellow-worker ' (*synergon*) or ' fellow-worker with God' (*synergon tou theou*), a favourite Pauline idea (cf. 1 Cor. iii. 9 ; 2 Cor. vi. 1). Whichever it is, this elaborate title is not designed to emphasize Paul's act of sacrifice in parting with him, but to enhance the importance of Timothy's visit—perhaps also with a side glance at Timothy's shyness and diffidence (1 Cor. xvi. 10, 11). Paul, unable to go himself, had not sent them some underling apprentice, but his dear brother Timothy, a fully qualified **minister of God in the gospel of Christ, for your strengthening and encouragement in the faith**—i.e. to strengthen and encourage you in your Christian belief and practice.

The Thessalonians needed strength and encouragement **to** 3 **prevent anyone from being disturbed by these troubles.** The background which these words imply is a continuation of the Gentile opposition to the mission in Thessalonica inspired by the ill-will of the local Jews. During these troubles—which are in this case not Paul's troubles—the new converts needed someone to steady them. Moffatt translates : they were liable to be *disturbed* (A.V. moved) by the opposition. The word is only found here, and this is the general view of its meaning. Another possible meaning is, however, if anything more suitable. Homer uses the word of a dog wagging its tail (*sainein*)—something therefore in the nature of fawning, flattering, cajoling, is suggested. This would better fit in with the tactics of the Jews in Thessalonica. The real danger to the Thessalonians was not so much that they should be shaken in their faith by persecution, but that during the Gentile opposition the Jews were losing no opportunity of sowing distrust in the converts' minds by their smooth talk (cf. ii. 1–12). The Thessalonians were in danger of being ' led astray ' or ' lured away.' One of the old commentators remarks : ' The devil is often more to be feared when he fawns than when he roars. . . . David vanquished Satan in the battle field ' (1 Sam. xvii. 49) ' but was vanquished by him in the cool of the evening on the housetop ' (2 Sam. xi. 2).

4   Then in parenthesis Paul adds : (**Troubles are our lot, you know that well ; for we told you beforehand, when we were with you, that ' we Christians are to have trouble '—and, as you know, it has been so**). It sounds as if one of the Jewish arguments must have been that any religion that aroused such opposition must be unwholesome and perverse. Paul's reply to this is that as they knew very well—how often had the missionaries not warned them ?—it was the inevitable lot of a Christian to face opposition and suffering in a hostile world. Paul now includes himself as sharing in the common lot of Christian suffering—and rightly. He had been the first victim of anti-Christian persecution in Thessalonica himself. For **troubles are our lot** (literally, we are appointed to (bear) this). This may be a reminiscence of our Lord's own words (e.g. Matt. v. 11–12) ; at all events, as Calvin points out, it amounts to saying : ' This is the law of the Christian life.' Certainly in Thessalonica and the early Church generally there was no chance of avoiding open hostility. The danger came, not so much from the Roman authorities, as from the pagan priesthood, jealous and outraged Jewish fanatics, financial interests, and the ignorance and stupidity of the masses. All these would conspire to make life at times a bitter trial. Social pressure and mob law were more dangerous weapons than Government action.

When Paul told the Thessalonians that ' **we Christians are**

to have trouble,' did he mean only this obvious kind of opposition or did he mean something more ?   Apart from anything
else, the strong word ' we are appointed ' suggests rather the
vocation than the inevitability of suffering for Christian converts.   It is like the compulsion implied in Acts xiv. 22 : ' It
is through many troubles that we must enter the Kingdom of
God,' and the general view of the Gospel events as having
been already planned by God (e.g. Luke ii. 35 ; Mark viii.
31).   While the words have universal applicability in the
Christian life—' there is no need of Purgatory for anyone who
loves sufficiently a sufficient number of people' (quoted by
Anderson Scott, *Footnotes to St. Paul*, p. 211)—there may have
been in Paul's mind the close connexion between troubles of
all descriptions and the impending end of the world.   It had
been foretold by Jesus (Mark xiii. 7 ff.), and the Messianic
Woes which should precede the Messiah's coming were a
postulate of Jewish theology.   Before the Kingdom could be
fully realized there must be violent opposition and much
travail for Christians to endure (see 2 ii. 3).   There may also
be that profound insight of Col. i. 24, that the true member of
the Body of Christ is in some measure bearing Christ's suffer-
ings for him.   In this sense all Christian suffering is *Stigmata
Christi*.   This has been—and still is—the experience of many
devout souls within the Church.   But the unreality of the
experience in the Church as a whole in our own country to-day
is perhaps at the root of our complacency and the measure of
our failure.

Paul now repeats his words of verse 1.   It is not, as some   5
have thought, a different messenger that Paul refers to here.
As is clear from verse 6, Timothy is the only emissary in
question.   **Well then, unable to bear it any longer, I sent to
find out about your faith.**   Concerned about the possible effect
of Gentile opposition and Jewish guile upon the loyalty of the
Thessalonians, he sent Timothy to report back, **in case the
Tempter had tempted you and our labour had been thrown
away.**   As well as the primary purpose of strengthening and
encouraging the Thessalonians, Paul had as a secondary object in sending Timothy the setting of his own mind at rest.

Paul was, as we have seen, in unusually low spirits and, probably, bad health at this point, and perhaps more ' on edge ' than was normal. The **Tempter** is, of course, Satan (see note on ii. 18), the prime mover behind the evil designs of the Jews, who are certainly referred to here, and probably also in ii. 18. In this case the Tempter—with a Jewish accent—had been suggesting to the Thessalonians that this Christianity was hardly worth what it cost them, and that all things considered —the indifference of Paul and the opposition of their own kith and kin—they would be much better to drop it. **In case the Tempter had tempted you**—Paul knew very well the Tempter had, in fact, been extremely busy. What he could not bear was the thought that all the work of the campaign might have been for nothing. The whole sentence might equally well and with added vividness be translated as a question in Paul's mind spoken aloud : had the Tempter perhaps tempted you, and would our labour be thrown away ?

(3) TIMOTHY'S REPORT (iii. 6–10)

6 But when Timotheus reached me a moment ago, on his return from you, bringing me the good news of your faith and love and of how you always remember me kindly, longing

7 to see me as I long to see you, then, amid all my own distress and trouble, I was cheered—this faith of yours en-

8 couraged me. It is life to me now, if you stand firm in the

9 Lord. How can I render thanks enough to God for you, for all the joy you make me feel in the presence of our God?

10 Night and day I pray specially that I may see your faces and supply what is defective in your faith.

A new topic is now introduced, and there is a break in the narrative. Paul has just described the despatch of Timothy and the anxious thoughts which had accompanied him from Athens and had followed him ever since. Now he describes Timothy's return. The apostle has by this time moved on to Corinth, and he is engaged in synagogue disputations with the Jews, in the interval of plying his trade under the auspices of Aquila and Priscilla, when Silvanus and Timothy arrive from Macedonia (Acts xviii. 1–5). It seems as if, unnerved

and ill, as he probably was, after his Athenian experience
(1 Cor. ii. 3), the arrival of Silvanus and Timothy gave him
new life. He forthwith adopted much more aggressive tactics—turned his back on the obdurate Jews—and launched a
Gentile mission. It does appear that in the apostle's mind
much more turned on what kind of news Timothy would
bring back than just the welfare of the Thessalonian Church.
Paul's approach at Athens had been wrong. If in addition
the Thessalonians, who had been such exemplary converts,
and whose mission had been attended with such notable tokens
of the presence of the Spirit, could not stand up to the wiles
of the Devil for such a short time, then perhaps the whole
missionary plan of action must be changed. Paul's subdued
behaviour at Corinth until the Macedonian reporters arrived
indicates something of this kind. But now Timothy had returned and set his fears at rest. All was well at Thessalonica
—indeed, so much better than he expected that the apostle's
delight knows no bounds and he ends on a high note of thanksgiving to God running into a prayer for the continued welfare
of the young Church.

But when Timotheus reached me a moment ago—a pardon- 6
able exaggeration, it may have been a day or two—**on his
return from you, bringing me the good news of your faith and
love. . . .** Paul is so delighted with Timothy's report on
Thessalonica that he uses the technical word for ' spreading
the Gospel ' (*euangelizomai*)—only here in the New Testament
used in a non-technical sense—for the **good news** about
Thessalonica that Timothy brings. But what Timothy told
him was in fact the Gospel in action—the seed bearing fruit.
Their **faith and love** is Paul's way of summing up their Christian witness, what Calvin calls : *totam pietatis summam.*
Faith, or trust, is the Christian's relation to God : **love** com-
prehends his ethical obligations to his fellows (cf. 1 Cor. xiii.).
The third ingredient of the triad in i. 3 is lacking, namely,
hope. As so much of the rest of the letter is concerned with
questions about their ' hope,' the two others are here emphasized.
  Timothy reports also, as Paul notes gratefully, that
apart from their Christian faith and conduct, their personal

affection for the apostle himself is unabated—**how you always remember me kindly**—not necessarily a reference to prayer, but simply ' as a pastor and friend,' as he likewise remembers them (i. 3)—**longing to see me as I long to see you.** Paul is obviously not concerned about what the Thessalonians think of him for his own sake. As a good psychologist, however, he recognizes that an affectionate personal relationship between pastor and people is the foundation of a successful ministry in the best sense. It may be that it is only the foundation, but certainly a pastorate without that foundation achieves very doubtful results for the Kingdom.

7 When all this accumulated good tidings reached him— news that the Thessalonians were standing firm despite all Gentile opposition—and that their affection for Paul remained unchanged despite all Jewish slanders—**then, amid all my own distress and trouble, I was cheered**—**this faith of yours encouraged me.** **Distress** here means ' privation,' and **trouble,** as before, means ' persecution.' The result of this cheering news was seen in the new zest Paul displayed in the Corinthian mission (Acts xviii. 5 ff.). His own hardships and tribulations there were forgotten in his delight over the report that the Thessalonians had stood fast in what mattered above all, their **faith.** This, as he was later to develop in the epistle to the Romans, was always for Paul the fundamental postulate of the Christian life.

8 How much this news from Thessalonica meant to him can be seen in the vehemence of his next words. **It is life to me now, if you stand firm in the Lord.** Paul meant every word of it. It was no idle talk or tea-table gossip, this interest in the successes and failures of the Churches he founded. It was a passionate concern. They were his life in the sense that the only thing that made life worth living was the successful propagation of the Gospel. He was prepared to lose his life at any time amid **distress and trouble** (cf. 2 Cor. xi. 24 ff.) for his Master's sake, because he had already found the only life that mattered, and the news from Thessalonica revived this new life within him.

To stand firm **in the Lord** was to remain steadfast in Christian belief and practice, through being in the same relationship to Christ as the branch is to the vine. But now, characteristically, Paul's instincts direct him to the fountain-head. He is overflowing with thankfulness for what, judged by secular standards, was a personal triumph. It was a tribute to Paul above all, that in spite of all sorts of discouragements, the Christian foundations had been so truly laid during the Thessalonian campaign that the converts remained unshaken. It was only slightly less a tribute to the Thessalonians that they had been so surprisingly loyal amid so many difficulties. But Paul does not for a moment doubt where the real *fons et origo* lies. As a Christian, he gives God the glory.

How can I render thanks enough—not to you Thessalonians, 9 or to myself—but **to God for you**—and not ' on your behalf ' but ' on your account '—**for all the joy you make me feel in the presence of our God ?** Paul's rejoicing is consecrated. He lifts up his natural gladness over Timothy's report and offers it to God. The grace of God has made this thing possible : to Him alone be the glory. ' The more grace abounds, the more thanksgiving may arise and redound to the glory of God ' (2 Cor. iv. 15). This very thanksgiving itself is the work of the Spirit (Rom. viii. 26). For Paul, God's grace is equally seen in the conversion of the pagans, in the gift of the Spirit, in the successes of the mission-field, and in the thanksgiving of His people for these blessings. They are only giving God back His own. The Greek word for **render** (*antapodidōmi*) means to ' return what is due.' How can anyone hope, says Paul, to return the thanks that are God's due ?

But Timothy's report was not to the effect that the Thessalonian Church was a garden of roses. Paul's Christian realism, while it enables him to put first things first, does not allow him to wear blinkers. He is rightly filled with rejoicing to hear that the little Church has remained true to its faith—that is primary. But Thessalonica has its problems, to which Paul turns now and which occupy him to the end of the letter.

It is in the light of this that he says in winding up this 10 section of the epistle : **night and day**—not, of course, ' at two set hours daily ' but ' continually '—**I pray specially that I**

may see your faces and—not now merely to renew our friendship but to—**supply what is defective in your faith.** His eagerness to see them again is intensified by what he has heard from Timothy. Their faith is strong enough : what it lacks is moral content and doctrinal instruction. This is what chapters iv. and v. and the second epistle supply. The Thessalonians were faithful to Christ and loyal to His apostles, but they needed guidance and direction. Calvin's comment is worth while : ' From this it is clear how much we must devote ourselves to teaching. For teachers were not ordained only that in one day or in one month they should bring men to the faith of Christ, but that they should bring to completion the faith that has just begun.' Although Paul's own conversion was ' sudden,' he would be the last to say that that was enough, or that conversion was the culmination of the Christian life. Rather is it only the beginning. ' Sudden ' and ' gradual ' conversions alike must be followed by instruction. Teaching is as important as preaching.

Some words of Denney are worth quoting in this connexion : ' In one sense faith is a very simple thing, the setting of the heart right with God in Christ Jesus. In another it is very comprehensive. It has to lay hold on the whole revelation which God has made in His Son, and it has to pass into action through love in every department of life. It is related on the one side to knowledge and on the other to conduct. . . . In its earliest stage it is compatible with a high degree of ignorance, of foolishness, of insensibility in the conscience ; and hence the believer must not forget that he is a disciple : and that though he has entered the school of Christ, he has only entered it, and has many classes to pass through, and much to learn and unlearn, before he can become a credit to his Teacher ' (ad loc.). To provide this enlightenment on moral and theological matters is in fact one of the main purposes of the epistle. What we have read so far, it transpires, are only the ' preliminaries.' They are rounded off by a prayer (iii. 11–13) which recapitulates what Paul has just said. Verse 11 echoes verse 10*a*, and verses 12 and 13 echo verse 10*b*. The phrase about ' the deficiencies in their faith ' is the bridge between the first and the second half of the letter. Having tactfully praised the Thessalonians, Paul now goes on to deal with their shortcomings.

V. PRAYER
(iii. 11-13)

May our God and Father and our Lord Jesus direct my way to 11 **you! And may the Lord make you increase and excel in** 12 **love to one another and to all men (as is my love for you), so as to strengthen your hearts and make them blameless** 13 **in holiness before our God and Father when our Lord Jesus comes with all his holy ones. (Amen.)**

This short passage marks another stage in the formal arrangement of the epistle. The Greeting (i. 1) is followed by the thanksgiving (i. 2-10). Then a general review of the Thessalonian situation (ii. 1-iii. 10) issues in this prayer (iii. 11-13) for the continued progress of the Church. But it would be a mistake to regard this prayer as purely a formal division in a prescribed method of letter-writing. It is a devotional outburst occasioned by the thoughts that have been passing through the apostle's mind. Like the psalmists, Paul finds the evidence of the Living God at work in his own life at times overwhelming.

Realizing that after all it is God Himself alone who can 11 turn our desires into reality, Paul sums up his own thoughts and hopes now in a prayer. **May our God and Father and our Lord Jesus direct my way to you !** It is worth noticing that Paul uses here the singular of the word **direct.** Our God and Father and our Lord Jesus are not two but one. No doubt this is not a theological statement (cf. note on i. 9), but it is an indication that the apostle regarded God and Jesus as a unity to whom he addressed his prayers. **Direct** means in one sense ' make straight ' (cf. Ps. xxxvi. (xxxvii.) 23— LXX), i.e. by removing the obstacles. There may be here an allusion to ii. 18 in that the hindrances put in Paul's way by Satan can only be removed by a power greater than Satan's.

The first part of Paul's petition is that it may please God to allow him to revisit Thessalonica ; the second is that He would bless the Church there and make it more like what the Church ought to be.

12 **May the Lord make you increase and excel in love to one another and to all men (as is my love for you).** Whether his own visit ever takes place or not, this is his prayer for them. **The Lord** here is surely Jesus. In Paul's mind there was no real distinction. It was only when he came to know Jesus that the word *Kurios*—the ordinary word for the Lord in the Old Testament—came to have a real vital content. His prayer is that they may **increase and excel in love.** ' Love ' they had already (i. 3), but in Bacon's words : ' Love is the only thing that cannot be carried to excess,' and in a wonderful phrase Chrysostom calls this a prayer for ' the unchecked madness of love.' It was not, however, only to be **love to one another**— that was no more than the Gentiles practised, as the Master had said (Matt. v. 46 ff.)—but the much more difficult demand of **love to all men**—even their enemies and persecutors. Such love could only come as a gift from God.

As a pattern of what their attitude should be, he cites himself : **as is my love for you.** He could ask for them no greater power of selfless concern for the good of others than his own devoted consideration for them. It may be that this special emphasis on **love** indicates that there was particular need of such an intercession on their behalf. The other Macedonian Church at Philippi suffered from a tendency to quarrelsomeness and backbiting (Phil. ii. 1–11, iv. 1–2). But there is nothing elsewhere in the letter to indicate that the ' monstrous regiment of women ' which apparently caused the trouble at Philippi (iv. 2) obtained also at Thessalonica.

13 The purpose of the prayer concludes this part of the letter. The abundance of love that Paul asks to be granted them is **so as to strengthen your hearts and make them blameless in holiness before our God and Father when our Lord Jesus comes with all his holy ones.** Once again (cf. ii. 4), the Biblical use of **heart** takes the place of what we should call the inner self, the whole personality, will and thought as well as emotion.

The Lord's grace is to produce in them such a measure of selfless love that their whole lives will be transformed in readiness for the Great Day when He appears. **Love** is the basis of their achievements in character. They will be true Christians only if the love of Christ dwells in them ; it is that that **strengthens** their will to obedience. Perfect moral achievement would produce **blameless** characters : perfect moral achievement, recognized as obedience to the will of God, i.e. inward purity, as well as external compliance, would produce characters **blameless in holiness.** The word used for ' holiness ' here (*hagiōsune*) does not mean ' sanctification ' (*hagiasmos*)—the process of becoming holy—but the state of holiness itself, ' sanctity.' Since selfishness is the essence of sinfulness, love, which turns the self away from itself and towards God, is the condition of holiness, which is the antithesis of sinfulness. **Before our God and Father** means in God's sight. A man may be morally blameless without being holy, and a man may be ecclesiastically ' holy ' without being moved by love. But to be blameless in holiness **before God** demands the inwardness of consecrated service—the ' heart ' must be pure as well as the outward behaviour, and the motive must be love to God and one's neighbour.

The whole thought is, of course, eschatological, leading up to the last clause. Paul prays that the Thessalonians may be so richly blessed that they will be able to be presented spotless before God **when our Lord Jesus comes with all his holy ones.** As before (ii. 19), and elsewhere in these letters (iv. 15, v. 23 ; 2 ii. 1, 8), the reference is to the Second Advent of Christ, which is regarded as not far off. The word translated here ' holy ones ' is the ordinary word for ' saints ' (A.V.)—*hagioi*— which in the early Church was a synonym for Christians (2 i. 10 ; Rom. i. 7 ; 1 Cor. i. 2 ; 2 Cor. i. 1 ; Eph. i. 1 ; Phil. i. 1 ; Col. i. 2, etc.). The ' saints ' are therefore generally neither the canonized saints of our stained-glass windows, nor even the faithful departed, but ordinary Church members. Clearly this cannot be the meaning intended here. For Christ at His coming is to bring the ' saints ' with Him. But the Thessalonian ' saints ' in the ordinary New Testament sense are to be presented blameless in holiness before God when Christ appears. Who, then, are the ' saints ' that Christ will bring with Him ? (*a*) If they are angels, it is odd that Paul does not say so, since he uses the word *angeloi* later on (2 i. 7) when he refers to Christ coming with His angels. (*b*) It may be that he means the faithful departed in this case. He certainly speaks in the next chapter of their return from the dead with Christ when He comes (iv. 14). (*c*) It is also possible that he means both the blessed dead and the angels. Of the three this seems the most likely. The preferences of the commentators are almost equally divided among them.

Another possibility not to be ignored is that Paul had none of these in particular in his mind at all. If, as looks very probable, the passage is more an echo of conventional liturgical phraseology, the words **with all his holy ones** would attach themselves to the thought of the Parousia almost automatically and without clear definition in Paul's own mind. The expression follows closely the words of Zech. xiv. 5 (LXX) : ' And the Lord my God will come and all the *Hagioi* with Him.' There the prophecy concerns the great Day of Jehovah, and the *Hagioi* are obviously the angelic retinue of the Lord when He comes to judge the world. A significant indication of the adaptation of features of the Old Testament Day of Jehovah to the Second Advent is that the Zechariah passage (xiv. 5) is quoted literally in the later ' Teaching of the Twelve Apostles ' (xvi. 7) and applied to the Second Coming of Christ with the resurrected saints. Similar language is used in the Old Testament (LXX) of the descent of Jehovah at Sinai ('on His right hand were His angels with Him '—Deut. xxxiii. 2), and in the gospels of the Coming of the Messiah in Judgment (Mark viii. 38) (' when He (the Son of Man) comes in the glory of His Father with the holy angels'). (Cf. also Matt. xxv. 31 : Jude 14.) Some MSS. at this point add Amen—perhaps a liturgical response.

VI. PRACTICAL PROBLEMS
(Chaps. iv.–v.)

(1) MORAL INJUNCTIONS (iv. 1–12)
(a) *General Exhortation* (iv. 1–2)

Finally, brothers, we beg and beseech you in the Lord Jesus to 1
follow our instructions about the way you are to live, so
as to satisfy God ; you are leading that life, but you are
to excel in it still further. You remember the instruc- 2
tions we gave you, on the authority of the Lord Jesus.

Paul might quite well have finished the letter at the end of
chapter iii. The ' Amen ' inserted in various MSS. perhaps
indicates that the copyists thought so too. He set out on
Timothy's arrival from Macedonia to express the gratification
he felt at the heartening news of their loyalty and steadfastness, and to defend himself against Jewish intrigues. This he
has now done, but there are some matters to be cleared up
before he stops. It is not necessary to assume that Paul is
from now on replying to points raised in a letter sent by the
Thessalonians. The sequence of topics explains itself equally
well as points which Timothy had mentioned in conversation
and which now occur to the apostle as he addresses them. It
is not even necessary to assume that all that is contained in
the next two chapters of this letter is designed to meet special
problems that had arisen at Thessalonica. Much of it may
simply be, as in the first part of the letter, echoes of the
original campaign—reminders of the kind of instruction the
converts were given during the apostles' visit.

Finally, brothers, when there is almost half of the letter yet 1
to come, seems a trifle reminiscent of some sermons. Paul
uses the same word (*loipon*), however, in the middle of the
Philippian letter (iii. 1) as well as near the end (iv. 8). It
seems to have been used in secular literature to mark a transition to practical exhortation. **We beg and beseech you in the**
Lord Jesus to follow our instructions about the way you are to
live, so as to satisfy God; you are leading that life, but you
are to excel in it still further. Moffatt's paraphrase, though
giving the sense, conceals an interesting sidelight on Paul's

handling of his converts. The sentence, literally translated, reads : ' Finally, then, brothers, we beg and beseech you in the Lord Jesus, that, as you have received instructions from us how you ought to live so as to please God—and indeed you are so living—that you increase (in it) more and more.' Paul's original thought was clearly : ' As you were instructed by us how to live . . . so you must live.' Tact and politeness compel him to soften the suggestion that they were not in fact complying with his instructions. He therefore changes the admonition to a word of praise, ' and indeed you are so living ' ; having done which he has to finish the sentence by urging them to do even better.

We **beseech you in the Lord Jesus**—not by our own authority but by the authority that both you and we acknowledge as supreme—**to follow our instructions** (literally, as you have received (instructions) from us). The word for ' to receive by hearsay or tradition ' (*paralambanō*) is, as in ii. 13, the technical word in the Christian mission for the handing on of information and instruction pertaining to the Gospel. (Cf. 1 Cor. xv. 3, xi. 23.) The instruction which had been given to them at Thessalonica, to which Paul now claims to add nothing new, was the common teaching of the Christian missionaries **about the way you are to live so as to satisfy God.** ' Live ' is the real meaning of the word, common in the Old Testament, translated ' walk ' in the A.V. To ' walk with God ' as the patriarch did (Gen. v. 22) is to live in accordance with God's will. This is to **satisfy** or please God, a frequent criterion in this letter. (ii. 4, ii. 15.) **You are leading that life,** says Paul kindly, **but you are to excel in it further.** ' You are doing very well, but try to do even better.'

2   **You remember the instructions we gave you on the authority of the Lord Jesus.** Paul's message to the Thessalonians had not been merely Good News of God's mighty acts, but the moral obligations of believers—teaching as well as preaching, *didachē* as well as *kērygma*. We may assume that by this time there was a fairly clearly formulated body of moral instruction on the Christian life which was imparted to new converts. The substance of it would be the sayings of Jesus.

The word here for ' instruction ' (*parangelia*) means significantly enough a word of command given by a superior officer
to be passed down to others, e.g. Acts xvi. 24. Paul
reminds his readers of some of their obligations now. None
of his injunctions was a private opinion or an invention of his
own, he had delivered them **on the authority of the Lord Jesus.**
The apostles had been only the Lord's messengers in the sense
of handing on the accepted teaching of the Church as the
Church had received it from Jesus. Where Paul gave his own
opinion he said so (cf. 1 Cor. vii. 10 with 1 Cor. vii. 12 ; 1 Cor.
vii. 25–6). Nor was this the dead hand of past tradition, for
behind the authoritative teaching of the missionaries was the
greater authority of the ever-present indwelling Christ.

(b) On Sex (iv. 3–8)

It is God's will that you should be consecrated, that you abstain 3
    from sexual vice, that each of you should learn to take a 4
    wife for himself chastely and honourably, not to gratify 5
    sensual passion like *the Gentiles in their ignorance of God—*
    no one is to defraud or overreach his brother in this mat- 6
    ter, for *the Lord avenges* **all these sins, as we told you**
    already in our solemn protest against them. God did not 7
    call us to be impure, but to be consecrated ; hence, he 8
    who disregards this, disregards not man but the God who
    gave you his holy Spirit.

One might ask at this point whether the raising of this topic
first by the apostle indicated that sexual laxity had assumed
large proportions among the Thessalonians. It does not
sound, from the general congratulatory tone of the letter, that
any vice was prevalent to great extent, though at the same
time Paul has just recognized that in some respects the life of
the new Church is not all that it might be (iii. 10). It is
possible, but not likely, that Timothy had reported cases of
immorality—Paul's handling of actual misdemeanours might
perhaps have been more trenchant (cf. 1 Cor. v.). It is more
likely that the advice given here is prophylactic. Timothy
may well have brought back news of the difficulties experienced by the Thessalonians of living up to Christian moral

standards in a pagan environment, and to Paul living in Corinth this would be no news.

Much speculation has arisen—largely as a result of some observations by Lightfoot (*Biblical Essays*, p. 257)—about the cult of the Kabeiroi at Thessalonica. We know so little about this apart from the fact that it was a mystery-religion second in popularity only to the Eleusinian Mysteries, and practised in Thessalonica, that Lightfoot's supposition that it included ' foul orgies ' may be questioned. Lightfoot suggests that the charge of impurity brought against Paul by the Jews (ii. 3), which he indignantly repudiates, is connected with these practices. If there were this concentrated sex-laden atmosphere in Thessalonica, it would certainly explain Paul's emphasis on its dangers. But even without it, his own knowledge of Greek cities, especially the one from which he was writing, would make this part of the moral instruction of the converts the one that most needed repetition—especially to people living in a cosmopolitan seaport. The pagan attitude to sex-relations was extremely tolerant (see Lecky's *History of European Morals*, i, pp. 104 ff.)—in some religious societies sacramental fornication was part of the worship. It must have been particularly hard for ex-pagans, who had not the moral discipline of the Jewish Law behind them, to break the attitude or habits of a lifetime and to live up to the Christian standard in sex-behaviour. This is enough reason for Paul now to put this important matter in the forefront of his ethical injunctions. He now makes explicit what he had meant by ' living so as to satisfy God,' and the ' instructions ' he had given them.

3 **It is God's will that you should be consecrated.** This is the primary demand upon the Christian, that he should live his life in all respects as a servant of God, setting himself apart to His service. The literal translation is : ' For this is the will of God, (namely) your sanctification.' The word (*hagiasmos*) is related to ' holiness ' (*hagiōsunē*) in iii. 13 as the gradual process which leads up to the final state. ' Consecration ' or sanctification beginning here and now points forward to ' blameless holiness . . . at the Coming of our Lord Jesus.'

From this basic attitude it follows **that you abstain from sexual vice.** The Thessalonians—and all ex-pagans—had to learn this when they became Christians. In our own semi-pagan society it needs to be stated again as firmly as Paul does here. ' Affairs ' are not a source of easy laughs for radio or variety comedians, but—more properly described as promiscuous fornication—are one of the Seven Deadly Sins.

It also follows **that each of you should learn**—not as Moffatt 4 translates : ' To take a wife for himself,' but—' to possess his own body ' **chastely and honourably.** The interpretation here turns on the meaning of the Greek word *skeuos*, translated in the A.V. and R.V. as ' vessel.' Is a man's ' vessel ' his wife or his body ? Much may be said on both sides. In favour of the meaning ' wife,' supported by many modern commentators—and St. Augustine !—it is held that *skeuos* is used in this sense in rabbinical literature, and that it is not used in this way of ' body ' anywhere else in the New Testament, but is definitely used of a ' wife ' in St. Peter's famous reference to the ' weaker vessel ' (1 Pet. iii. 7). Against this meaning and in favour of ' body ' are the Greek commentators generally and some Reformation and present-day authorities. Their contention is that to translate *skeuos* ' wife ' is to lower the whole conception of Christian marriage, which Paul would hardly want to do at this juncture ; that the frequent use of *skeuos* in Greek to denote the body, the vessel of the soul, is paralleled in Paul himself : ' We have this treasure in earthen vessels ' (2 Cor. iv. 7) ; that the argument from 1 Pet. iii. 7 rather supports ' body,' in that both the man and his wife are spoken of as ' vessels,' the wife being the weaker of the two ; and that, in fact, the quoted examples from rabbinical literature of the word *skeuos* do not necessarily mean ' wife ' at all, but have the normal meaning of ' vessel ' or ' instrument.'

A difficulty in making ' vessel ' mean ' body ' is the word that precedes it. Moffatt translates it as ' take ' (*ktasthai*), which is the orthodox meaning. Obviously if this word can only mean ' take,' it would be awkward for those who favour the ' body ' theory, and favourable for those (like Moffatt) who prefer ' wife.' The papyri, however, reveal that the present tense of this verb could also be used in a perfect sense as 'to have taken,' i.e. 'to possess' (Moulton and Milligan's *Vocabulary*). There is therefore no reason why the more attractive translation of the whole sentence should not also be the thought that was in Paul's mind, namely, that the Thessalonians should regard their bodies as the temple of the Holy Spirit (1 Cor. vi. 19 ; Rom. xii. 1), and therefore learn, instead of being possessed by their passions, to possess them.

The whole passage, therefore, is not an injunction to married men to treat their wives as objects of respect instead of lust, or to unmarried men to get married to prevent fornication on the *pis aller* basis of 1 Cor. vii. 2, 9. It rather sustains the initial note of consecration. The whole question of sex-relationships has to be viewed in this light, that for the Christian the body is to be offered to God as completely as the mind and the spirit. It makes little difference to the sense if, as some commentators suggest, we translate the verb 'to learn' (*eidenai*) in this sentence as 'to respect or reverence,' which is what it means in v. 12. This would mean 'that each of you should reverence his own body, controlling it, literally, "in holiness and honour ".' 'Holiness' (*hagiasmos*) is used here like *hagiōsunē* in iii. 13, meaning the 'state' of inward purity or consecration, and not, as in iv. 3, meaning the 'process' of sanctification.

5　The man who looks on his body in this light uses it **not to gratify sensual passion like** *the Gentiles in their ignorance of God*. This is the opposite of 'mastering the body in chastity and honour '—it means that a man is a slave to his own lusts. 'It is not I who do the deed, but sin that dwells within me ' (Rom. vii. 17). Love and reverence for man and woman disappear, and they become, not sons and daughters of God, but things to be made use of for purely selfish ends. This was the popular pagan view (see Rom. i. ; 1 Cor. vi.), and it is a view that has been condemned not only by Christian moralists. Burns, in his 'Epistle to a Young Friend,' speaks from the heart when he says : 'But och, it hardens a' within and petrifies the feeling.' It almost seems as if Paul were writing to Jews, since he refers here to the Gentiles. But for Paul

Gentiles include all pagans outside the Church, while those Christians who were once pagan are now part of the Israel of God. It is clear, from his references to past idolatry (i. 9), that most of his readers came into this category.

The phrase ' the Gentiles who know not God ' is found almost *verbatim* in Jer. x. 25 (LXX) and the same thought in Ps. lxxviii (lxxix.) 6. Paul uses it to account for the evil state of the world. Although the pagans had been given a certain natural perception of God and His ways, they had refused to recognize it. They had preferred idolatry, and idolatry had given rise to immorality (Rom. i. 20 ff.). Paul has no doubt that Christian doctrine and Christian ethics are inseparable. Rejection of God in Christ inevitably leads to sexual laxity. Conversely, the Thessalonians, having welcomed the new faith, have automatically a new criterion, namely, the consecration of the body to God.

No one is to defraud or overreach—better, perhaps, ' disregard and take advantage of '—**his brother in this matter** (literally, in ' the ' matter). The question is : in which matter ? Moffatt obviously—and probably correctly—refers it back to the matter which has just been discussed—namely, sexual intercourse. The A.V., however, translates as ' in any matter '—i.e. not only in sex-relationships but in affairs generally. This seems the least likely of any interpretation. But it points to another possibility which superficially has much in its favour. The word translated ' matter ' is *pragma*, which can mean also—in the plural at any rate—' business.' It has therefore been suggested that Paul breaks off the topic of Sex and introduces a new one, Greed. Certainly it makes sense to read : ' No one is to defraud or overreach his brother in business.' It has the authority of the Vulgate, and the fact that sensuality and avarice were the recognized twin vices of paganism. The difficulty is that *pragma* in the singular does not generally mean ' business,' and the next few words, dealing with ' uncleanness,' seem to be still referring to sexual matters. Another possibility is that *pragma* means ' a dispute,' as it does in 1 Cor. vi. 1. It seems on the whole most reasonable to regard this section iv. 3–8 as a unity, dealing

6

with Christian teaching on the relation between the sexes, and to regard *pragma*, in the sense of ' matter,' as a euphemism for the sexual promiscuity—normal and abnormal—of paganism. The whole clause then is a reminder of the Christian's obligation not to treat anyone as less than a person in this respect—married or unmarried—least of all a fellow-Christian, man or woman. The word **brother** is here used in its widest sense.

For *the Lord avenges* **all these sins, as we told you already in our solemn protest against them.** This is the first of three reasons that the apostle gives why pagan licence in sexual matters could not be shared by Christians. (1) There is a judgment on sin ; (2) our calling as Christians involves personal consecration (ver. 7) ; (3) it is an injury done to God Himself (ver. 8). The sanction given here is one of fear of the consequences. Sin will be punished **for** *the Lord avenges.* The thought of the avenging Lord is so common in the Old Testament that there is no need to look here for a specific allusion. If there is one, it is probably an echo of Deut. xxxii. 35. In the Old Testament and Apocrypha, Judgment is the function of Jehovah, here of Christ at His Second Advent, as in 2 i. 7 ff. It is clear from this how closely related in the early missions were the moral demands of Christianity and the impending Judgment on those who disregarded them, not only on Gentiles, but on Christians who relapsed into pagan ways.

It is, of course, possible that Paul's idea here is of the same impersonal inevitability of judgment upon sin as in the corresponding idea of the Wrath (see note on i. 10, ii. 16). But it seems less likely that he is thinking here of the physical and psychological consequences of moral laxity, than of the actual Day of Judgment itself. It is, of course, in a real sense true that both aspects are indistinguishable. The crucial point in Paul's mind is that there is judgment on sin. It is both present and future. Sin brings its own nemesis in mental and moral corruption and insensitiveness, but there must be some moment of confrontation when we come fully face to face with the Holiness of God and are made to recognize how far we have come short of it. This can only take place, as Paul

cléarly saw, in an eschatological setting. The pictorial image
which he had of such an Assize is immaterial—any we have
ourselves is equally speculative. What is important is that
we realize there is Judgment, and that fear of it is a wholesome
Christian emotion. **All these sins** may refer either to all the
varieties of immorality implied in the earlier part of the verse,
or it may refer to a standard moral catechism which the
missionaries had left with the Thessalonians, comprising
among other things injunctions on sexual matters. At all
events Paul bases his present observations on teaching which
the Thessalonians have already received during the campaign
—as we told you already in our solemn protest against them.
This condemnation of laxity had been necessarily an important
feature of the missionary teaching. Calvin's comment is :
' Such is the sluggishness of men that without vehement blows
they are touched with no sense of the Divine Judgment.'

7   The second ground on which a Christian must be distinguish-
able from a pagan in his attitude to sex is that **God did not call
us to be impure, but to be consecrated.** Here the emphasis is
on the Christian's vocation. He is chosen by God to serve
Him, to grow in grace into the stature of true sonship. For
such a one all uncleanness such as the pagans practised must
be anathema.

8   **Hence, he who disregards this, disregards not man but the
God who gave you his holy Spirit.** This is the third and deepest
reason why pagan lust and Christian liberty must not be con-
fused. The word translated here ' disregard,' is the word that
Jesus uses when He says to the Seventy : ' He who rejects
you rejects me, and he who rejects me rejects him who sent
me ' (Luke x. 16). The thought is the same. The man who
rejects or disregards this call to live a life free from licentious-
ness in every form is not rejecting some human voice but the
voice of God. Paul is perhaps saying : ' These are not my
orders, but God's. It is Divine authority you are flouting,
not man's. It is not merely an offence against human relationships—it breaks your relationship with God.'

   Moffatt translates the last part of the sentence : **God who
gave you his holy Spirit** (A.V. ' hath given '). But the best MSS.

(cf. R.V.) give the present tense : ' God who gives you his holy Spirit.' And this is a better meaning. ' To reject God's call is not to offend against Him who at one time bestowed the gift of His Spirit, but it is to sin against the living presence within you of the Holy Spirit which God is giving you every day.' Paul generally speaks of God's gift of the Spirit in the past tense—as a gift once bestowed (Rom. v. 5 ; Gal. iv. 6). Here surely it is rather in line with 1 Cor. vi. 19 : ' Your body is the temple of the Holy Spirit within you.' To abuse the body, to engage in sexual affairs which degrade the body is to sin against the indwelling Spirit of God which is continually enabling us to meet these very temptations. The phrase is perhaps based on Ezek. xxxvii. 14 (LXX), where Jehovah says to the Dry Bones : ' I will give you my spirit and you shall live.' Paul points the Thessalonians away from the thought that the presence of the Spirit is to be associated only with the distinctive manifestations of the early days of the mission—giving rise to speaking with tongues and other strange portents—and rather to the dynamic presence of the Spirit in each one of them, enabling them to obey God's commands.

(c) *On Brotherly Love in Action* (iv. 9–12)

9 You need no one to write to you upon brotherly love, for you
10   are yourselves taught by God to love one another, as indeed is your practice towards all the brothers throughout all Macedonia. We beseech you, brothers, to excel in
11   this more and more ; also, endeavour to live quietly, attend to your own business, and—as we charged you—work
12   with your hands, so that your life may be correct in the eyes of the outside world and self-supporting.

It may be that once again (see notes on i. 9, ii. 13) Paul refers to some letter which Timothy had brought back from Thessalonica in which this point is mentioned. It is certainly introduced in the same way as replies to specific points raised in the letter from the Corinthian Church (1 Cor. vii. 25, viii. 1, xii. 1, xvi. 1, etc.). On the other hand, the advice given is so general that it may well be—like the previous passage—an echo of the good counsel the Thessalonians had been given at the beginning, without any particular reference to present conditions at Thessalonica.

Paul addresses them as a real Father in God, kindly and 9 encouraging. **You need no one to write to you upon brotherly love.** This is indeed no idle compliment, but an honest recognition of one of the gladdening features of the Thessalonian Church (2 Cor. viii. 1). The word for brotherly love (*philadelphia*) is always used in the New Testament, not of natural family affection, but of the wider family of Christian brotherhood. Denney says : ' The early Christian Churches were little companies of people where love was at a high temperature. . . . Men were drawn to them irresistibly by the desire to share this life of love ' (ad loc.)—a sobering comment on our Churches to-day. **You are yourselves taught by God to love one another.** This is not a reference to any instruction the Thessalonians might have had on this subject (cf. iv. 2), or to any passage of Scripture, or to any words of Jesus, but to the presence of the Holy Spirit within them. ' You are God-taught ' (*theodidaktoi*), says the apostle. No other explanation could account for the remarkable way in which they evinced this fundamental characteristic of their new faith. As Calvin says : ' Love had been engraved on their hearts so that there was no need to write about it on paper.' Their love for each other came from the love of each one for God.

Nor was it confined to their own fellowship, it was as wide- 10 spread as it could be—**as indeed is your practice towards all the brothers throughout all Macedonia.** When he says **all Macedonia**—i.e. the Roman province of Macedonia—Paul either indulges in pardonable exaggeration (cf. i. 8), or else he prophetically sees a Christian Macedonia like a Christian Achaia (2 Cor. i. 1). We are told of only two other Churches being founded in Macedonia apart from the one at Thessalonica, namely, Philippi and Beroea. It may be, however, that individual Christians and Christian families from these places had by this time already settled in other towns and villages as well, or, living in neighbouring places, had come under the influence of the missionaries, perhaps on market days. The practical evidence of their brotherly love in this case would be hospitality to visiting Christians and charitable help to any who needed it. The Macedonians were apparently still noted for their hospitable ways in St. Jerome's day (Milligan, p. xlvii.). Then, in words that are reminiscent of iv. 1, Paul goes on to urge them to continue their good work and do better still. **We beseech you, brothers, to excel in this more and more.** Their example of Christian love in action is not to expend itself only in works of charity and friendly hospitality, but, as the apostle now points out, in other practical ways as well. Some commentators divide these verses (9–12) into two distinct topics—Brotherly Love and Hard Work. But surely these connecting words indicate that Brotherly Love is the subject of the whole passage, issuing firstly in hospitality, secondly, in every man recognizing his Christian duty to contribute his share of honest work to the community as a whole.

If the Thessalonians had written to Paul, we must assume that one of the things they asked his advice about was what to do with some of their members, who were so excited about the impending Parousia (iv. 13–v. 11) that they had thrown up their ordinary jobs, and were quite prepared to live off the other members of the congregation until the Great Day. If there were no letter, some such situation may have been outlined by Timothy—certainly the problem was acute at a later point in the history of the Thessalonian Church (2 iii. 6 ff.). But we must not exclude the possibility that this passage—which is, after all, couched in very general terms, and is at no point specific—may simply be as before (iv. 3–8), prophylactic counsel. It appears to be again an echo of the campaign teaching. Paul reminds them of what he had told them before, and the necessity for repeating it here may arise more from his appreciation of the situation at the time of the mission and his knowledge of the kind of problems that would naturally arise from it.

11 He urges them to be calm—**endeavour to live quietly**—literally, be ambitious to be quiet ; almost ' be ambitious to be unambitious,' at all events paradoxical counsel. It is an appeal to them not to let their enthusiasm get the better of

them, but to direct their energies to an unusual kind of ambition—namely, to behaving like ordinary citizens. The warning is the kind of deterrent needed where revivalism and religious excitement generally tend to produce an unhealthy restlessness.

The cure is to **attend to your own business.** Later it appears that one of the problems of the Thessalonian Church was the existence of ' busybodies ' (2 iii. 11). Whether something of that kind is meant here, or whether it is simply an admonition like 1 Cor. vii. 20 to each Church member to carry on with the job in life that God had given him is not clear. If it is the latter, it is a further necessary caution against the unsettling effect of the Second Advent expectation. The temptation was to throw over all the ordinary commitments of daily life and wait in a state of suspended activity for the End. The same thing happened as the year 1,000 A.D. approached, which was supposed to bring the end of the world. Moffatt quotes a fairly modern example of the same phenomenon in Tripoli in 1899, where the report that the end of the world would come on November the 13th of that year produced ' an amazing state of affairs.' The *Westminster Gazette* recorded as follows : ' The Israelites are sending their wives to pray in the Synagogues and most workmen have ceased work. Debtors refuse to pay their debts, so that trade is almost paralysed ' (*E. G. T.*, ad loc.). Paul's advice is eminently sane : **work with your hands.** That is their duty whether the End is approaching or not. The community life must go on. The story is told in New England of a day during one of these times of excited expectancy of the end of the world when a sudden darkness at noon interrupted the session of Assembly. Some cried fearfully : ' It is the coming of Christ : it is the end of the world.' But the old President ordered lights to be produced : ' Bring in candles,' he said, ' and get on with your work. If the Lord is coming, how better can He find us than quietly doing our duty ?' This is in the spirit of Paul's advice to the Thessalonians (quoted by Paterson Smyth, *Life and Letters of St. Paul*, p. 124).

Further, the words emphasize that Christianity has no

place for drones. On the contrary, it demands an honest day's work from all who take their faith seriously. For modern Christian thought, work is a vocation—it is the service of God.

> ' *A servant with this clause*
> *Makes drudgery divine ;*
> *Who sweeps a room as for Thy Laws*
> *Makes that and the action fine.*'

But St. Paul does not explicitly cite this argument here. The reference to **hands** points not only to the fact that the Thessalonian Church was mainly an artisan community—possibly of weavers of the cloth for which the town was noted—but also to the difference between the Jewish and the Greek attitude to manual labour. To the Greek it was degrading—a slave's task ; to the Jew it was an essential part of human dignity. Paul himself was their pattern in this respect (ii. 9). All of this was nothing new. It was part of the missionaries' teaching—**as we charged you.**

12 The motive for this gospel of hard work is twofold : a third has been already mentioned (ver. 11), namely, to keep them out of mischief—**so that your life may be correct in the eyes of the outside world and self-supporting.** Paul stresses the importance of Christian witness. It is not enough that they should be inwardly convinced of the truth of the faith, or endowed with the Spirit—particularly if the Spirit manifested itself in abnormal ways. They must behave reasonably, and be an example to the rest of the non-Christian community— they must be letters of recommendation (2 Cor. iii. 2)—and set the highest possible standard as honest hard-working citizens. The apostles had been accused at Thessalonica of being men who turned the world upside down (Acts xvii. 6, 7). Their followers must leave no opening for such a charge again. As Anderson Scott comments, this is the ' scriptural sanction for the English standard of " behaving like a gentleman " ' (*Footnotes to St. Paul*, p. 212). Further, there must be no question of parasitism. Every man must stand on his own feet. If there are wealthy members in the fellowship, it is not their duty to sup-

port idlers. All must work. Paul's recipe for slackers was short but effective : ' If a man won't work, he doesn't eat ' (2 iii. 10). Paul did not want to see the failure of ' Christian communism ' at Jerusalem repeated in Thessalonica (see note on 2 iii. 6 ff.).

(2) THE SECOND COMING OF CHRIST (iv. 13–v. 11)
(*a*) *The Dead will not be Forgotten* (iv. 13–18)

We would like you, brothers, to understand about those who 13 are asleep in death. You must not grieve for them, like the rest of men who have no hope. Since we believe that 14 Jesus died and rose again, then it follows that by means of Jesus God will bring with him those who have fallen asleep. For we tell you, as the Lord has told us, that we the living, 15 who survive till the Lord comes, are by no means to take precedence of those who have fallen asleep. The Lord 16 himself will descend from heaven with a loud summons, when the archangel calls and the trumpet of God sounds ; the dead in Christ will rise first, then we the living, who 17 survive, will be caught up along with them in the clouds to meet the Lord in the air, and so we shall be with the Lord for ever. Now then, encourage one another with these 18 words.

The underlying thought of the last paragraph was the unsettlement in society caused by anticipation of the Second Advent. What follows is much more directly concerned with the Parousia itself and the problems it raised. This important passage, forming with v. 1–11 a block of eschatological teaching, gives the epistle its characteristic note (cf. i. 10, ii. 12, ii. 19, iii. 13, etc.). The approaching end of the world is depicted with great vividness, and Paul as much as his readers is keyed up with expectancy. The problem for him—as is seen from the necessity for a second letter—was to clarify the correct nature of that expectancy. For Paul, the coming end of the world was an adjunct to the vital event, namely, the Triumph of Christ and the Consummation of the Kingdom. For the Thessalonians, naturally enough, the emphasis tended to be on the cataclysm itself. Thus it would be quite wrong to regard the primary purpose of the passage as a detailed factual description of what the apostle expected to happen. He is much more concerned with the practical questions involved—the necessity to reassure the Thessalonians that, come what may, their loved ones who have died are in God's hands (iv. 13–18), and the Christian's obligation to live always in such a way that he is ready at any time to face his Lord in judgment (v. 1–11). Up to a point the apostle is covering travelled ground. This is not so much a wholly new theme upon which he embarks as the application of an old one. The Parousia is assumed as part of the missionary message (i. 10, iii. 13, v. 1). All that is necessary here is to deal with two specific problems connected with it. The two sections are very similar in style. Each states a question (iv. 13, v. 1), gives an answer (iv. 14–17, v. 2–10), and ends with an exhortation (iv. 18, v. 11).

The first problem which Paul deals with in iv. 13–18 was one which had become acute in the period between his departure from Thessalonica and the time of writing this letter. It was apparently assumed by the apostles and their converts alike in the first instance that all who received the Gospel and the gift of the Spirit would, as the fulfilment of their Christian election, take part in the imminent Second Advent of the Lord. They would be alive at the Lord's Coming, they would see His Glory, and they would share in His Triumph. So confident were they of the nearness of the Advent, or rather so intense was their sense of already living in the New Age, that the climax seemed liable to take place at any moment. The possibility, therefore, was not discussed that all who renounced paganism and embraced the new faith might not in fact live to see the Great Day ushered in.

This is apparently what had in fact happened at Thessalonica after Paul had left. Some members of local Christian families had died and the missionaries had said nothing about what would happen to them. So it would not be surprising if their pagan background (Acts xvii. 32)—assisted by the cynical observations of their late co-religionists—made some of those who remained wonder if the consummation of the Christian hope was, after all, a myth, as some of their Corin-

thian brethren did later on (1 Cor. xv. 12 ff.)—or think it was
already past, like Hymenæus and Philetus (2 Tim. ii. 17–18).
If they did not doubt that, there was the disquieting thought
that the promises of the missionaries' preaching seemed to be
breaking down : Christ had risen, the New Age had begun in
earnest, the Spirit was at work among them, the fulfilment was
at hand when the Lord would return in glory to judge the world
and destroy the power of evil ; those who had repented and
believed the Gospel would share in the full triumph of His
Kingdom. What, then, of those who did not live to see the
Great Day ? Had God withdrawn their election ? Had they
missed their chance of sharing fully in the Lord's Coming ?
Were they being punished in any way that they were being
deprived of the climax to their hopes (cf. 1 Cor. xi. 30) ? The
question was very acute. There was until now no doctine of
an intermediate state between death and the final Judgment.
That the problem was not confined to Thessalonica is shown
by 1 Cor. xv. 29. Apparently at Corinth the practice had
arisen whereby Christians who lost members of the family
circle—not, however, members of the Church—had themselves
baptized as their representatives ' to ensure their final bliss '
(Moffatt, *E.G.T.*, ad loc.). At Thessalonica, however, the dead
in question are Christians. Here, then, is Christian theology
in the making, as, out of this practical difficulty, Paul supplies
new doctrinal teaching. The occasion is in all probability
part of Timothy's report on the state of the Thessalonian
Church.

So Paul begins : **We would like you, brothers, to understand** 13
about those who are asleep in death. (Literally, ' But we do
not want you to be ignorant, brothers, about those who are
asleep ' or ' the sleepers.') The words with which Paul introduces the topic are paralleled elsewhere (e.g. Rom. i. 13,
xi. 25 ; 1 Cor. x. 1, etc.), and seem to be used to emphasize
particularly what follows, which is usually something new. In
this case he is not recalling to them something he had said
before, as previously in this chapter (vers. 1–2, 6, 9, 11), though
it is not likely that this is the first time Paul had ever considered the problem. There had been deaths among the

Christians before this (Acts xii. 2), but it is the first extant written reference in the epistles to the resurrection of the dead, and in part it is apparently new teaching to the Thessalonians.

The phrase **those who are asleep** is a peculiarly fitting euphemism for death among Christians who believe in an awakening. But it was also used by Jews and pagans who had no such belief, because of the obvious similarity of death to sleep. The Old Testament metaphor of 1 Kings ii. 10, ' So David slept with his fathers,' is paralleled by Homer's death of Iphidamas : ' He slept an iron sleep ' (*Il.* 11, 241). It was possible to have on the same grave the inscription, ' His sleep is in peace ' and ' No man is immortal ' (Dibelius, ad loc.). The meaning of ' cemetery ' is ' a sleeping place,' and it comes from the same word as Paul uses here (*koimaomai*), nor was this used exclusively by Christians (see Milligan, ad loc.). Paul doubtless employs the word here because it was in everyday use and not with any theological reference to the intermediate state of the soul. Whether he shared the Jewish eschatological view that the dead go on to lead a shadowy existence in Sheol is not clear from this passage. What is clear is that he is certain that the believer who dies ' in Christ ' remains ' in Christ ' (ver. 16). The fate of non-Christian dead is not under consideration. **You must not grieve for them, like the rest of men who have no hope.** The point here is not that Christians should grieve less than others who have no hope, but that they should not grieve at all. At once we must say that this is, humanly speaking, impossible. And Paul is obviously not saying that it is unchristian to shed tears over the loss of a loved one. He would say, as we should, that where there is no regret there can have been little love. He is partly, no doubt, thinking of the frenzied manifestations of grief among certain contemporary cults, and, partly, insisting as strongly as possible that, in fact, the death of loved ones is no reason for Christian sorrow, but rather for rejoicing. We may sorrow over our own loss, but not over theirs.

The **rest of men** are the non-Christians **who have no hope.** It was not true, of course, that non-Christians had no hope. Plato taught immortality, the Pharisees believed in the resur-

rection of the body, and the worshippers of the various mystery-religions—possibly even of the Thessalonian Kabeiroi as
well—were guaranteed victory over death (see Angus, *Religious Quests of the Graeco-Roman World*, pp. 90–91). There
are two possible ways, therefore, in which Paul's apparently
sweeping statement might be meant. He is speaking presumably particularly of the rank and file of ordinary pagan
working folk of the same social background as the Christians.
To them possibly the esoteric speculations of the philosophers
gave little comfort, and the Mysteries, with no anchor in
history, carried little conviction. We do not know enough
about the mystery-religions in Paul's day to know how much
they affected the average pagan, or how far their ideas had
percolated into popular thinking. What we do know from
classical writers and inscriptions on tombstones generally is
that to all intents and purposes death for the pagan was the
end of everything. We must also give full weight to Paul's
own testimony here and in Eph. ii. 12. He knew the pagan
outlook—as did the people to whom he was writing. It had
been their own outlook too.

Frame quotes two contrasting viewpoints on death—pagan
and Christian—which illustrate Paul's statement. The pagan
one is from a second-century papyrus : ' Irene to Taonnophris
and Philo, good cheer. I was as sorry and wept as much over
Eumoiros as over Didymas. I did all that was fitting, as did
all my family . . . still there is nothing one can do in the
face of such trouble. So I leave you to comfort yourselves.'
The Christian comment is from a contemporary apologist,
Aristides : ' And if any righteous man among them passes
from the world, they rejoice and offer thanks to God ; and
they escort the body as if he were setting out from one place
to another near.' The note of one is despair and of the other
complete confidence. Paul then may have been thinking
here of the Gentile masses he knew so well. When they died
they ceased to exist. The darkness of the tomb was the last
word. It was right that such a fate should be mourned and
lamented by those who remained. ' Of a man once dead there
is no resurrection,' said Aeschylus (*Eum.* 651), while Catullus

(**V.** 5) beautifully but pathetically adds : ' Suns may set and rise again. When once our brief life has set, one unbroken night of sleep remains.' On the other hand, is it not more likely that for Paul, if a man was not ' in Christ,' he was without any real hope ? Immortality and resurrection, or for that matter the Parousia, were not for Paul the essence of the Christian's ground for optimism, but his mystical union with the Risen Christ. To die is for the Christian to be with his Lord (ver. 17 ; cf. 2 Cor. v. 8)—the ' how ' is of much less moment than the fact that this is the real fulfilment of his calling.

14 Paul now proceeds to give the foundation of the Christian hope—the anchor in history which differentiates Christianity both from speculative philosophy and religious mythology : **Since we believe that Jesus died and rose again.** It is interesting to note that Paul uses the word *apethane* for ' died,' not part of the word *koimaomai* to ' fall asleep ' as in the previous verse and a few words later. Chrysostom's comment is : ' Since Christ came and died for the life of the world, death is no longer called death but a slumber and a sleep.' Because Jesus's death was utterly real and final, death for those who live and die in Him is turned into a sleep with an awakening. The very use of the word in this context is consolation to the mourners. Jesus's death, as the Fathers say, was ' the death of death.'

Then it follows that by means of Jesus God will bring with him those who have fallen asleep. The meaning of this sentence turns on the relation of the words translated here ' by means of ' and ' with ' (*dia* and *sun*). If they are parallel expressions, then the A.V. and R.V. translations are nearer the mark than Moffatt or Weymouth. Nothing very much can be learned from the order of the words in the original. The sentence can be read either as in A.V.—' Even so them also which sleep in Jesus will God bring with him ' or as in Moffatt above. The difference is that A.V. takes the words *dia Iesou* to mean ' in Jesus ' and attaches them to the word ' sleep,' i.e. in modern English the A.V. would read : ' Then it follows that God will bring with him those who have fallen asleep in Jesus.' Whereas Moffatt associates the phrase *dia Iesou* with ' will bring.' That is, the A.V. suggests that the point is that the faithful departed, because they die in mystical union with Christ, will be brought back with Him at His Coming, while Moffatt's translation really says that God will at the Parousia bring back the dead along with Christ through the agency of or by means of Christ. On the face of it the A.V. translation is theologically more Pauline—and more profound (cf. the same idea in 1 Cor. xv. 18). If ' with ' and ' by means of ' are simply referring to the same event, one of them is surely redundant. The words become much more significant if both *dia* and *sun* are here taken to be parallel expressions for the union between Christ and the Christian, meaning more or less the same as ' in Christ.' On this view, the translation ought to be : ' Those who have fallen asleep through (= in) Jesus will God bring (again) with Him.'

As it now stands, it should be noted (1) that it appears from this that the Thessalonians were not principally in doubt about the resurrection of their dead so much as about their share in the Parousia. Paul does not say, as we might expect, God will ' raise up ' (2 Cor. iv. 14). That is passed over, taken as a matter of course, and the word used ' will bring ' (with Him) points to the Thessalonians' real problem. The resurrection of the dead is taken for granted as a prelude to the Second Advent. (2) The thought is not expressed in full. Expanded, it would read something like this : ' Christ died and rose again. That is an historical fact that we know. Through faith in Him we die as far as our old selves are concerned and rise to a new life (Gal. ii. 19–20 ; Rom. vi. 3 ff. ; Col. ii. 20, iii. 1–4). That new life is life in Christ. His Spirit lives in us, so that when we die " in Him " or " through Him " we remain " in Him " (ver. 16) until the great day of His Coming, when we shall be raised from the dead to be for ever " with Him." ' Since in this particular case Paul's chief concern is to comfort people who are concerned about the future of their friends and relatives who have died, and not with opponents who need to be convinced by argument, he does not deal in detail with the nature of the resurrection. It is, after all, not in question. We do not know, therefore, whether at this early date he had formed the views on the nature of the Resurrection-body which he expresses briefly in Rom. viii. 11 and fully in 1 Cor. xv. 35–55.

Is there any special significance in the phrase ' through Jesus ' ? One suggestion is that it refers to dying a martyr's death, with a probable confirmation of such a situation in Thessalonica in ii. 15—' You have suffered from your compatriots just as they have suffered from the Jews who killed the Lord Jesus and the prophets.' While this is possible, it is more likely that the phrase has precisely the same meaning as in verse 16—the dead in Christ. Christ's death and resurrection are for Paul not to be treated as two distinct things but as one Divine act.

The mystical union of the believer with Christ, which begins at baptism, is binding for eternity. He becomes part of the Body of which Christ is the Head. It is a fellowship which persists through life, through death, through resurrection, and is consummated in its final fulfilment as life together with Christ for ever in glory. This conception, which is fundamental in Paul's thinking, finds not only its guarantee, but its dynamic in the events of Jesus's life. It is because Jesus died and rose again that the Christian who dies in Him will likewise rise (2 Tim. ii. 11), and it is because the risen Christ will come again soon that the Thessalonians will shortly see their own loved ones brought back with Him. Paul is not only assuming their knowledge of the missionary presentation of the Gospel as far as the Resurrection and Second Advent are concerned—the only new factor being that the missionary preaching had not linked up this teaching with what would happen to any who died before the Parousia—but possibly also farther back still their upbringing in a background formed by the mystery-cults. The idea that the worshipper through mystical union shared the fate of his god was acknowledged. Paul sees this as fulfilled and given historical reality in Christ. What Christ has done, that will His people be enabled to do (cf. Phil. iii. 9–11). It is an argument the pagan world can understand. The agent behind the whole conception is **God**.

It is He who will bring both Jesus and the faithful dead at the
Parousia. The idea is surely of the return to a new earth of
Christ with the saints, i.e. He will ' bring ' them with Him,
and not, as Frame suggests, when accompanied by His saints
He finally ' leads the way heavenward to hand over the Kingdom to God the Father.' In the Ascension of Isaiah—mostly
first century according to Charles—there occurs the following
comparable picture : ' But the saints will come with the Lord
with their garments which are (now) stored up on high in the
seventh heaven : with the Lord they will come whose spirits
are clothed, they will descend and be present in the world,
and He will strengthen those who have been found in the
body together with the saints, in the garments of the saints,
and the Lord will minister to those who have kept watch in
this world ' (iv. 16).

Paul has now met the real point at issue : the dead will not 15
be deprived of their part in the Parousia. He now goes on to
strengthen his statement by adducing a ' word of the Lord '
in confirmation. **For we tell you, as the Lord has told us, that**
. . . (literally, in (= by means of) a word of the Lord).
Moffatt's translation suggests that the information which
Paul passes on has been imparted to him personally. And
this is a possible explanation. The word of the Lord came to
the prophets in vision, trance, and ecstasy, and so it came to
Paul too (Gal. i. 12, ii. 2 ; Eph. iii. 3 ; 2 Cor. xii. 7). One
might have expected some special reminiscence of the occasion, as when he quotes specific words of the Lord to him in
2 Cor. xii. 8-9. Alternatively, there may have been some
special vision of the Parousia granted to Silvanus (Acts xv. 32)
or some other Christian prophet in which these words were
spoken. It seems, however, more likely that Paul is alluding
to some definite pronouncement going back in the last resort
to Jesus's own words. The difficulty is, of course, to say which.

It is not satisfactory either to say that the following words
give the gist of some cryptic saying of Jesus like Mark ix. 1—
' There are some of those standing here who will not taste
death till they see that God's reign has come with power '—
which is more likely to refer to the Resurrection than to the

Second Advent ; or that they point to some saying apparently in the teaching tradition of the Church, but not found in the gospels (e.g. Acts xx. 35). A further difficulty is to decide whether Paul intends verse 15 to be the ' word of the Lord ' and verse 16 an amplification, or vice versa. In favour of the former is its position immediately following the introductory words. Against its being a quotation, however, is the use of the word ' we.' On the other hand, in favour of verse 16 is its impersonal nature. It reads like a pronouncement. But the inclusion of the words ' the Lord Himself ' makes it unlikely that it, any more than verse 15, is a verbatim word of Jesus. Further, in none of the Parousia passages in the gospels (e.g. Matt. xxiv. 30 = Mark xiii. 26 ff. = Luke xxi. 27 ; Matt. xvi. 27) is there anything resembling the statement made here.

We are left with the following alternatives : (1) Paul gives in verse 15 the substance of some teaching on the Parousia attributed to our Lord, and amplifies it in verses 16 and 17 with traditional imagery, taken either from Jewish apocalyptic literature or from Old Testament descriptions of the Day of Jehovah. (2) The thought of the whole passage, verses 15-17, is appropriated by Paul from Jewish apocalyptic or Old Testament sources and adapted to this particular occasion—verse 16 giving the nearest approach to the original and verses 15 and 17 supplying a Pauline paraphrase. This adaptation, written under the guidance of the Lord's own Spirit as a prophetic revelation (cf. 2 i. 7 ff.), Paul could then call a ' word of the Lord.' On the other hand, if the imagery of the whole passage is regarded as derived from Old Testament sources exclusively, would not Paul regard it all as the ' Word of the Lord,' just as we should say : ' As the Word of God says. . . .' ?

Now comes the summary of the ' word ' : **We the living, who survive till the Lord comes, are by no means to take precedence of those who have fallen asleep.** There is obviously no question in Paul's mind at this time but that he—and his readers—would live to see the Coming of the Lord (see note on ii. 19). The older commentators, eager to safeguard Paul's infallibility on all matters, had their ingenuity taxed to explain this sentence away. Calvin suggests that of course Paul knew that the Parousia would not happen in his day, but that he is anxious to keep the Thessalonians up to scratch ! Paul's views on the subject changed as time went on. Like the other New Testament writers, he never lost his belief that the Parousia was not far away (1 Cor. x. 11, xvi. 22 ; Rom. xiii. 11 ; Phil. iv. 5 ; cf. 1 Pet. iv. 7 ; Heb. x. 25 ; Jas. v. 8 ; 1 John ii. 18). But he later recognized the possibility that he might die before it happened. He still thinks of himself as alive at the Second Advent at the time of writing the first Corinthian letter, probably five years after this in A.D. 55 (1 Cor. xv. 51), but apparently dating from his serious illness in Asia (2 Cor. i. 8, 9) he begins to think otherwise, and approximately five years later still, in the letter to the Philippians in A.D. 60, he has given up hope (Phil. i. 20 ff.).

By no means (are we) **to take precedence of those who have fallen asleep.** This is the kind of categorical assurance that the Thessalonians want. It seems an odd matter to be so anxious about, but it was apparently very real. Their anxiety was, of course, encouraged by the old Jewish idea that those who happened to be alive at the Great Day were especially blest (Dan. xii. 12). Paul now assures them that this will not be the case. The quick, as the A.V. has it, ' shall not prevent them which are asleep.' It should perhaps be repeated that throughout this whole passage—especially in view of the following detailed account of the Parousia—the point that Paul is concerned to make has nothing to do with forecasting the manner of the Lord's Second Coming. All that is incidental though important. Paul's real interest and emphasis are much more on the fact that if a Christian dies in Christ he remains in Christ. Whatever happens after that ought to give those who loved him no anxiety at all. He is in his true home. Paul is primarily concerned to comfort sorrowing relatives, not to describe the Second Advent. What he says about that is second-hand information—the traditional picture familiar in part at least to all his readers—his own contribution is the underlying religious message. The important point for Paul is the last clause of verse 17 : ' So we shall be with the Lord for ever.'

The description of the Parousia now given is the fullest in the New Testament. It is a vivid pen-picture of the end of the world. With dramatic suddenness, heralded by appropriate celestial intimations, the Lord descends from heaven ; the faithful dead are raised to meet Him in mid-air, while at the same time the faithful who are still alive are caught up with them ; then living and resurrected dead, now joined with their Lord, remain in His presence for ever. It can be clearly seen, however, from the sketchy nature of the description—leaving so much unsaid and so many questions unanswered—that to give a full account of the Parousia was not Paul's intention. He says nothing, for example, about the Judgment, or the important question of the fate of non-Christians. He does not tell us anything about the dissolution of the present world or the nature of the bodies which rise, or how the living are fitted for their assumption. He does not make it plain whether, after the reunion, the Lord and His saints return to a transformed earth to inaugurate the Messianic Kingdom, or whether they proceed directly heavenwards. Some of these details he fills in in later epistles, e.g. the Judgment (1 Cor. iv. 4, 5 ; cf. 1 Thess. v. 1–11), the Messianic Kingdom (possibly 1 Cor. xv. 22, 24 ; more possibly xv. 28 ; but see Charles' *Eschatology*, pp. 389–90), the nature of the Resurrection-body (1 Cor. xv. 35 ff.). But we would do well not to press this imaginative sketch into a literal prophecy. How far Paul himself accepted this picture as literally true we cannot say, any more than we know how far our Lord used the language of His times symbolically. What we can say is that Paul's chief interest in the Parousia was theological, not speculative. We must bear this in mind in the passage that now follows.

16 **The Lord himself will descend from heaven with a loud summons, when the archangel calls and the trumpet of God sounds.** The impression given by the whole sentence is of the awe-inspiring nature of the Second Advent. In the forefront is **the Lord himself**, as if Paul would say : this same Jesus our

Lord, in whom we live, now risen and glorified, He it is and
none other who on the Great Day will come again. He **will
descend from heaven**—as He ascended in the disciples' sight
into the sky, so He will come down again (Acts i. 10–11),
leaving His seat at the Right Hand of God (Col. iii. 1), where
He has been enthroned since His Ascension. What is the
nature of the **loud summons** ? Is it the voice of God, or of
Christ, or of the archangel ? Paul does not say. The word is
used in classical literature of the shout of command given by
an officer to his men, by a huntsman to his dogs, by a boat-
swain to the oarsmen, by a charioteer to his horses, etc. The
nearest suggestion would seem to be of a battle-shout or a
signal to a fleet or an army. The three sounds are presumably designed to awaken the sleepers. They may all indeed
represent one sound : the loud summons may be the archangel's voice, which is regarded as the trumpet of God. Voice
and trumpet are identified in Rev. i. 10, 12, iv. 1 ; and it is
' a mighty angel ' who is God's spokesman in Rev. v. 2, vii. 2.
When the archangel calls may refer to Michael, the only archangel mentioned in the New Testament (Jude 9), and who
appears in the apocalypses of both Testaments (Dan. x. 13,
21 ; xii. 1 ; Rev. xii. 7). In Jewish apocalyptic literature
Michael's rôle was to summon the angels and sound a trumpet
heralding God's approach to judge the world. In Christian
apocalyptic, the Lord when He comes is surrounded by His
retinue of angels (Matt. xxv. 31), led presumably by the archangel mentioned here.

And the trumpet of God sounds. . . . This feature of the
Last Trump heralding the Last Day, which has long been in
popular use, is referred to twice again by Paul in his fuller
treatment of the Resurrection of the Dead (1 Cor. xv. 52).
The passage may be compared with Matt. xxiv. 31 : ' And he
(the Son of Man) shall send his angels with a great sound of a
trumpet.' If this is a ' word ' of Jesus, Paul's imagery here
may be based upon it ; on the other hand, the possibility must
not be overlooked that both may have a common source.
Mark xiii. 27, on which Matt. xxiv. 31 is based, has no reference
to a trumpet. The loud summons may not be so much a

shout to waken the dead as something of the same type as God's command to Christ to descend into the world (Ascension of Isaiah x. 3), and the angelic voice may be rather a heavenly shout of triumph as in Rev. xix. 1. Trumpet blasts either awaken the dead or herald the Parousia in Psalms of Solomon xi. 1 ; 2 Esdras vi. 23, and elsewhere. If Paul's mention of the Last Trump seems to introduce an unnecessarily materialistic element, it is perhaps worth comparing a Jewish description of the same feature. There are seven peals of the trumpet ' which is a thousand ells long according to the ells of God. At each peal a certain result follows ; at the first peal the world is awaked, and at the others the various parts of the human body are collected and reorganized.'

The general view is that this picture of the descent of the Messiah from heaven is to be sought in the increasingly supernatural conception of the Messiah which developed in later Judaism—perhaps by a combination of an extraneous Redeemer-motif with the old prophetic political Deliverer. Whatever Dan. vii. 13, 14 originally meant, it undoubtedly came to be used as the authority for the descent to earth upon the clouds of ' one like a Son of Man.' It is almost certain, however, that this is not the meaning of Dan. vii. 13, 14—that it is not a descent but an ascent, an enthronement, an investiture ; and not of a Messiah but of a man as opposed to beasts (cf. Frame ad loc. and Glasson, op. cit., pp. 13 ff.). Nevertheless, the later identification of this figure with a supernatural Messianic figure, the Son of Man, became part of Jewish and later of Christian apocalyptic tradition. Paul does not use the title ' Son of Man ' himself (though the ' last Adam ' (1 Cor. xv. 45) means the same thing) ; but when he speaks of the Second Advent it is generally held that the descriptive detail is an adaptation of the Messianic prophecies of late Jewish apocalyptic (e.g. Dibelius, ad loc.).

There is much to be said, however, for the view that for these ideas—and indeed for this whole conception of the Parousia—we need look no farther than the Old Testament, where in one form or another most of this imagery is to be found, sometimes associated with the Day of Jehovah, but always with a manifestation of Jehovah Himself to men. In the Greek version the language is often identical. Thus the parallel for **the Lord himself will descend from heaven** is Micah. i. 3 : ' For behold the Lord comes forth out of His place and will descend.' **The loud summons,** or shout, and the **trumpet** both appear in the descent of Jehovah to earth at Sinai (Exod. xix. 16 ff.).

> *The Son gave signal high,*
> *To the bright minister that watched ; he blew*
> *His trumpet heard in Oreb since perhaps*
> *When God descended : and perhaps once more*
> *To sound at general doom.*
>
> (MILTON.)

While in Joel ii. 1 appears the following description of the Day of Jehovah : ' Blow ye the trumpet in Sion . . . for the Day of the Lord cometh, for it is nigh at hand.'

When all this has happened, **the dead in Christ will rise first.** This is once more the point on which the Thessalonians needed assurance. The dead would not be at a disadvantage —on the contrary their turn would come before the living. It is abundantly clear from this that Paul is not imparting systematic doctrine. There is here no teaching about an intermediate state of purgatory, no statement of what happens to the dead between ceasing to draw breath and the Last Day. Paul simply says they are **in Christ.** He goes a stage farther than verse 14 in that **those who have fallen asleep in Jesus** continue ' in Jesus,' while to all appearances their bodies lie lifeless in the grave. Through Him they are not dead but asleep. Nor is he concerned here with what happens to those who do not die in Christ. He is replying to a specific question, not writing dogmatics. Because of this mystical union with Christ, then, the Christian believer is assured that at the Last Day, when the same Christ comes down from heaven, the grave will have no power to keep him from Him. ' Neither death nor life . . . can separate us . . .' (Rom. viii. 38).

In speaking of the resurrection of the body, Paul is speaking of something which was part of his Pharisaic upbringing (cf. Acts xxiii. 8), but which only became real on the Damascus road. As an example of the Pharisaic view of resurrection at its best, Milligan quotes a passage from the Psalms of Solomon iii. 16 : ' But those who fear the Lord will rise to everlasting life, and their life will be in the light of the Lord, and He will never leave them.' It is perhaps worth noting that in the principal Old Testament passage where the resurrection of the body is postulated (Dan. xii. 2—the only other passage is Isa. xxvi. 19), and which formed the basis of the Pharisaic belief, the situation is not unlike that of Thessalonica. At the Last Day, while those remaining alive whose names are ' written in the book ' shall be delivered, ' many ' (as with Paul, not ' all ') shall be raised from the dead to share in everlasting life (or everlasting punishment). They are not to be deprived of their place in the coming salvation through the mere fact of death. **First** here has, of course, no reference to the First Resurrection of Rev. xx. 5.

17 The primary stage in Paul's eschatological picture has been reached : the Lord descends from heaven, the dead rise from their graves. Now comes the further development. **Then we the living, who survive**—this is a repetition of the words in verse 15—**will be caught up along with them in the clouds to meet the Lord in the air.** Paul's conception of the second stage of the Parousia would seem to be that the resurrected dead and the living, now a great company of saints assembled on the earth, are seized by Divine agency and taken upwards together, as it were on a chariot of clouds, until they reach the spot between heaven and earth where the Lord in His descent has arrived. It is not clear from the description how much of verses 16 and 17 takes place simultaneously. It is, however, all part of one connected act, presumably with no hiatus. No mention is made here of the change that must take place in the bodies of the dead to enable them to rise, and in the bodies of the living to enable them to soar into the heavens. Paul deals with this fully in 1 Cor. xv.—as fully as the human mind can deal with it.

At the time of writing 1 Cor. xv. he was clear that the body that is buried and the body that rises are not the same body. The flesh-and-blood structure that we call the body disintegrates, but the individuality, the self, who is united to Christ, remains alive. It is that that returns from sleep at the Last Day. Similarly, the flesh and blood of those who are then alive are presumably transformed, at all events it is the ' real ' body that enters the new sphere of existence. It is not a crude picture of the rattling bones of the saints reassembling, nor a mere survival of the soul. It is a serious conception of the resurrection of the self, individual, recognizable, ' the real man,' entering into the fullest union with his Lord. Here this change is omitted, and the thought is cast in more primitive and presumably more traditional form.

After the Resurrection comes the Rapture—we **will be caught up**—' caught up ' literally like Philip (Acts viii. 39) and the Messianic child (Rev. xii. 5), and also like Paul himself in a spiritual experience (2 Cor. xii. 2). **Along with them** implies that they will be individually recognizable—that it is not only a union with Christ, but a reunion with one another. Again the emphasis is that the living will have no advantage over the dead. **In the clouds** introduces a common motif in apocalyptic writing. The basis is the obvious one of a bridge between earth and heaven ; something that is at once solid in appearance and yet in fact unsubstantial. Particularly appropriate is the shrouding, enveloping effect, contributing to the atmosphere of mystery and awe (cf. Dan. vii. 13 ; Matt. xxiv. 30, xxvi. 64 ; Rev. i. 7, etc.). The Ascension is depicted as Jesus's disappearance in a cloud (Acts i. 9), and His return is foretold as happening ' in like manner ' (Acts i. 11).

As He comes with the clouds, His people rise in the clouds **to meet the Lord in the air.** According to the cosmology of the time, the earth is flat, and is separated from the seven heavens, which are in tiers above it, by the air. The air is therefore a suitable meeting-place between earth and the pure ether of heaven. Enoch (Secrets of Enoch iii. 1 ff.) describes his journey to heaven as follows : ' It came to pass when I had spoken to my sons, these men (the angels) summoned me and took me on their wings and placed me on the clouds. And lo the clouds moved. And again going still higher I saw the ether and they placed me in the first heaven.' The word used here for meeting the Lord (*apantēsis*) means a reception—the kind of reception given to royalty. It is the word used in Matt. xxv. 1, 6 of the Wedding Guests going out to meet the Bridegroom—a parable of the Second Advent. So the saints go forth to receive their Lord.

What happens then is not obvious. Paul says.: **and so we shall be with the Lord for ever.** Many would be content to say with Moffatt (*E.G.T.*, ad loc.) : ' This is all that remains to us in our truer view of the universe from the naïve *logos kuriou* of the Apostle, but it is everything.' It is indeed obviously the chief point in Paul's own mind. But others will ask : where does this happen ? In the air, or on earth, or in heaven ? It is certainly not very clear what Paul meant if, indeed, he gave the matter thought at this point. The dwelling-place of the Lord and His saints can hardly be the air, which was in those days within the power of Satan and his demons (Eph. ii. 2 ; Asc. Isa. vii. 9). The normal sequel to the appearance of the Lord at His Advent is the establishment of the Messianic Kingdom on a new earth. This seems to fit in much better with the idea of the royal reception than that the Lord should then return to heaven with those who have gone to receive Him. We should therefore now expect the saints who have joined the retinue of the Lord to come down with Him as His ' holy ones ' (iii. 13) and to assist in the Judgment (1 Cor. vi. 2). There would then follow the Messianic Kingdom to which there is a possible reference in 1 Cor. xv. 28 (if 1 Cor. xv. 22, 24 refers to pre-Parousia events). This Kingdom could, of course, only be shared by those who have put on ' incorruption,' and not by flesh and blood (1 Cor. xv. 50). But it is more than likely that Paul did not at the time of writing consider the point at all. They were to be ' with the Lord for ever '—whether on a transformed earth for a spell or immediately in heaven made no difference. There is an interesting similarity of thought in Isa. xxvi. and xxvii., where, in a description of the Day of Jehovah, several of the features of verses 16–17 occur : ' Thy dead shall live : my dead bodies

shall arise (Isa. xxvi. 19). And it shall come to pass in that
Day that the great trumpet shall be blown (Isa. xxvii. 13)
. . . and ye shall be gathered one by one, O ye children of
Israel ' (Isa. xxvii. 12) (Glasson, op. cit., p. 170).

Augustine's comment on the conclusion of the passage is : 18
' Let sorrow perish where there is so much consolation.' It is
another way of saying what Paul himself says : **now then,
encourage one another with these words.** Paul has not left
the Thessalonians to comfort themselves like the pagan writer
of condolence. He has given them in these verses, not only
an answer to their problem, but also a real message of hope
and encouragement. The question is, is it any encouragement to us ? It can only fail to appear relevant if we approach the passage with a false attitude and with false questions. If we seek information as to the actual procedure to
be gone through by believers after death, or the events that
will accompany the end of time and history, our own guess is
as good as Paul's or the apocalyptists'. If, however, we are
to look beneath the traditional superstructure of eschatological
imagery, we arrive at the conviction which was uppermost in
the apostle's mind, and which was indeed our Lord's own concern to show (John xiv.), that those who die in Christ live in
Christ, Who is the Resurrection and the Life, and Who comes
again to receive us unto Himself that where He is we may be
also.

(b) Be Wakeful and Sober (v. 1–11)

As regards the course and periods of time, brothers, you have 1
no need of being written to. You know perfectly well that 2
the day of the Lord comes like a thief in the night ; when 3
' all's well ' and ' all is safe ' are on the lips of men, then
all of a sudden Destruction is upon them, like pangs on a
pregnant woman—escape there is none. But, brothers, 4
you are not in the darkness for the Day to surprise you
like thieves ; you are all sons of the Light and sons of the 5
day. We do not belong to the night or the darkness.
Well then, we must not sleep like the rest of men, but be 6
wakeful and sober ; for sleepers sleep by night and drunk- 7

8   ards are drunk by night, but we must be sober, we who belong to the day, *clad in* faith and love as *our coat of*

9   *mail,* with the hope of *salvation as our helmet*—for God destined us not for Wrath but to gain salvation through

10   our Lord Jesus Christ, who died for us that waking in life or sleeping in death we should live together with him.

11   Encourage one another, therefore, and let each edify the other—as indeed you are doing.

In the second half of this eschatological block (iv. 13–v. 11) Paul deals with another aspect of the Thessalonians' concern about the Second Advent, namely, when it would happen. One of the shortcomings to which he referred earlier (iii. 10) seems to have been a restless and unsettled mood of expectancy that the Parousia was at any moment due to take place. The practical result of this was, as we have seen (iv. 11), and as Paul is to emphasize again (v. 14), that the ordinary business of living was disrupted. This he strongly condemns. Work must go on. Society cannot afford drones. But here he goes to the root of the problem and addresses some words to the Thessalonians on the fundamentals. It may be true that the Parousia will not be long delayed ; but if they are believing Christians, the Second Advent is not something at which they should be alarmed or disturbed : they have nothing to fear. Their chief concern ought rather to be to be ready for the Lord's Coming when it does happen. Paul is not now telling them anything new, he is reminding them of what they already know and calling their attention to its implications. The fact that Jesus specifically discouraged such questions, and that people knew that He had discouraged them, seems never to have prevented men from asking them (Mark xiii. 22 ; Matt. xxiv. 36).

1 **As regards the course and periods of time, brothers, you have no need of being written to.** The phrasing is almost identical with iv. 9. (A.V. translates ' times and seasons ' where Moffatt gives **the course and periods of time.** A.V. is neater but less accurate.) The difference between ' times ' (*chronoi*) and ' seasons ' (*kairoi*) is strictly a difference of quantity compared with quality—the length of time con-

trasted with certain critical moments within it. The two questions underlying the words might be distinguished as : ' How long will it be before the Lord comes ? ' and ' What will happen before His coming ? ' But as the phrase ' times and seasons ' is almost a standard term (e.g. Dan. ii. 21 ; Acts i. 7 ; Wisd. viii. 8), it is likely that Paul is simply using it in this popular sense. **You have no need of being written to :** This, as in iv. 9, is not flowery language, but a statement of fact. In this case it is a reference to the missionary teaching, which doubtless had made it plain that the Coming of the Lord was not a date that could be marked on the calendar. There is no real contradiction between the fact that the Parousia will be unexpected, as Paul goes on to say, and his indication of the events that should be recognized as its forerunners in 2 ii. 3 ff. The suddenness of the Judgment upon the evil-doers is a favourite theme of the apocalyptists. Unlike the righteous, they are unable to read the signs of the times.

You know perfectly well that the day of the Lord comes like a thief in the night. 2 The Day of the Lord (*hēmera Kuriou*), here meaning the Second Coming of Christ, is the traditional Jewish expression for the day when God would intervene in history to vindicate His chosen people, destroy their enemies, and establish His Kingdom. Amos, who is the first prophet to use the word (v. 18), obviously treats it as an already established idea. His contribution is to warn the nation that when the Day comes it will not be a day of national deliverance for the Jews, but one of Judgment upon them for their sins. This insistence that the Day will be essentially a vindication of God's justice is characteristic of the highest prophetic insight. In the apocalyptic speculation that followed, the Day took on more of the traditional character of a Judgment on the enemies of Israel and on renegade Jews. Supernatural phenomena of the most terrifying description would herald its coming and usher in the Kingdom of God (2 Esdras iv. 51– v. 13, vii. 39–42). In the New Testament the Day of the Lord is the Second Advent—the prelude to the visible fulfilment of the Kingdom in triumph and glory for the just, and in retribution and torment for the wicked. The Synoptic gospels speak of the Day, the Judgment (though not specifically the Day of the Lord), or the Day(s) of the Son of Man, sometimes clearly with reference to Jesus (e.g. Matt. vii. 22), sometimes with arguable reference (e.g. Luke xvii. 22 ff.).

Paul, however, makes the identification explicit in harmony with the rest of his thought where Jesus is Lord, and the phrase 'Day of the Lord (Jesus)' becomes interchangeable with 'Day of Christ' (cf. 1 Cor. v. 5 ; 2 Cor. i. 14 with Phil. i. 10, ii. 16). Here, and in 2 Pet. iii. 10, the expression 'Day of the Lord' is used as in the Old Testament. In both cases it is followed by the same comparison **like a thief in the night.** This would seem to be a standard use in missionary teaching. The Thessalonians are reminded of it almost as if it were a quotation. It origin is probably to be found in the words of Jesus Himself. In Luke xii. 39 (Matt. xxiv. 43) He speaks of the Coming of the Son of Man as an event which will be as unexpected as a housebreaking. In Jesus' mind this was not a nocturnal visit to appropriate some pieces of jewellery and decamp, but 'to steal, to kill, and to destroy' (John x. 10). Echoes of this are found in Rev. iii. 3 and xvi. 15, where the Lord is spoken of as coming like a thief. Here (as in ver. 4 and 2 Pet. iii. 10) the simile is transferred from the Lord to the Day of the Lord. The idea that the thief comes **in the night** springs naturally from the gospel passage, or from the parable of the Wise and Foolish Virgins when the Bridegroom comes at midnight, and gave rise to the common belief in the early Church that the Parousia would take place at midnight, especially on Easter Eve, as Jehovah came to Egypt on the night of the Passover.

3 At such a time, **when 'all's well' and 'all is safe' are on the lips of men, then all of a sudden Destruction is upon them, like pangs on a pregnant woman—escape there is none.** The whole sentence clearly refers, not to the Ecclesia, but to the unredeemed world. This vivid and terrifying picture of the crack of doom is paralleled in Isa. xiii. 6–8, where the coming of the Day of the Lord is with more graphic detail likewise compared with a woman's labour pains. The suddenness and

unexpectedness of the Advent, as of the Flood (Matt. xxiv. 38, etc.), is marked by the fact that it is just when men are comforting themselves that they have nothing to fear from God or man that the Judgment falls. Ezekiel's warning to Jerusalem (xiii., 10) prophesying disaster upon those who said ' Peace ' when there was no peace, is in similar vein (cf. Jer. vi. 14 ; viii. 11). Our Lord used the same word for **all of a sudden** in Luke xxi. 34, when He exhorted the people in the Temple to be ready for the Day lest it come upon them and find them roystering and wantoning.

The **Destruction** will be overwhelming, complete, and cataclysmic, as it was in the days of Noah, when the Deluge obliterated an evil world, or when God destroyed Sodom and Gomorrah for their wickedness. This was the Old Testament view of what would happen at the Day of the Lord (Isa. xiii. 6 ff. ; Ezek. xxx. 3 ff. ; Joel ii. 1 ff. ; Zeph. i. 14 ff. ; Zech. xiv., etc.), and it is likewise the New Testament view of the Day that is impending (Luke xvii. 22 ff. ; Acts. ii. 20). Disaster for the enemies of God ; salvation for His faithful servants. It would seem, however, from 2 i. 9, where the same word is used for Destruction (*olethros*), that Paul is thinking, not so much of annihilation, as of the eternal spiritual destruction which is separation from Christ. This, behind the apocalyptic framework, is his real assessment of what the penalty for sin means. Kennedy (op. cit., pp. 124–5) points out that the question of existence or non-existence was one that held no interest for Paul. What counted was existence in touch with God—i.e. life, or existence without God— i.e. destruction. **Pangs** of childbirth are a common Biblical way of describing sorrow and suffering in general (Jer. iv. 31 ; Hos. xiii. 13 ; Mark xiii. 8). Here the point is not, however, the pains of the guilty at the Judgment or the severity of the preliminary visitations, but the suddenness with which the Judgment comes. That is, it is not a description of the Messianic Woes that precede the Judgment, as in Mark xiii. 8.

The thought of the Day of the Lord coming like a thief in the night (ver. 2), and the fate of the unbelievers, leads Paul

4

now, in verses 4 and 5, to contrast with them the situation of those who are already in Christ. He does so in a word-play on the Day (of the Lord), equating it with the light in which Christian people already live, and the Night (of the Last Judgment) which he compares with the present darkness of the unregenerate ; the new light through Christ, which, but for sin, illuminates every part of the Christian's being, compared with the dark corners and hidden secrets of the soul that knows not God—the soul that loves darkness instead of light because its deeds are evil. **But, brothers, you are not in the darkness for the Day to surprise you like thieves.** You, brothers, are believers ; therefore you know there is a Judgment coming, and you are ready to meet your Lord when He comes. The Day of Reckoning will not find you in ignorance and spiritual darkness, and strike terror to your hearts, as it will for the unredeemed, who will be like thieves in the night, surprised in their evil-doing by the coming of daylight. The R.V. marginal reading **thieves** is more striking than A.V. thief —a repetition of verse 2.

5 Paul now uses the same metaphor positively instead of negatively : **you are all** (yes, all of you, Paul would say, even including those of you who are now a little timorous of what the Day may bring for you) **sons of the Light and sons of the day.** That is, you are not living in the ignorance and moral depravity of heathens, which is darkness, as once you did, but in the full enlightenment of the Christian Faith. Light should be taken in its widest sense, meaning the mental, moral, spiritual enlightenment which Christ has brought into the world and made available for His people. He is Light, Life, and Salvation for all who are members of His Body. The ordinary rabbinical teaching was that this present age is black night : the Age to Come is day and light. For the early Christian, however, the Age to Come was already here : he lived in the New Age. He had therefore already stepped out of darkness into light. Having said this, however, Paul would no doubt have agreed that the Thessalonian Church consisted no less of a mixture of saints and sinners than any of the other Churches or than the average congregation to-day.

But weak, ignorant, foolish though they were, they were still sons of the Light *in posse* through Christ.

Paul employs a common Biblical idiom when he calls the Thessalonians **sons of the Light.** A man is a son of anything which completely dominates and determines his character. Jesus contrasts the Sons of This World with the Sons of Light (Luke xvi. 8), and calls James and John the Sons of Thunder (Mark iii. 17). In the Old Testament, Son of Belial is a frequent description of the evil-doer (1 Sam. ii. 12), who is also called the Son of Wickedness (Ps. lxxxix. 22). Those who are in Christ partake of His nature. They do not simply live ' in the light,' they are themselves part of His light who is the Light of the world (John i. 9). **Sons of the day** is not a repetition of the same thought, but is again part of the word-play. Because they are Sons of Light they are also Sons of the Day of the Lord, i.e. they will be partakers in its glory, and, unlike the Sons of Darkness, who will be taken by surprise, they should look forward to it with joyous expectation and untroubled minds. The promise is, of course, not unconditional. Baptism into the faith does not automatically guarantee that the Christian has nothing to fear from the Judgment. If he is to be saved from the Wrath to Come (i. 10), he must, as Paul goes on to say (vers. 6 ff.), fulfil the conditions of the Christian life (cf. iii. 13). The only ground for his confidence and his hope of sharing fully in the coming glory (ii. 12), is that Christ already dwells in him and enables him, so far as his sinful nature allows, to meet the moral obligations of his calling (cf. Eph. v. 8 ff.). To such men the Day will be like the sunrise after a long night of darkness. The connexion between Light and the Day of the Lord is true to Old Testament thought : ' My Judgment will go forth as light,' says Jehovah (Hos. vi. 6—LXX).

The next sentence is a tactful preparation for the admonitions which follow. **We do not belong to the night or the darkness.** Having called the converts Sons of Light who have nothing to fear from the Day of the Lord, Paul has perforce to remind them that that does not mean that they have nothing to do but to sit back and fold their hands. On the contrary, Christian people must be alert and active, fitting themselves for their future rôle. Before saying this, however, he hastens to identify himself (and Silvanus and Timothy) with the converts. What he has said and what he is about to say applies to all members of the Body of Christ, teachers and learners alike.

6   **Well then,** if we are children of the Light, **we must not sleep like the rest of men, but be wakeful and sober.** Sleep is here taken to be the characteristic attitude of the non-Christian—**the rest of men.** It is suggested by the fact that they are by definition creatures of darkness. Their ' sleep ' then betokens that they are not alive to the possibilities of Light and Life in Jesus Christ. However shrewd and alert they may be where business is at stake, when it comes to the possibilities of their immortal souls their minds are dulled and drowsy. The world that seems real to them, Paul would say, is a dream world ; though their own view would be that it is the Christian who lives on unrealities and visions. They are like men who, when a thief breaks into their house, are startled out of slumber when it is too late, just as the Day of the Lord will shock the worldling into wakefulness (cf. Mark xiii. 36). As Paul explains in the following verse, he is also using **sleep** as a figure of speech for moral obtuseness and insensibility, the blunting of moral perception, the blurring of the distinction between right and wrong.

The exact opposite of this is the attitude of the Christian man, who must **be wakeful and sober.** **Wakeful,** so that he will not be taken by surprise like the thief of the night: mentally alert, and keeping a close watch on himself. The exhortation to watch or be wakeful was frequently on our Lord's lips (Matt. xxiv. 42, xxv. 13 ; Mark xiii. 35). To watch and to pray appeared to Him to be the characteristic duty of a disciple (Mark xiv. 38). It is the sign of a man who is ready to meet his Lord in Judgment at any moment, who not only is looking for Him, but is looking at himself with a critical eye and a penitent spirit. To be **sober** is not so much to avoid alcoholic excess as to keep an even stability of mind and spirit. It is the sobriety of men who have peace of mind through their trust in God, who do not allow themselves to be deflected from the path of Christian obedience by the whims of the moment or the waywardness of the senses.

The metaphor is continued in the words **for sleepers sleep by night and drunkards are drunk by night.** Sleep and drunkenness—the opposites of Christian wakefulness and sobriety—belong properly to the night and therefore to the Sons of Darkness. They have no place in the programme of the Sons of Light and of the Day. Both of them are used figuratively —'sleep' as in the previous verse, meaning lack of moral perception, a slumbering conscience, a suspension of self-control, and 'drunkenness' typifying moral irresponsibility. Chrysostom, for example, says : 'For wealth and the lust of possession is a drunkenness of the soul ; and so is carnal lust, and every sin you can name is a drunkenness of the soul.' **7**

All this has been leading up to the conclusion (vers. 8–10), although the word-play on darkness and light, sleeping and waking, is continued right to the end. **But we,** i.e. we Christians, **must be sober, we who belong to the day**—'sober' is used as in verse 6 and 'day' in the double sense of daylight and the Day of the Lord as in verse 5—*clad in* **faith and love as** *our coat of mail*, **with the hope of** *salvation as our helmet*. Once again the traditional triad of Christian virtues appears (cf. i. 3), combined this time with what is probably a more ancient metaphor of the 'panoply of God.' There is a picture in Isa. lix. 17 of Jehovah coming in Judgment in which He 'clad' Himself in righteousness as 'a coat of mail,' and put a 'helmet of salvation' upon His head (cf. also Wisd. v. 17 ff.). It seems as if Paul, adapting this to the Christian warrior, substitutes the distinctively Christian characteristics, faith, hope, and love. Christian 'faith' and 'love,' replace Old Testament 'righteousness' quite naturally ; 'hope,' because of the primarily eschatological tone of this epistle, slips in before 'salvation.' Paul uses this picture of the Christian warrior more than once, notably—and more fully—in Eph. vi. 11 ff., where he retains the Old Testament 'righteousness' and omits 'hope.' The point here is that as sober and wakeful children of Light, who must be ready to meet our Lord when He comes, **8** we need protection. Perhaps the thought of the vigilant Christian suggested the weapons of defence of the vigilant sentry. At all events, we are protected against every assault of the world, the flesh, and the Devil, since we are armed with a supernatural armour, namely, Christian faith, love, and hope. Faith and love—the religious and moral aspects of Christianity—are bound up with the ultimate hope of salvation. Without faith and without love there can be no hope of salvation, which here means salvation from the Destruction (ver. 3) or the Wrath (ver. 9) which will fall upon the wicked at the Day of the Lord.

It would seem from this that Paul is putting a rather negative value on faith and love ; but he corrects this in the following verses 9 and 10 by showing that salvation means also ' living together with Christ.' Paul would add to both these aspects of salvation—deliverance from the consequences of sin and eternal fellowship with Christ—the hope of the transformation of this body into the likeness of Christ's glory at His Coming (Phil. iii. 20). He rightly makes this hope conditional upon living the Christian life (cf. iii. 12). We all—Christians and non-Christians—must face the Judgment (Rom. xiv. 10 ; 2 Cor. v. 10), though by virtue of our calling we have more reason to hope that we may sustain it. It is hardly likely that Paul, in describing the spiritual armour of the Christian, is thinking of the great struggle with Antichrist (cf. 2 ii. 3 ff.), which, according to Daniel xi. and Jewish apocalyptic, was to precede the End. The armour is purely defensive—as in Eph. vi.—and is designed to fortify the believer against the stratagems of the Devil : the coat of mail protecting his heart and the helmet his head. The ideas of the whole passage are singularly paralleled in Rom. xiii. 11–13, where the antithesis of day and night, sleeping and waking, darkness and light, sobriety and drunkenness, are coupled with the image of the Christian soldier.

9 Having stressed the point that the Christian must be alert and disciplined, using the defences that only the new man in Christ possesses against the power of evil, Paul now goes on to show why the Christian has more reason for hope than fear

as he looks towards the Judgment that will search all men—firstly, because he has been called out of the world into the Church ; secondly, because Christ died for him ; thirdly, because Christ lives with him. This is indeed the answer to the whole problem of v. 1–11. It does not matter when the Lord comes, what matters is that when He does come the Christian has an assurance of salvation which is based on the saving acts of Jesus Christ in history. **For God destined us not for Wrath**—otherwise He would not have called us out of this pagan world into His Church (i. 4, ii. 12). The word used is less specific than ' called,' but clearly means the same thing. **Wrath** is, as in i. 10 and ii. 16, the condemnation of the wicked at the Day of Judgment. That is the negative side of the Christian hope. The positive side is that God destined us **to gain salvation through our Lord Jesus Christ.** Christ is the Christian's anchor in history. Salvation is no religious theory or pious expectation, it is a certainty, because on this earth at a certain point in time Jesus Christ was born, lived as man, died on a cross, and rose again. God has called us, says Paul, i.e. those of us who are now within the Ecclesia, **to gain salvation** by entering into our true relationship of sonship to God which the work of Christ has made possible.

This means a renewal of life by the grace of God through membership of the Body of Christ, with, on the part of the Christian, the exercise of faith and love and hope and constant self-examination, as Paul has just made plain. This can only happen by the indwelling power of Christ, i.e. **through our Lord Jesus Christ.** But it is active, not passive ; i.e. the Christian must **gain** salvation by making his contribution. God, by forgiving his sins, by bestowing His grace, by giving him victory over death, again **through our Lord Jesus Christ,** confirms his future salvation. For this new life, the condition of being saved is only fully realized in the eschatological sphere, beyond the world as we know it, and it is to this salvation in the ultimate sense that God has destined us. Salvation here, then, the hope of the Christian, is the opposite of Wrath, the fate of the pagan: both are realized in the context of the Day of the Lord (cf. Rom. ii. 5–11, and see note on ii. 16).

10 The particular aspect of the redemptive work of Jesus which Paul mentions here is His Death : our Lord Jesus Christ **who died for us**. This is noteworthy for various reasons. It is stated rather baldly (cf. Gal. i. 4 ; Col. i. 20 ; 2 Cor. v. 18 ff., etc.) ; it is the only place in these epistles that the Death of Christ for us is mentioned ; and it is not associated with the Resurrection as is generally the case (cf. i. 10, iv. 14 ; Rom. iv. 25, v. 10, etc.). But it is not therefore to be assumed that this is an early stage of Paul's theology, that at this time he was more concerned with the work that Christ was soon to do at His Coming than with the Cross. In the first place, he could not have referred to the doctrine so casually, and assumed that it would be understood, if it had not been a prominent part of the teaching of the Thessalonian mission, as indeed of all the missions. It was in fact the heart of the *kērygma* (1 Cor. xv. 3 ff.). Secondly, where the redemptive work of Christ is mentioned in this epistle, the full Pauline doctrine is implied (i. 10, iv. 14). Thirdly, as we learn from the Corinthian letters, he was busy preaching a full theology of the Cross at the time when this letter was sent to Thessalonica (1 Cor. ii. 1 f., i. 17 ff.). The explanation is surely that this is an occasional letter ; that the main problem is eschatological, and that the characteristic Pauline insistence on Christ's death as reconciliation between God and man is simply not at issue. What he does say here is that Christ **died for us**, died on our behalf, i.e. for our sins, which already says a great deal. The words that follow, however, imply even more. Christ died for us **that waking in life or sleeping in death we should live together with him.** The text has simply ' whether we wake or sleep.' Moffatt adds ' in life ' and ' in death ' as, plainly, the words are not used here in the same sense as in the previous verses (6 and 7), but as equivalent to ' alive ' or ' dead.' Here the apostle goes back to the first half of the eschatological block (iv. 13–18), where he was concerned to show that those who had fallen asleep in death would in no way be at a disadvantage at the Lord's Coming. Now he comforts them on similar lines but from a different standpoint.

The faithful departed are as close to Christ as the faithful

who are still alive. Life with Him is possible for both because Christ died for us and rose again, ascended into heaven,
and from His place at the Right Hand of God constitutes the
Head of the Body of which we are all members. There is
thus here involved as full a theology as in, say, Rom. vi. 1-11
—not a transactional theory of Atonement, centred exclusively on the Cross, but a declaration of a new relationship
made possible by the Cross, and this relationship one which
death cannot touch. Christ died for us in order that this new
relationship might be effected (cf. Rom xiv. 8-9). At His
Coming, Christians, both living and dead, will enter into it in
all its fulness (iv. 14, 17). It is a relationship which makes
possible a present moral renewal, and has its future consummation in the hereafter. Above all, it is not a private relationship—Paul is no supporter of individualist salvation—for
we shall **live together**, i.e. reunited in fellowship also with those
we have loved and lost and the whole company of the saints
as well as **with him** (cf. the same combination of ' together '
or ' along ' and ' with ' in iv. 17).

On this note of comfort Paul ends the whole passage iv. 13–
v. 11. **Encourage one another, therefore, and let each edify** 11
the other. **Edify** must be taken here in its literal sense ' to
build up.' What he has just said is not simply to be regarded
as consolation for the faint-hearted who are concerned about
the coming Judgment, but is to be used as material for
strengthening the faith of the whole Church—possibly, by
public exhortation, which was then not the function of one
man, but of all members (cf. 1 Cor. xiv. 31), but certainly by
a recognition that the Church member's rôle is not one of
passive absorption, but of active evangelism (Eph. iv. 16).
The metaphor of ' building up,' a favourite with Paul, may
follow from his thought of the Church as the Temple of the
Spirit (Eph. ii. 22 ; 1 Cor. xiv. 4), or may go back to our Lord's
own words about the Church in Matt. xvi. 18 or vii. 24–7. It
is at all events emphatically a pointer to the Ecclesia as a
body of believers and not a group of individuals. Then with
characteristic tact (cf. iv. 1, 9, 10) he tempers admonition with
praise—**as indeed you are doing.**

The real point of this whole paragraph, whose motto, Watch and Pray, should be graven on the shield of every Christian warrior, is the paradox so difficult to us, but much less difficult to minds schooled in the prophets, of stressing the imminence of the Parousia while denying its immediacy. To Paul this clearly presented much less of a problem than it did to the Thessalonians. The Lord is at hand—the End of this Age is upon us—Paul could use expressions like these, and at the same time discountenance an immediate cataclysmic end of the world without being conscious of any inconsistency at all. The important matters for Paul were the correct attitude of the Christian man in this world, and the certainty that life was lived here on the threshold of the world to come. Whether a man entered the new world as an individual at death, or according to apocalyptic expectations, was in a real sense secondary. There is thus no fundamental change with the passing of the years in Paul's mind on the Parousia. If in his later epistles the apocalyptic framework is less in evidence, it is merely the outward form that has altered ; the inner conviction, which is that a man once ' in Christ ' remains ' in Christ,' is unchanged. Anderson Scott, in pointing out that our main difficulty in a matter of this kind is in detaching ourselves mentally from the time-process, says rightly that ' God must be thought of as outside the time-process, so that events which, occurring in the stream of time, appear to men as past, present or future, are all eternally present to Him.' He quotes von Hügel, in his essay on *The Apocalyptic Element in the Teaching of Jesus*, as saying : ' The very suddenness springs from the need to express a junction between the Simultaneity of God and the Successiveness of man ' (*Footnotes to St. Paul*, p. 214).

3. CHURCH LIFE AND CONDUCT (v. 12–22)

12 Brothers, we beg you to respect those who are working among you, presiding over you in the Lord and maintaining dis-
13 cipline ; hold them in special esteem and affection, for the sake of their work. Be at peace among yourselves.
14 We beseech you, brothers, keep a check upon loafers,

encourage the faint-hearted, sustain weak souls, never
lose your temper with anyone ; see that none of you pays   15
back evil for evil, but always aim at what is kind to one
another and to all the world ; rejoice at all times, never 16,17
give up prayer, thank God for everything—such is his will   18
for you in Christ Jesus ; never quench the fire of the Spirit,   19
never disdain prophetic revelations but test them all, re- 20,21
taining what is good and *abstaining from whatever* kind *is*   22
evil.

These next verses contain sundry admonitions and regula-
tions for the conduct of congregational life and private piety.
The whole section resumes the tone of iv. 1–12, which then
passed into the two eschatological problems, and the first
words follow naturally on v. 11, where the Thessalonians have
been exhorted to ' edify each other.' This seems to have
suggested to the apostle that there was another side to the
story, and he proceeds to deal with the deference due to certain leaders in the community.

Brothers, we beg you to respect (A.V. ' know ') those who are   12
working among you, presiding over you in the Lord and maintaining discipline. These leaders, as Moffatt makes it clear,
are not of three types (cf. A.V.). Whatever they were, they
were a class of people who are here described as being active
in three ways : working among the members, presiding over
them, and maintaining discipline. It is unlikely that there is
any special significance in the word working (*kopiao*), though
it is the word Paul uses for his own physical toil (ii. 9 ; 2 iii. 8),
as well as for his herculean efforts in evangelism (iii. 5 ; 2 Cor. x.
15). Here, as in i. 3, it refers to a ' labour of love,' and does
not draw a distinction between the ' workers,' who take their
Christian duties seriously and translate their Christian Faith
into action, and the ' idlers,' whose concern about the imminence of the Parousia makes them not only ' down tools,' but
sow discord in the congregation (cf. iv. 11, v. 13–14). It is
almost equally unlikely that at this stage in the growth of the
Church there was a clearly defined official ministry whose three
functions were so specifically circumscribed.

In the letter to the Philippians (i. 1)—approximately ten

years later—Paul makes his first clear reference to official orders ; viz. Bishops and Deacons. It is generally agreed that even at this stage, and for a long time after, bishops (*episkopoi*) and elders (*presbyteroi*) were different names for the same officials (cf. Acts xx. 17, 28, where both words are used of the same people). From an early point in his missionary journeys Paul had made a practice of appointing elders— as in the Jewish synagogue—to each Ecclesia (Acts xiv. 23), but that was far from being an official ministry of presbyter-bishops. Something of this unofficial nature seems to be indicated here. The Thessalonian community is young ; organization is fluid. The leaders of the community—presumably the elders—Moffatt suggests the names of Jason (Acts xvii. 5), Secundus (Acts xx. 4), and Demas (2 Tim. iv. 10), as examples—were those who worked hardest in the congregation's interests, who presided at their meetings, and who maintained discipline. It may be that the word here translated **presiding over**—though found with reference to official positions in the papyri—means no more than ' looking after you,' as in 1 Tim. iii. 4 ; Titus iii. 8, 14, and Rom. xii. 8. In 1 Tim. v. 17, however, the word is used of presbyter-bishops who ' rule ' as their official function. The phrase **in the Lord** suggests the difference between this kind of relationship in a Christian setting and in any other. Those who ' preside over ' and ' look after ' the others do so, not from personal motives of ambition, but because Christ bids them.

Similarly, the translation **maintaining discipline** suggests rather more an appointed ministry than is justified. The A.V. word ' admonish ' is perhaps better, suggesting something much more elastic and personal—though ' practical counsel and guidance ' is what is meant as much as anything. The picture is not of a strictly regulated community with a definite official hierarchy towards whom Paul now urges a fitting obedience. He is much less concerned with our problems of valid orders and much more with the smooth running of the Church. It is to this end that he asks for co-operation from the rank and file with those who find themselves—as some will in any society—the naturally constituted leaders, and whose concern it is, by their own hard work, supervision, and guidance, to bind the congregation together and make it a real fellowship in Christ.

As for such men, he adds, **hold them in special esteem and 13 affection, for the sake of their work.** The point here is that the ground of respect and esteem in a Christian congregation for its office-bearers is not their status, but their Christian service. It seems that there is some suggestion of tension which Paul is anxious to dissolve. Maybe the natural independence of the Macedonians, or the particular class of society from which the Thessalonian Church was mainly recruited, resented any assumption of authority on the part of some members of the Church. The only solution is, as the apostle points out, to deal with the situation in the spirit of Christian love, conquering human prejudice and perhaps personal dislike by trying to see the welfare of the community as a whole. Also **be at peace among yourselves,** an echo of our Lord's own words (Mark ix. 50). It is possible to take this simply as the kind of advice any pastor would address to any congregation— advice which no Christian congregation could ever say was unnecessary. It is also possible to construct a particular situation in Thessalonica, by referring back to iv. 11 and forward to v. 14 ; 2 iii. 13–15, whereby we see in these words suggestions of friction between the ' workers ' and the ' idlers ' ; the ' idlers ' expecting the ' workers ' to keep them in idleness ; the ' workers ' treating the ' idlers ' with scant ceremony. So the ' workers '—being in control in spiritual and financial matters, are opposed by the drones (see Frame, ad loc.) But all this seems to be giving imagination free rein and the words make sense without it. A third and more unlikely possibility is that the sentence should read : ' Be at peace " through them " ' (reading *autois* instead of *heautois*), i.e. maintain peace within the congregation by being loyal to your leaders.

It is further confirmation that verse 12 does not refer to 14 clerical orders, as distinct from the laity, when we consider the language of verse 14. The whole congregation is obviously being addressed—' brothers ' in verses 12 and 14 attests that

—and here they are exhorted to perform what might more properly be called the duties of the clergy—to admonish, encourage, and help. Paul is setting a very high standard of Christian service for the ordinary Church member, and placing upon his shoulders duties which we tend now too much to regard as ' the parson's job.'

We beseech you, brothers, keep a check (literally, admonish) **upon loafers.** This is once more a reference to the peculiar Thessalonian situation where Second Advent expectations so upset some that they threw up their normal employment and became a burden on the more stable members of the community (iv. 11 ; 2 iii. 6). It is the duty of all the brethren to take a firm hand with them. In classical Greek the word translated ' loafer ' (*ataktos*) is generally used of a soldier breaking ranks, or an army in disarray, hence the A.V. reading ' unruly,' and R.V. ' disorderly.' In a contemporary papyrus, however (A.D. 66), an interesting use of the word occurs in a contract of apprenticeship, where a father undertakes that his son will serve the specified time, with the proviso that if at any time the boy should ' play truant ' (*atakteo*) from his work, the loss of time will be made up after the period of the contract expires. In this sense the word would clearly apply to the absenteeism which constituted a special Thessalonian problem (Milligan, op. cit., pp. 152–4).

Secondly, all are to **encourage the faint-hearted.** This may be a general appeal to be especially gentle with what Wycliffe calls the ' men of litil herte '—the easily discouraged, less-robust type of Church member whose faith is barely strong enough to withstand the buffets of life and the crises of the times (i. 6). In the case of the early Church, Gentile-Jewish hostility and family opposition were factors everywhere present which only stout hearts could face unflinchingly. Again, however, there may be a special reference to the Thessalonian situation, this time to those who are despondent over the fate of their loved ones (iv. 13–18) or of themselves (v. 9–11).

Thirdly, they are to **sustain weak souls**—and this is no Thessalonian peculiarity. Mostly it is a case of the weak supporting the weak, for the **weak souls** are the normally frail human stuff of which the Christian Church consists. But, by the grace of God, some are better able to resist temptation than others, and it is to them that Paul addresses these words. He lays upon them the Christian duty of strengthening the wills of those who are more liable to wander in the broad way— falling back into pagan habits, sharing the easy standards of the worldly wise, forsaking the Christian life through sheer despair of ever being able to approach the Gospel ethic. ' Put your arm round them,' says Paul (*antechesthe*). Perhaps there is a special plea here for help to the waverers of iv. 2–8. But should the loafers be stubborn, and the faint-hearted be still despondent, and human frailty fall from grace, then, as the A.V. has it, ' be patient toward all,' or as Moffatt translates with less dignity but more literally : **never lose your temper with anyone.** This patience or long-suffering is of the very nature of God (Rom. ii. 4, ix. 22), and Paul defines it else- where (Eph. iv. 2) as ' bearing with one another lovingly.' It is both one of the fruits of the Spirit (Gal. v. 22) and one of the attributes of Charity (1 Cor. xiii. 4).

The next words appear to have a wider reference than just 15 the congregation. **See that none of you pays back evil for evil, but always aim at what is kind to one another and to all the world.** Paul would not exclude the possibility that even an exemplary Thessalonian might be provoked beyond en- durance, and think of revenge rather than forbearance. There- fore this applies in the first instance to the internal life of the community. But in view of the last words of the sentence, and what we know of the local situation, it would appear to refer also to the hostile Jews and pagans who were making things so difficult for the Church (cf. ii. 14, iii. 5). Human nature, as well as Jewish law, says ' an eye for an eye,' though the Old Testament could rise to something very much higher, e.g. Prov. xxv. 21–2. Bacon calls revenge a kind of wild justice, and, as Denney says, men will hardly be persuaded that it is not just (ad loc.). But the Christian must take his lead from the Master who said : ' Love your enemies ' (Matt. v. 44), who Himself made these words come alive, and who now en- ables members of His Body to fulfil them. The Christian's duty, as Paul sees it, is not only not to take revenge himself, but to see that no one else does—to act the difficult part of peacemaker in the Church and in the world.

Their motive must be, as Paul says, literally, to ' pursue the good ' (*to agathon*) of each other and of all men.   In a parallel passage in I Cor. xiv. I he says : ' Make love your aim.'   Here, therefore, in all probability ' pursuing the good ' does not mean simply performing little acts of kindness, as opposed to little acts of retaliation, but means making Christian charity the mainspring of all activity.   ' The good ' would be the *summum bonum*, the ideal moral standard, which for the Christian is Love.   The whole thought is expressed more fully in Rom. xii. 17–19 (cf. I Pet. iii. 9).

16– There follows a characteristically terse sequence of general
18 injunctions, which Moffatt calls ' diamond drops ' and Denney calls ' the standing orders of the Christian Church ': **Rejoice at all times, never give up prayer, thank God for everything.** They strike the three notes of joy, prayer, and thanksgiving to God (cf. iii. 9–10)—for **such is his will for you in Christ Jesus.** These last words are the operative factor which controls the rest—possibly even as far back as verse 14.   This is not a series of commandments in the Jewish style, but, like the Sermon on the Mount itself, rather a picture of the transformation that comes over common life when men live in the new relationship of the Kingdom.   For anyone but a New Man in Christ the prescription that Paul has just given in verse 15 and which he now continues in the following verses is fantastic—to rejoice always, to pray without ceasing, to gives thanks constantly.   How can the natural man fulfil such an assignment ?   Nor can we pretend that even the Christian man comes anywhere near it.   But it is again, as in the Sermon on the Mount, the impossible which demands fulfilment, and to which the only approach is by the supernatural power of the indwelling Spirit, but which reaches fulfilment only in the full fellowship of the Lord and His Saints hereafter. For this reason the controlling words are in verse 18*b*.   This is the kind of conduct that God expects from men who have been redeemed by Christ.

Rejoice at all times—the keynote of Philippians—is a 16 word often on Paul's lips. No one by human standards had less reason to rejoice (cf. 2 Cor. xi. 23 ff.), yet no one more clearly saw the paradox of Christian joy through suffering. Nothing that men could do to the early Christians was comparable to the glory that awaited them (Rom. viii. 18 ; 2 Cor. iv. 16–18). It was no mere emotionalism—though Paul was a deeply emotional man—but a strange, joyous exhilaration that possessed them, a sense of having thrown off a great weight, of having stepped out of darkness into light, of living already in the fulness of the Age to Come. This early Christian joy—founded on fellowship with Christ (John xv. 11, xvi. 24, xvii. 13), and testified to by the works of the Spirit— which induced them to call their children Hilaritas, Gaudentius, Victor, which took them through fire and sword in spiritual exaltation, which made the persecutions of the Emperors look adolescent, must have been one of the most remarkable evidences to the pagan of the new order that had begun. Paul himself was the most striking witness that sorrows borne for Christ's sake are by His power transformed to joy (Acts v. 41, xvi. 25 ; Rom. v. 3–5 ; 2 Cor. xii. 10), and he can therefore speak with authority to the Thessalonians, whose own lot was sorely troubled (i. 6, ii. 14, iii. 2–4 ; 2 i. 4).

A second characteristic of the man in Christ is that he must 17 **never give up prayer,** literally, ' pray incessantly.' This is not an injunction to emulate the Importunate Widow, though private petition ought to be a large part of any man's prayer life, and no inhibitions about bringing our personal trivialities to God ought to deter us if we take our Lord's words seriously. Paul's own life was not one of monastic seclusion, where meditation and the daily offices formed the major part of his day. But his whole life was a prayer, in that all that he did was offered to God, all the good that came to him he accepted with thanksgiving to God, and in all things subordinated his own will to God's : doing justly, loving mercy, and walking humbly. It is in this sense that he now exhorts the Thessalonian community to make their lives, their work, and their leisure, an offering of worship. In this sense he writes elsewhere :

whether you eat or drink or whatever you do, let it all be done
to the glory of God (1 Cor. x. 31). The truth is surely two-
sided. We never reach the stage when we can dispense with
saying our prayers, and we can never eat and drink to the glory
of God unless the I–Thou relationship is kept constantly alive
through the dialogue of prayer. As John Donne has it :

> *In none but us are such mixed engines found*
> *As hands of double office ; for the ground*
> *We till with them ; and them to heaven we raise ;*
> *Who prayerless labours, or without this, prays,*
> *Doth but one-half, that's none.*

Paul's letters, where every now and then he breaks into thanksgiving, indicate how largely this kind of occasional ejaculatory
prayer must have bulked in his own experience.

18   Perhaps it is in this sense that he charges them next to
thank God for everything, though indeed we can be thankful
to God without an uttered prayer. Christian thanksgiving
is even more fundamental to Paul's thinking than Christian
joy. It is the acknowledgment of the creature's dependence
on the Creator—the primary recognition of the Christian life
(cf. Eph. v. 20 ; Col. iii. 17). And it is itself made possible
only by God's grace, for ' everything ' here would include the
opposition and persecution which the Church had to endure.
Only God's grace enables us to give Him the glory for what
appears to us the seamy side of our experience, even suffering
and bereavement. These three, then—joy, prayer, and thanksgiving—are the products of the new life, and **such is his
will for you in Christ Jesus.** This is what God expects and
demands of you. He has shown you the Life of the Kingdom
worked out in familiar surroundings in the Life and Death of
Jesus. There is your pattern. But not only in that sense is
His will to be ' seen ' in Christ Jesus, it can only be ' realized '
in Christ Jesus. Only by the transformation of a man's life
that comes from keeping company with Jesus can the joy,
prayer, and thanksgiving, which were the keynotes of His own
life on earth, become a reality for members of His Body.

Finally, in this series of exhortations (vers. 12–22) comes a 19 pertinent word on the place of the gifts of the Holy Spirit in the life of the Church (vers. 19–22). Paul has been holding up a picture of the New Man and a kind of life which is only possible for those who draw on the supernatural power of the Holy Spirit. He now goes on to deal with the more obvious—and often less admirable—manifestations of the Spirit : the ' gifts ' of the Spirit as opposed to the ' fruits ' of the Spirit. Both are God-given, but the latter, though less startling, are always for Paul the more excellent way (1 Cor. xii. 31), and according to him it is only in so far as the gifts of the Spirit subserve the fruits of the Spirit, summarized as the highest Christian demand of love, that they are of any value at all.

Among other ' gifts ' enumerated in 1 Cor. xii. 8 ff. two are relevant here : (1) unintelligible babbling under the influence of religious emotion (*glossolalia*, or ' speaking with tongues ') which was characteristic of the early Hebrew prophetic bands (1 Sam. x. 10–13), and is still a recognized feature of certain types of revivalism, was equally with (2) intelligible ecstatic prophecy, of the order of the classical Hebrew prophet, reckoned to be due to the direct agency of the Spirit (Acts ii. 17, xix. 6). The difference was considerable. In the one case there was an incommunicable experience which had the doubtful value of arousing varied reactions among the by-standers ; in the other, a distinct utterance which, though it might be delivered in an ecstatic condition, was often intui-tively recognizable by the hearers as a word from God. Such magnificently inspired passages in Paul's writings as the Hymn of Charity (1 Cor. xiii.) or Rom. viii. 18–39 may, it is thought by some, have originated in such an ecstatic experience. As Moffatt rightly explains, this whole section refers to the mani-festations of the Spirit, and not, as in the Authorized Version, to a mixture of that (in vers. 19–20) with general counsel (in vers. 21–2). This is indicated by verse 20 and confirmed by the fact that verse 18 rounds off the moral and religious in-struction, and verse 23 begins the closing prayer. The five crisp injunctions in verses 19–22 may therefore be referred to the lengthier passage in 1 Cor. xii. and xiv. for clarification.

Here, as there, the subject is charismatic gifts, but here the only one specified is the gift of prophecy, which, of course, as in the Old Testament, has much less to do with the prediction of future events than with declaring the present Will of God for men. Early Christians, like Old Testament prophets, were more forth-tellers than foretellers. It is probable that the objections in the Thessalonian community were more against ' speaking with tongues,' with which criticism Paul himself was largely in agreement (1 Cor. xiv.). But he wants to make it plain that it is one thing to frown on ' tongues ' and another thing to condemn supernatural manifestations entirely. As distinct from the situation at Corinth, where Paul had to subdue an excess of charismatic utterance, it seems that the trouble at Thessalonica was of the opposite kind. It looks as if some of the more critical members were inclined to frown on any kind of supernatural manifestation. Possibly the prophets of 2 ii. 2 were already upsetting the community.

At all events, Paul urges them strongly : **never quench the fire of the Spirit.** The metaphor of quenching a fire is in keeping with the conventional symbolism of the Spirit which came as tongues of flame at Pentecost (Acts ii. 3), and always brings, as Findlay says, ' Warmth for the heart, light for the mind, and power to kindle the human spirit ' (*Thessalonians : Cambridge Bible*, ad loc.). Paul would say that even if some particular varieties of religious enthusiasm are distasteful to us, we must be very hesitant about damping down real fervour, and must always recognize in them the work of the Holy Spirit. He would also remind us that the Holy Spirit can be quenched.

20 The Thessalonians must, in particular, **never disdain prophetic revelations.** Prophesying ranked first among the spiritual gifts in Paul's thinking (1 Cor. xiv. 1). The prophet, next in importance to an apostle (Eph. iv. 11), utters words from God that edify, encourage, and console (1 Cor. xiv. 3). Those who fancy that any particular prophet does none of these things must yet remember that it is not a human but a Divine message that they are hearing. It is possible—but doubtful—that once again the apostle is dealing with the

' workers *v.* idlers ' question. If this is the case, Frame suggests that the idlers had been abusing the gift of prophecy to persuade the workers to give them money. In any event Paul's counsel is that while they must always be ready to acknowledge real religious fervour, and be very chary about dismissing charismatic gifts, especially of the prophetic variety, still they must be critical, wary of impostors, and must discriminate between true and false.

They must **test them all**, retaining **what is good** *and ab-* 21 *staining from whatever* **kind** *is evil.* It is in harmony with this 22 that in 1 Cor. xii. 10 he lays it down that the ability to distinguish between true and false manifestations is also one of the ' gifts of the Spirit,' and that only two or three should prophesy, while the others are to be ready to pass judgment on what they say (1 Cor. xiv. 29). The fact that a man is in the grip of what appears to be religious ecstasy does not necessarily mean either that it is in fact religious or that what he says while in that condition is worth heeding. He may be a case for the psychiatrist : his words may be his own, not God's. The extraordinary charismatic gifts, says Paul, must be brought to the bar of the no less charismatic gifts of Christian conscience and understanding. The well-being of the Church, the furtherance of the Gospel, and the supreme law of Love are the ultimate criteria. But the critics must not be content with negative criticism. **What is good** must be retained. The word for ' good ' here (*to kalon*) is not the same as in verse 15 (*to agathon*). Here the meaning is ' good ' in the sense of being ' genuine '—like a coin which rings true.

The early commentators connected the whole sentence with a traditional saying of Jesus : ' Show yourselves approved money changers.' This would be more likely if verses 21-2 were intended to be a general admonition, i.e. test everything by the Spirit ; hold to the true metal and reject the base. But almost certainly the meaning is not general, but particularly concerned with the testing of charismatic utterances. The last clause from the Greek may mean ' abstain from every appearance of evil,' i.e. only from what is visibly recognizable as evil, not necessarily from all evil. This is obviously not what Paul means (cf. Matt. xxiii. 5). Or it could mean generally : ' abstain from every kind of evil '—i.e. avoid wickedness entirely. This is possible only if the last verse refers to ' good ' in general and does not particularly refer to charismata. But Moffatt's translation is both possible and better suited to the specific problem with which Paul is dealing. Anything, even charismatic manifestations, which upsets the congregation instead of edifying it, is to be banned.

VII. FINAL PRAYER AND FAREWELL
(v. 23–28)

23 May the God of peace consecrate you through and through ! Spirit, soul, and body, may you be kept without break or
24 blame till the arrival of our Lord Jesus Christ ! He who
25 calls you is faithful, he will do this. Pray for us too,
26 brothers. Salute every one of the brothers with a holy
27 kiss. I adjure you by the Lord to have this letter read aloud
28 to all the (holy) brothers. The grace of our Lord Jesus Christ be with you. (Amen.)

23 Paul's last words in this letter are, as we should expect, a prayer for God's blessing upon his readers. May the God of peace (Himself) consecrate you through and through, i.e. ' only in His strength can you contemplate the strenuous life of a citizen of the Kingdom which I have been outlining.' The God of peace is a favourite expression with Paul as he draws to the close of his letters (Rom. xv. 33 ; 2 Cor. xiii. 11 ; Phil. iv. 9 ; 2 iii. 16). It is therefore not used here with reference to the possible tension within the congregation (v. 12–13), though it is not inappropriate. The peace which the Christian man enjoys is restored fellowship with God through the reconciling work of Christ. It is only when this right relationship has been achieved through penitence and forgiveness that the work of sanctification or consecration can begin (see note on 1 i. 1). Paul prays that the God who gives that peace may consecrate them through and through, i.e. make them utterly His children, filling them wholly with His Grace,

enabling them to grow ' unto the measure of the stature of
the fulness of Chiist ' (Eph. iv. 13).

Then, with added emphasis, Paul enlarges on what he has
just said : **Spirit, soul, and body, may you be kept without
break or blame till the arrival of our Lord Jesus Christ !**
Moffatt's alliterative pattern in the phrase **without break (or
blame)** makes his translation a trifle obscure. The word
(*holoklēros*) means ' entire ' or ' perfect,' and the American
R.S.V. rendering is more intelligible : ' sound (and blameless).' In the Old Testament (LXX) it is used of the perfection of the stones which are to build the altar (Deut. xxvii. 6).
Had Paul some thought of the connexion with the ' living
sacrifice ' (Rom. xii. 1) ? The question of what is in the apostle's mind when he uses the combination of three words to
define ' through and through,' namely, **spirit, soul, and body,**
is surely clear. Firstly, it is obvious that the spirit referred
to is man's own spirit (Rom. viii. 16 ; 1 Cor. ii. 11), and not
the Holy Spirit or part of Him, in some way conceived of as
detached from the whole and bestowed upon the individual
Christian. Paul would neither give man's soul and body
equal place with ' spirit ' if it were the Holy Spirit, nor would
he pray that He should be preserved sound and blameless till
the Parousia. Secondly, it is not an attempt to establish a
trichotomy in respect of man, as an organism divided into
three well-defined compartments. The effort, therefore, to
distinguish what Paul describes as ' spirit ' (*pneuma*) from
what he calls ' soul ' (*psyche*)—the one as the organ of our
' spiritual life,' the other of our ' instinctive life '—is beside
the mark.

He is speaking rhetorically, not theologically, as Moffatt
makes plain by the exclamation marks. A modern preacher
would urge his congregation to put their ' hearts and souls '
into an evangelistic mission, with an equal disregard for psychological exactitude. Here Paul is simply underlining the prayer
of the previous verse in popular language, that the Thessalonians may be completely and utterly God-possessed men.
The triple combination may indeed have been a current liturgical formula in Christian or Jewish circles. At all events,

Paul is certainly as unconcerned about psychology as was our Lord when He gave as the chief commandment to love God with heart, soul, mind, and strength (Mark xii. 30). If there were anything more than this in Paul's mind, it would not imply a departure from the normal New Testament conception of man as a unity of spirit (or soul) and body. In this case ' spirit ' would refer to the God-ward side of man's activities, his devotional life, while ' soul ' would include his normal manward activity—his thoughts, emotions, conscience. Thus the prayer is that the readers may be reached in every aspect of their being by the vital transforming power of God.

The word for **without blame** (*amemptōs*), which appears only in this letter, has oddly enough· also been discovered in inscriptions upon tombs at Thessalonica. The prayer, though different in detail, is similar in intention to that in iii. 13. Both are requests that God may preserve and sanctify the converts so that they may be ready for the **arrival of our Lord Jesus Christ** in Judgment.

24   The next words are simply a reminder that Christians need have no fear : their trust for the future is in God. **He who calls you is faithful, he will do this.** Once again Paul is writing as a missionary and not as a dogmatic theologian. This is not a statement upon which we can base the view that once a Christian receives the call of God and the gift of His Spirit, he is beyond all further concern or obligation ; that he has God's grace and can never fall from it ; that his eternal salvation is assured. Paul has just told his readers that, Chosen Children of the Light though they be, they must be wakeful and sober, and arm themselves with the panoply of God (vers. 7, 8). He assumes, therefore, that the two-sidedness of the New Covenant is understood, and speaks now to men who are soberly conscious of the dangers that beset them without and within, which may end in personal catastrophe. Notwithstanding, he urges them to go forward undaunted in hope: God who has brought them into His Kingdom will strengthen them and enable the apostle's prayer (ver. 23) to be fulfilled.

He who calls—as in ii. 12 (see note) a present participle—

may mean ' He who is constantly calling men into his Church,' i.e. new converts ; or more probably God's call is thought of as something that is timeless—purposed and consummated in eternity, though given and recognized in time, and including justification and glorification (Rom. viii. 30 ; see note on 2 ii. 13). The main point is that God does not give men a fore-taste of life in the Kingdom without making its full realiza-tion the goal which He is constantly enabling them to reach. Finally come three short requests before the Benediction.

Pray for us too, brothers, i.e. as we have just been praying 25 for you. Paul needs the intercessions of his Churches as much as they need his (cf. Rom. xv. 30 ; Eph. vi. 19 ; Col. iv. 3), and here no doubt us definitely includes Silvanus and Timothy. It is a reminder, too, to the Thessalonians that life in Corinth was not without its depressing features and problems, and that their sympathy and prayers were needed.

Salute every one of the brothers with a holy kiss. The point 26 in specifying **every one of the brothers,** instead of the more usual ' each other ' (Rom. xvi. 16 ; 1 Cor. xvi. 20 ; 2 Cor. xiii. 12), does not imply that these words are specially ad-dressed to the leaders of the Church, but that the fellowship of the Church is to be all-inclusive, and that no one is to be left out. The suggestion in this and the following verse is that some were for some reason either absenting themselves from the meetings of the community, or through their own short-comings (cf. ver. 14 ff.) were rather frowned on by the rest of the congregation. Paul's emphasis in both cases is on the unity of the fellowship.

What part the **holy kiss** played in Christian religious prac-tice at this time is not known. In all probability when they met in Church at this stage, the men greeted each other with a kiss, similarly the women kissed each other—presumably on the cheek—as a sign that they were members of one family in Christ. The custom, whatever its origin, was practised in ordinary pagan circles and taken over by Christianity. The ' kiss of peace ' later became a standard practice during pub-lic worship, and was exchanged between men and women, which gave rise to scandalous talk among anti-Christian critics.

135

Even Clement of Alexandria complained of the ' resounding kisses in Church which made suspicious and evil reports among the heathen.' As a result, the practice was restricted to what was believed to be the early custom, and eventually became, in the West at any rate, largely a symbolical part of the liturgy, though it has been retained as a custom among the laity to a limited extent in the Eastern Churches to this day (*Dictionary of the Apostolic Church*, II, p. 443). Paul is saying, as we should to-day : Give everybody a kiss from me, just as he writes to the Corinthians : My love to you all in Christ Jesus (1 Cor. xvi. 24). Some such greeting was the ordinary way of closing a letter then as now.

27   The third request is more of a command. **I adjure you by the Lord to have this letter read aloud to all the (holy) brothers.** (' Holy ' (*hagioi*) has most likely crept in by mistake from the expression ' holy kiss ' in the previous verse. Christian ' brothers ' are by definition already ' *hagioi* ' ; cf. note on iii. 13.) The vehemence of the first words of this verse is astonishing. To ' adjure ' anybody by the Lord is to put him on his oath as a Christian. Why should Paul need to do this ? It would be easily accounted for if one could assume either that those who got the letter were the kind of men who might want to keep it to themselves, or exclude part of the congregation from hearing it ; or if, on the other hand, some members had let it be known that they proposed to pay no attention to anything the apostle might have to say. But even allowing for the tension already noticed between 'loafers' and 'workers,' the praise which the apostle has lavished on the Thessalonians—at times almost fulsome—makes nonsense if there were any deep-seated violent antagonisms between members of the congregation. The explanation must be rather (1) that the apostle wants this letter to be the fullest possible substitute for the visit which he cannot undertake, and to set at rest any doubts about his concern and love for the brethren (cf. ii. 17 ff.), and (2) that he wants the anxieties of the bereaved members to be comforted (iv. 13 ff.). He uses this strong language—plus the first person singular (cf. ii. 18, iii. 5)—to make perfectly certain that every one of the Church members,

whatever his particular situation and need, should hear what
he had to say. The practice of reading aloud was normal in
classical times (cf. the incident of Philip and the Ethiopian
Eunuch—Acts viii. 30). But if ' reading ' here means reading
in public, Paul is establishing an important precedent. It
was through reading his letters aloud during Church worship,
though not necessarily at this early stage, that they came to
form part of the New Testament. In the present instance
what may be in the apostle's mind is to have the letter taken
to the homes of those who do not hear it at a service. Some
of the members may not have been able to read in any case.
The last words of the letter are the Pauline form of the 28
ordinary Farewell ! (Acts xv. 29). **The grace of our Lord
Jesus Christ be with you. (Amen.)** Closing benedictions vary
in Paul's letters, from the very short ' Grace be with you '
(Col. iv. 18) to the full Trinitarian blessing of 2 Cor. xiii. 14
(cf. i. 1). The ' Amen ' which Paul added to some of his
letters is, according to MSS. evidence, doubtful here.

THE SECOND EPISTLE TO THE
THESSALONIANS

I. GREETING

(i. 1–2)

Paul and Silvanus and Timotheus, to the church of the Thessa- 1
lonians in God our Father and the Lord Jesus Christ :
grace and peace to you from God the Father and the Lord 2
Jesus Christ.

THE only difference between this greeting and that in 1 i. 1 1
(q.v.) is that God is called **our** Father, and that the ending
found in all the other epistles is added **from God the Father**
and the Lord Jesus Christ. (Col. i. 1 omits ' and the Lord
Jesus Christ '.) This second epistle, therefore, while expressing Paul's views, is, like 1 Thessalonians, intended to
incorporate the greetings, prayers, and lively concern of the
other two missionaries. Where the plural is used—everywhere except ii. 5—the sense will have to determine how much
is written personally and how much is more than a merely
courteous association of the names of Silvanus and Timothy.
God our Father emphasizes rather the fact that God is the
Father of all Christians than that he is ' *the* Father '—the first
Person of the Trinity. The **grace and peace** of the previous 2
greeting (1 i. 1) are here defined as coming **from God the Father**
and the Lord Jesus Christ. Although it would be true to say
that Paul generally regards grace as the gift of Christ (Rom.
xvi. 20, etc.), and peace as being bestowed by God (Phil. iv. 7 ;
Rom. xv. 33)—i.e. through the grace of Christ we know the
peace of God—here no distinction is made. The power of
new life which restores the broken harmonies is the gift of
God as we know Him in Jesus Christ.

139

II. THANKSGIVING AND PRAYER
(i. 3–12)

3 We are bound always to thank God for you, brothers—it is
proper that we should, because your faith grows apace and
4 your mutual love, one and all, is increasing. So much so,
that throughout the churches of God we are proud of you,
proud of the stedfastness and faith you display through all
the persecutions and the troubles in which you are in-
5 volved. They are proof positive of God's equity ; you
are suffering for the realm of God, and he means to make
6 you worthy of it—since God considers it but just to repay
7 with trouble those who trouble you, and repay you
who are troubled (as well as us) with rest and relief,
when the Lord Jesus is revealed from heaven together
8 with the angels of his power *in flaming fire, to inflict
punishment on those who ignore God,* even on *those who
9 refuse obedience* to the gospel of our Lord Jesus, men who
will pay the penalty of being destroyed eternally *from the
10 presence of the Lord and from the glory of his might, when
he comes to be glorified in his saints* and *marvelled at* in all
believers *on that day* (for our testimony has found con-
11 firmation in your lives). In view of this we always pray
for you, asking our God to make you worthy of his calling
and by his power to fulfil every good resolve and every
12 effort of faith, *so that the name* of our Lord Jesus *may be
glorified in you* (and you glorified in him), by the grace of
our God and the Lord Jesus Christ.

As in the first epistle, there follows now a prayer of thankfulness—shorter and apparently more formal than before
(vers. 3–4), introducing an eschatological pronouncement
(vers. 5–10), before being rounded off on a note of intercession
for the welfare of the young Church (vers. 11–12).

3 **We are bound always to thank God for you, brothers** : this
is on first sight an oddly stilted expression for the writer of
I i. 2–10. But it is not such grudging praise as it seems. The
words **we are bound** do not mean ' we are obliged ' to thank
God, i.e. whether we want to or not, nor are they used in the

formal liturgical sense of ' it is very meet, right, and our bounden duty ' ; but ' we owe it to God to give thanks.' Similarly, **it is proper that we should** may suggest half-hearted praise, but it is in fact the contrary, as can be seen by comparing the same kind of expression in Phil. i. 7. It means : ' It is no more than you deserve.' If Paul has, in the interval between sending off the first letter and the despatch of this, received an answer either in writing or a verbal message, one of the topics raised may well have been a protest by the Thessalonians at what they considered too flattering a tribute to their progress in the faith. Paul, as we have seen, did not spare his praise in the first letter—and unquestionably meant every word of it. He never blinded himself to a congregation's failings, but at the same time he never forgot what they had been like in their pre-Christian days, and never forgot to thank God for what He had achieved in them. It is a fair assumption that the Thessalonians, among other things, modestly and sincerely deprecated these tributes and accused Paul of flattery. In reply he now says : ' I was neither flattering you nor indeed was I thinking at all of what effect my words might have on you. We are not thanking you but God. There is so much to thank Him for that it would have been wrong not to express it as we have done.'

The point at issue is, of course, more than that of accounting for the apostle's apparent change of mood. The view of many scholars has been that 2 Thessalonians was not written by St. Paul, or if it was that it cannot have been written to the same people as 1 Thessalonians (see Introduction, pp. xix. ff.). Among other grounds for questioning the epistle is this alleged difference of tone in the opening verses for which no adequate reason is given. It is not by any means certain, however, that there is a marked change of tone—certainly not enough to make us question the letter's authenticity or seek a new body of readers. The words of verses 3–4, if read without preconception, could not be more complimentary. Indeed, they go farther than what Paul said in 1 i. : **Because your faith grows apace and your mutual love, one and all, is increasing.** In other words, he has more reason to praise them now even than he had before. Their present Christian witness, of which he has since heard, marks an advance even on their excellent showing when last he wrote.

Here, as in 1 i. 3, he stresses their **faith** and **love,** but without adding the third grace of the triad—hope. ' Patience,' however, with which ' hope ' is combined in 1 i. 3, and which here takes its place, appears in the next verse (Moffatt : ' stedfastness '). In the first letter Paul had spoken of their ' active faith '—that is, their new Christ-centred relationship as it affected their daily living. Now he speaks of that relationship as even deeper and stronger, issuing in a correspondingly greater consideration for each other. Previously he had spoken of their ' labour of love ' (1. i. 3) and prayed that they might ' increase and excel in love to one another ' (1 iii. 12). Now he acknowledges that this has happened. The prayer has been answered. His words are emphatic, literally, ' the love of each one of you all towards one another '—nobody is left out : they are a model Christian community.

4   **So much so, that throughout the churches of God we are proud of you.** If this is what Paul meant, well and good. But Moffatt does not include the emphatic ' we ourselves ' (cf. A.V.) which appears in the Greek. Literally, the sentence reads : ' So that we ourselves boast about you in the churches of God.' By implication the measure of the Thessalonians' achievements is that even the founders of their Church themselves cannot but talk about them. This might sound quite natural if it were not that in 1 i. 8–9 Paul's comment on what at that time was a less notable example of Christian living was not that he boasted about it to others, but that he had no need to, since other people started to talk about it to him of their own accord. Is Paul therefore less enthusiastic about Thessalonica after all ? Moffatt side-tracks rather than solves the difficulty. Perhaps the parallel is rather 1 ii. 20, where Paul writes : ' You are our glory and joy.' It was an unusual thing for Paul to boast (1 ii. 6 ; Gal. vi. 14 ; 2 Cor. xii. 1–6) ; but even he and the other missionaries could not forbear to praise—and share the credit for—the mighty Christian witness of the Macedonian Church. His sense of thanksgiving to God

makes him willy-nilly glory and rejoice before men. **The churches of God** are presumably not meant to be limited to the Church at Corinth and its adherents in the neighbourhood, who, if we take this literally, were probably the only Christian congregation outside Macedonia at this time to have heard of the Thessalonian mission—unless Paul had written to them. More likely Paul uses the same pardonable hyperbole as in 1 i. 8 when he says : news of their faith had reached every place.

He pictures all their Christian brethren everywhere as being proud of them : **proud of the stedfastness and faith you display through all the persecutions and the troubles in which you are involved.** **Stedfastness** or patience (*hypomenē*) is the word used with ' hope ' in 1 i. 3 (' patient hope '), and may suggest here, not only endurance of opposition, but the hope of a speedy end to it in the Second Coming. **Faith** is not necessarily faithfulness or constancy in this case, but has its normal meaning of trust and reliance on God in Christ through all adversity. It is their faith that gives them power to endure. Paul has already, in 1 ii. 14 and 1 iii. 3, made reference to outbreaks of persecution, in the first instance from the side of the Gentiles, but in all probability at the instigation of the Jews. That opposition continues. Life is still no easier for the young Church at Thessalonica than it had been for the apostle himself (Acts xvii. 5 ff.). But this is no reason for losing heart.

They are proof positive of God's equity. Moffatt's translation is as ambiguous as the Greek. What are ' proof of God's equity ' (literally, righteous judgment) ?—the fact that as Christians they suffer trouble and persecution, or the fact that God enables them to bear these troubles with stedfastness and faith ? The continuation of the sentence suggests that a combination of both ideas is in the apostle's mind—**you are suffering for the realm of God, and he means to make you worthy of it.** Paul wants to comfort them both with reference to the present and the future, and he points out how the equity (righteous judgment) of God shows itself in two ways : (1) they must recognize that the very fact that their faith has been strengthened rather than weakened by adversity, that they have been given power to endure all the ills that befall them, is the surest indication that there is a just God who cares for His people. He does not leave them comfortless. He is nearer to them in affliction than in prosperity, thus giving them proof of where His final judgment will fall between them and their persecutors. So it had been with Paul and Silvanus themselves as they sang praises to God in their prison cell, and with Stephen as he faced his murderers. God had given them a pledge that, however evil seemed to triumph, the real victory would be theirs. (2) Further, it is by these very hardships that they are being fitted to take their place in the full citizenship of the redeemed saints of Christ in His Kingdom. When the Day of the Lord comes, the humble and faithful who have borne the assaults of the world will find that worldly judgments are overturned, and that God's justice, of which even now they have proof, will vindicate those who have kept faith. This world is ruled by the power of darkness, therefore the righteous suffer. In the New World of Light— in which men in Christ already live and which is soon in all its splendour to break in upon the old world—the rule of darkness will be reversed. The wicked will suffer and the righteous will reap their reward.

6–   This is what Paul now proceeds to add : **since God considers**
7a **it but just to repay with trouble those who trouble you, and repay you who are troubled (as well as us) with rest and relief.** This appears to be such a forthright expression of the *Lex Talionis*, and the verses that follow so strongly echo the Old Testament, that some commentators have dismissed the whole passage as a Jewish interpolation, or have used it as a proof that the epistle is unPauline. There are, however, no real grounds for either of these suggestions. The Jewish law of an eye for an eye and a tooth for a tooth which Jesus supplanted with a new law (Matt. v. 38 ff.), was a plain matter of primitive justice between individuals, a means of exacting vengeance and retribution. The conception of God's justice in this verse is vastly different. It is not arbitrary, nor is it a matter of doling out punishments and rewards. It is, like

the Wrath of God (Rom. i. 18; cf. note on 1 i. 10), inherent
in the nature of a moral universe. Because God is ruler of
that universe, retribution for sin is a part of life either here or
hereafter (cf. Luke xvi. 25). In its deepest sense punishment
is separation from God and reward is fellowship with Him.
Paul sees this process at work in the world, but finds its ultimate fulfilment in an eschatological setting. In Rom i. 18 ff.
the emphasis is rather on the retribution that sin brings upon
itself in this present world. Here the emphasis is on the final
vindication of goodness and the punishment of evil at the Day
of Judgment.

This sentence, therefore, must be taken as a whole, i.e. including the words that follow : ' When the Lord Jesus is revealed from heaven . . . on that Day ' (vers. 7b–10). It is
then that those who have afflicted the weak and persecuted
the righteous—' those who refuse obedience to the Gospel '
(ver. 8)—will suffer the just punishment of God by ' being
destroyed eternally from the presence of the Lord ' (ver. 9).
Having by their evil deeds separated themselves from God in
this world, their punishment is to be separated from Him for
eternity. Those, on the other hand, who serve Him faithfully here and share His fellowship (cf. vers. 4 and 10) will
enjoy that relationship in all its eternal fulness as their reward,
for as Paul has described it before, it means to be with the
Lord for ever (1 iv. 17). **Rest and relief**—one word in Greek
(*anesis*) originally meaning the slackening of a taut bow-
string—is always used by Paul as a contrast with **trouble**
(*thlipsis*), and here clearly means rest and relief from the
afflictions of this world in the joy of life lived with Christ in
His Kingdom—as St. Chrysostom says : ' All but opening
heaven already by his word.' In this new life Paul associates the three missionaries with the converts—all are suffering, whether in Corinth or Thessalonica—**you . . . as well as
us.**

The next few verses (7b–10) complete the thought which 7b
began in verse 5 by giving a graphic picture of the Judgment.
The language is so reminiscent of the Old Testament (indicated by Moffatt's italics) and Jewish apocalyptic literature,

that it has been thought to derive either from a Jewish Psalm to which Paul has made some Christian additions, or to be a Jewish-Christian hymn which Paul uses. But it is just as likely that the picture comes from Paul's own mind, a Christian mind steeped in the thought and language of the Old Testament and later writings, which he adapts to suit his purpose. It may even be a prophetic revelation of the type which he refers to in I v. 20, and of which he himself possibly provides a specimen in I iv. 16–17—delivered in a state of spiritual exaltation in which Christian concepts are clothed in traditional Old Testament phrases. On Harnack's view that this second epistle was written to the Jewish Christians of Thessalonica, the Old Testament element in the following verse would be clearly explicable. Paul uses the traditional language of Judaism attached to the Great Deliverance of the Day of the Lord and applies it to the Triumph of Christ. Whether we can read out of it what Paul himself believed is like asking whether we ourselves use the language of the hymn-book and the psalter to express our theology. Particularly in the hymns that depict the glory of the life to come is this true. There is a popular traditional language of the hymn-book and there is a language of theology. When we are engaged in theological discussion we use the latter, when we sing hymns we can use language which conflicts in detail with our theology with no conscious insincerity. Paul is not here writing theology. Another parallel to-day is the preacher, revivalist or otherwise, who uses, probably unconsciously, traditional scriptural terminology much more freely as the emotional temperature rises.

The most notable feature is the reticence of the description. What in normal apocalyptic literature would have included a lurid picture of the tortures of the damned and the bliss of the righteous, in Paul's hands becomes a restrained background of Judgment with the light focused on the Person of Christ as Judge. Paul has been speaking of God's equity which, he says, will finally be plain **when the Lord Jesus is revealed from heaven together with the angels of his power** *in flaming fire*. Although this and what follows are variations played upon the theme of the Second Advent of Christ, there are strong similarities to various Old Testament theophanies. Christ is to appear at the Last Day accompanied by **angels** (cf. 1 iv. 16, iii. 13) and *flaming fire*. This recalls the appearances of Jehovah at Sinai (e.g. Deut. xxxiii. 2 ; Exod. iii. 2) or Isaiah's words in chapter lxvi. 15 : ' The Lord will come as fire.' ' Angels of Power ' are a definite class in apocalyptic eschatology. That Jesus is to be **revealed** suggests that what is now unknown will become plain. His glory, which is at present hidden from the mass of men—though glimpsed by faithful Christians—will become manifest. His presence, which is a reality for Christian men here on earth, will at His Coming be made known to all. The Second Advent is called a ' revelation ' also in 1 Cor. i. 7, and the first epistle of Peter (i. 7, 13, iv. 13). Involved in it are the ' revelations ' of the Sons of God (Rom. viii. 19) and of His righteous Judgment (Rom. ii. 5).

Literally regarded, the picture is of the descent from the sky of the Lord in a blaze of glory accompanied by the angelic host (Matt. xxiv. 31, xxv. 31)—symbol of His authority and charged to do God's will. Behind the material symbolism is the reality of the final climax of history, when the baffling reflections in the mirror become clear (1 Cor. xiii. 12). Jesus is to be revealed **from heaven.** Now He is in the presence of God in the realm of the unseen ; then men will see Him face to face in the company of the just made perfect and in the awful glory of His Divine majesty—a terrifying sight for the wicked.

This is surely what the apostle is thinking of when he speaks 8 of *flaming fire* rather than associating the words with the clause that follows : *to inflict punishment on those who ignore God.* The phrase to *inflict punishment* is a further echo of Isa. lxvi. 15. Paul uses the same words as the LXX. *Those who ignore God* are presumably the pagans who are spoken of in this way in 1 iv. 5 (see note). They will not be punished because as pagans they have not known the true God, but because they have wilfully disregarded what knowledge of God they possess. There is no punishment for ignorance as such. But God does not 'leave Himself without a witness' (Acts xiv. 17), and men are judged on their response to what light is given them. In Rome the wilful idolatry of the pagans brought its own nemesis—moral and spiritual corruption (Rom. i.). In Thessalonica the vindictive harrying of the Christian Church was no less a reckless disregard of God's eternal laws and would receive its deserts.

It is more likely that the next phrase describes a second group of evildoers who will be punished at the Last Day than, as Moffatt suggests by the word **even,** that they are the same people as the first. The translation would therefore read : 'and' (*kai*) **on** *those who refuse obedience* to the gospel of our Lord Jesus. It may be that the first class are a reminiscence of Jer. x. 25—' the heathen that ignore thee,' and the second of Isa. lxvi. 4—' when I spake they did not obey ' ; but if they are, they are no more than echoes. ' Those who refuse obedience to the Gospel ' is a phrase coined by Paul's own mind. He uses it of his recalcitrant countrymen in Rom. x. 16, and doubtless here of the Jewish instigators of the persecution. The pagans who flout God's natural laws and the Jews (as well as pagans) who reject the revelation of His Son—particularly in this case at Thessalonica—will alike suffer the penalty of their sin. In a real sense the Judgment has already begun. The condemnation is already upon those who love darkness rather than light (John iii. 18, 19). Paul sees the Last Judgment as the consummation of what has already begun. What will their punishment be ?

9 Paul describes their fate as that of **men who will pay the penalty of being destroyed eternally** *from the presence of the Lord and from the glory of his might.* There is a striking correspondence between these words and those of Isa. ii. 10, repeated in verses 19 and 21, where there is a description of the terror of the Day of the Lord. In the Greek version, twelve consecutive words—apart from one extra word in the Old Testament—are identical, as well as the words ' on that Day ' which appear in both cases in the following verse. Clearly this is a quotation—the only direct quotation from the Old Testament (or from Testimonia) in the passage—but it

need imply no more than that Paul, as one would expect from his training, had Biblical phrases woven into his thinking. Here again a Day of the Lord prophecy is transferred to the Second Advent.

The idea behind it, however, is more one of the inevitability of retribution for evil deeds than a prophecy of individual punishment being meted out in proportion to the sinfulness of the wrongdoer. Those who pay no heed to God's laws and flout the Gospel of Jesus Christ bring their own punishment upon themselves. The word **penalty** (*dikē*) does not mean so much punishment in the sense of 'chastisement' as in the sense of the 'execution of justice.' It is the root of the words for 'righteous' and 'righteousness.' There is inherent in it no arbitrary award or retaliation, but a just and inescapable consequence of defying God's will enshrined in the moral structure of the universe. The men in question are only a sample of the kind of men who bring upon themselves the penalty of **being destroyed eternally.** This does not mean annihilation or eternal torment. 'It is not the absence of being, but of well-being.' It means the opposite of eternal life. Eternal life is life lived in communion with the eternal God revealed in Christ Jesus—possible on earth and fully realized in the hereafter. Eternal destruction is separation from God for ever. There is no suggestion here of final deliverance. In the papyri and inscriptions the word used (*aionios*, literally, agelong) can mean 'lasting for a definite period' and not necessarily 'for ever.' But any qualification of this kind here is no part of Paul's theology. The 'age to come' replacing the present age will have no end (see Kennedy, op. cit., pp. 316 ff.). Rejection of the Light on earth means life in darkness **eternally.**

It is rather the absence of any positive content in life that Paul suggests—a negative vacuum which is banishment *from the presence of the Lord and from the glory of his might.* The *glory of his might* is the splendour of the power and majesty of the Lord before which mortal man must tremble, but which in some sense the believer shares hereafter (see note on Glory, I. ii. 12). In these Old Testament words—with the significant omission of the word ' fear '—cf. Isa. ii. 10 : ' From the presence of the fear of the Lord,' etc.—Paul describes the encounter with the Lord on the Last Day. The Lord will come then in power and glory, but for those who have merited His Judgment, it will bring sentence of expulsion from His presence for ever—the full realization of the deprivation of Life which they already suffer. It should be noted with what reticence Paul describes the fate of the wicked. He paints no lurid picture of their ultimate destiny—the horrors in which the Renaissance painters delighted. He writes symbolically and not literally. His emphasis is on the spiritual fact of separation from God, not on the material conditions. While he uses traditional language, his interest is not in the details in which the apocalyptists delighted, but in the essential contrast between the man who is in Christ now and for ever, and the man who by his rejection of Christ is for ever a lost soul.

What Paul has in mind is in fact something much more terrible than the most vivid imaginings of rabbinical theologians or Italian painters. It is failure to fulfil our destiny as Sons of God. For this we were created and put into this ' vale of soul-making.' In stretching out our hands to God through Christ, and committing our lives to Him, we reach the only true satisfaction in life and the fulfilment of personality. In this response of spirit to Spirit we know what Heaven means. To be in the Kingdom now—to be a follower of Jesus—brings its own reward, namely, to be always with Him (1 iv. 17). To turn our backs on God is to suffer Hell. Paul's solemn warning here is that Heaven and Hell are present possibilities which condition our eternal gain or eternal loss.

10   But while Heaven and Hell are realities which we may know here and now, the full realization is not yet. We shall know in all its fulness what life with Christ or life without Him means *when he comes to be glorified in his saints* **and** *marvelled at* **in all believers** *on that day. When he comes . . . on that day* refers of course to the Parousia (cf. 1 v. 2). That is the time when those who have merited eternal separation from God will realize their fate in all its horror, but it is also

150

the time when the Coming Lord will *be glorified in his saints.*
Saints mean here, as commonly, the rank and file of Christians,
now at the Parousia made perfect. Their excellence in faith
and virtue, wrought in them by the power of Christ, becomes
itself a tribute to the Advent Lord, as it would be in a lesser
degree to Paul himself (1 ii. 20). They reflect His Light and
share His Power. He does not merely receive honour among
His people and from His people, but because of them. The
Son's glory is the greater because of the witness of His Church
(John xvii. 10), as the Father's is by that of the Son (John
xiii. 31, xiv. 13).

Further, they are not only a source of praise but of wonder.
The Lord is also *marvelled at* **in all believers.** The emphasis
is here not so much on the wonder of the angelic host at the
holiness of the saints as on the inclusiveness of the sainthood.
It comprises ' all those who believe.' This surely is a word of
comfort for any despondent Thessalonians. They are assured
that their faith is real. They heard God's call and answered
it. Through all their stumbling and falling, their very sense
of unworthiness (cf. note on ver. 3) was the surest proof that
they were still Christ's people and would take their place
among His folk on His Day. As proof of their faith Paul adds
in parenthesis : **for our testimony has found confirmation in
your lives.** That would mean ' our preaching during the
mission has borne ample fruit since.' The more generally
accepted Greek text, however, though a trifle awkward
(cf. R.V.), would be translated : ' for our testimony to you or
among you was believed ' (*epistōthē* (Moffatt) and *episteuthē*
(R.V.)). Moffatt's preference does not seem to have any advantage over the other in meaning. The emphasis on the
Thessalonians' response of faith would be, if anything, more
Pauline.

The end of the first section, as in the first epistle, is a prayer 11
(cf. 1 iii. 11–13). **In view of this we** (also) **always pray for
you, asking our God to make you worthy of his calling and by
his power to fulfil every good resolve and every effort of faith.**
Paul has been reassuring the Thessalonians that their endurance of affliction will not be in vain ; their enemies will meet

their deserts, and they themselves will share in the triumph of the Lord when He comes. His prayer now is that the virtues they have may by God's grace be so perfected that they will add lustre to the Lord's coming. **In view of this** (i.e. your coming salvation) **we always pray for you.** Moffatt omits ' also,' which seems to fit in best after ' we.' Not only does Paul always thank God for them (ver. 3) and boast about them (ver. 4), he *also* prays for them. He asks God to make them **worthy of his calling.** The word (almost the same as in ver. 5) is more accurately translated to ' count ' than to ' make ' worthy—not so much a prayer that they may grow in grace as time goes on, but that they may have so grown in grace, that at the Great Day they will be counted worthy of their Master. **Our God** is again Paul's sympathetic identification of missionaries with converts—they are all God's people (1 ii. 2).

God's calling of men into the Christian fellowship is generally with Paul the decisive moment of encounter and conversion (cf. Rom. viii. 30 ; 1 iv. 7). He also regards it as in a sense an eternal act of God in the Christian life (cf. note on 1 ii. 12). Here His calling, first effected through the missionaries' testimony (ver. 10), is seen in its culmination. The end of it all, of the original summons and of the continuing work of sanctification, is to fulfil the true destiny of the Christian man at the Lord's coming. Only God can fit and equip His people by His grace to fill the rôle for which He has chosen them, namely, to glorify Him in the Kingdom of His Son at His Parousia and for ever. At the Great Day they can only hope to be deemed worthy of God's call to them if He has enabled them **by his power to fulfil every good resolve and every effort of faith.** Paul prays that every good impulse may be translated into action and not left as a pious intention, and that the acts of charity that their faith would suggest to them should not remain still-born. God plants any good resolves we have in us, and He alone can bring them to fruition. Through His grace we have faith, and only by the power of His Spirit does our faith issue in works of love. The lovely Easter Collect expresses a similar idea : ' We humbly beseech Thee that as by Thy special grace preventing us Thou dost put into our minds good desires, so by Thy continual help we may bring the same to good effect.'

Once again Paul makes it clear that there is nothing automatic about a man's salvation. He may be called and yet be lost by betraying his calling. He is in Christ only if he brings forth the fruits of Christian living. The test of the reality of a man's status as a Christian is essentially ethical. Paul cannot think that in the long run—so great is his conviction of the power of the indwelling Christ and the significance of His death—any Christian can fail to pass muster at the Great Day when he faces his Lord's Judgment, but he assumes that the inevitable accompaniment of life in the Spirit is the fruits of the Spirit.

And the fruits of the Spirit, i.e. the fulfilment of every good 12 resolve and every effort of faith, are directed to one end, namely, *that the name* **of our Lord Jesus** *may be glorified in you* (**and you glorified in him**), **by the grace of our God and the Lord Jesus Christ.** Once more Paul adapts an Old Testament phrase and concept. The Greek text of Isa. lxvi. 5 reads : ' That the name of the Lord may be glorified.' Here the Lord is the Lord Jesus. In the Old Testament the word **name** is used, not only in its ordinary English sense, but as involving the personality and character of the person named. The child whose **name** shall be called ' Wonderful, Counsellor, the Mighty God, the Everlasting Father, the Prince of Peace,' will in fact comprise all these things in His own nature (Isa. ix. 6). Jerusalem, after it has been cleansed from its iniquities, and has become the city of the redeemed in the Good Time Coming, ' will be called the city of righteousness ' (Isa. i. 26). *The name* **of our Lord** is, therefore, the Person of the Lord, so far as He has revealed Himself (e.g. Isa. lii. 6—' Therefore my people shall know my *name* '). In particular, like the expressions, ' the glory of the Lord,' ' the face of the Lord,' ' the angel of the Lord,' the phrase was used of manifestations of God as distinct from the essential unchangeable Being of God Himself (see Hastings' *Dictionary of the Bible* under Name).

Both ideas are involved here. It is the ' person ' of the Lord Jesus that is to be glorified by the Christian witness of

His people when He manifests Himself to men at His Coming. He will be seen then to be all that His Name implies—Messiah and Lord (Acts ii. 36), Firstborn of a great brotherhood (Rom. viii. 29). The climax of God's purpose will be reached when at the Name of Jesus every knee shall bow and every tongue confess that Jesus Christ is Lord (Phil. ii. 9–11). The Thessalonians' example of Christian behaviour will be a testimonial to the Lord on His Day. Men will marvel the more at the power and holiness of One who is able to effect such a change in His followers. The mutual relationship between Christ and His people is very striking. He will be *glorified in you* (**and you glorified in him**). To be known as Christ's men at His Coming will be to share in the honours paid to Him—' The servants come in for a share of the honour of the master whose livery they wear ' (Adeney, *Thessalonians : Century Bible,* ad loc.)—just as He is held in higher honour because of them. While it is with special reference to the Parousia that Paul speaks of this reciprocal reflected glory, it is a truism that here and now our Lord's good name is hindered or advanced by our witness, as much as we are saved from animated death by our communion with Him (John xvii. 9 f., 20 ff.).

Characteristically Pauline are the closing words of this chapter. The foundation, source, or motive power, of all that will reach its culmination at the Parousia is **the grace of our God and the Lord Jesus Christ.** But if the emphasis on **grace**—the Christian dynamic—is typical, not so is its combination with ' our God and the Lord Jesus Christ.' Grace is generally thought of by Paul as coming through Christ—the channel by which it flows from God the source of all. Here both Father and Son are regarded as the fountain-head of the love and favour which make possible the mutual glorification referred to in the previous words. (For **our God** see verse 11 and 1 ii. 2, iii. 9.) Dibelius thinks that this formal ending, together with the more formal tone of the whole chapter, indicates that this part of the epistle was originally designed to be read aloud to the congregation at Thessalonica.

III. ANTICHRIST

(ii. 1–12)

With regard to the arrival of the Lord Jesus Christ and our 1
muster before him, I beg you, brothers, not to let your 2
minds get easily unsettled or excited by any spirit of prophecy or any declaration or any letter purporting to come
from me, to the effect that the Day of the Lord is already
here. Let nobody delude you into this belief, whatever 3
he may say. It will not come till the Rebellion takes place
first of all, with the revealing of the Lawless One, the
doomed One, the adversary *who vaunts himself above and* 4
against every so-called *god* or object of worship, actually
seating himself in the temple *of God* with the proclamation
that he himself is God. Do you not remember I used to tell 5
you this when I was with you ? Well, you can recall 6
now what it is that restrains him from being revealed before his appointed time. For the secret force of lawless- 7
ness is at work already ; only, it cannot be revealed till
he who at present restrains it is removed.

Then shall the Lawless One be revealed, whom the Lord Jesus 8
will destroy with the breath of his lips and quell by his
appearing and arrival—that One whose arrival is due to 9
Satan's activity, with the full power, the miracles and
portents, of falsehood, and with the full deceitfulness of 10
evil for those who are doomed to perish, since they refuse
to love the Truth that would save them. Therefore God 11
visits them with an active delusion, till they put faith in
falsehood, so that all may be doomed who refuse faith in 12
the Truth but delight in evil.

As in the first epistle, the real business of the letter begins
in the second chapter after the introductory greetings and
thanksgiving are past, and Paul now comes to his main topic,
one of the most difficult passages in all the epistles—and one
which in the A.V. is quite incomprehensible. Part of the
difficulty lies in the fact that what he says here assumes considerably more that he had said already in person at Thessalonica, and which we have now no means of knowing, and part

lies in the nature of the topic. Augustine was perhaps the wisest of the commentators when he said : ' . . . we, who do not know what they knew, desire and yet are unable even with all our efforts to get at what the apostle meant, especially as the things which he adds make his meaning still more obscure '! Despite this, the attempts to find out what St. Paul did mean are unending. Excitement and unrest seem to have grown in Thessalonica since Paul's last letter. Parousia talk and expectancy appear to have completely unsettled their minds and habits. Since time was so short, some were saying : Why go on working ? Others were in a state of great trepidation, because they did not feel ready to meet their Lord. So after the customary word of greeting and disarming praise (i. 3 ff.), and before taking some of them sharply to task for their idleness (iii. 6 ff.), Paul deals with the signs which must precede the End. Until these things begin to happen, it is pointless to think of the Second Advent. Before the Last Day when the Lord comes, the Lawless One, who is at present held in restraint, must appear in the world as the antithesis of all goodness, yet likely to be mistaken for Christ Himself. Until then, as Paul had already told them, it is futile to talk as if the end of the world were already upon them. Such an outspoken apocalyptic utterance is peculiar to this epistle and presents a real problem of relevance to-day.

1　**With regard to the arrival of the Lord Jesus Christ and our muster before him.** Paul broaches the subject which is uppermost in his mind in writing this letter. He has led up to it by holding before his readers the certainty of the Lord's Coming and what it will entail. Now he turns to practical details, namely, When will all this happen ? The **arrival** of Christ and the **muster** are part of the same event. Paul has already described, in 1 iv. 16 ff., how at the Lord's Advent those believers who are still alive will be gathered to meet Him and the resurrected saints in the air. But the idea is older than that. In the Old Testament one of the promises was that at the Day of the Lord all the scattered tribes of Israel would be gathered together from the four corners of the earth (cf. Ps. l. 3 ff. ; Isa. xi. 11 ff., xxvii. 13). In the Apocrypha this is one of the marks of the inauguration of the Messianic Kingdom (2 Macc. ii. 7). In Mark xiii. 27, as here, it is part of the Advent of the Son of Man. An interesting use of the same word (*episynagōgē*) is to be found in Heb. x. 25, where the regular ' mustering ' of the people, presumably on the Lord's Day, is regarded as part of the preparation for the Day of the Lord. Paul, however, is concerned that the preparation of the Thessalonians for the Day is proceeding along false lines. They are behaving stupidly and irresponsibly.

He therefore continues : **I beg you, brothers, not to let your** **2** **minds get easily unsettled or excited by any spirit of prophecy or any declaration or any letter purporting to come from me, to the effect that the Day of the Lord is already here.** The Greek retains the plural *'we' beg you . . . from ' us,'* but it is obviously Paul speaking for himself. His problem is to restore order in a community which should be living and working soberly and prayerfully so that when the Lord came He should not find them off their guard. Instead of that (as the Greek word translated **unsettled**—*saleuō*—implies) they were behaving like ships that had been insecurely anchored, had broken from their moorings, and were now blown hither and thither with every rumour or chance remark that suggested that the end of the world had come. The same word for **excited** occurs in an eschatological context also in Mark xiii. 7 : ' When you hear of wars and rumours of war do not get excited.' It is a warning against ' nerviness.'

The most likely way to interpret the next words is that Paul is insisting that there is not the slightest reason to think that the end of the world is upon them, that they must allow nothing to persuade them that it is, and that certainly nothing that he himself had ever said or written lent colour to any such notion. He names three ways in which he thought it possible that his authority was being falsely cited through something he had said or written. It is not clear whether Paul knew exactly how the idea had arisen at Thessalonica that the End had come. He may simply be giving a comprehensive denial meant to cover any eventuality. On the other hand, it seems more than possible that it was as a result of further news from Thessalonica that this letter was written at all ; and as this part of it is the main topic, these three allusions may possibly refer to definite information that Paul had received.

The situation would then be that those who were upsetting the equilibrium of the Church at Thessalonica based their actions on a claim that (*a*) Paul had on some occasion, while in a prophetic ecstasy, proclaimed that the Day of the Lord was upon them ; or that (*b*) in one of his sermons or in conversation he had said so categorically ; or that (*c*) he had actually written it in a letter. This seems a more likely interpretion of the Greek text than that the **spirit of prophecy** (literally, spirit) (see notes on 1 v. 19, 21) refers to some inspired utterance of an unknown prophet in Thessalonica, and that Paul's authorization is claimed only in the case of the **letter** and the **declaration** or the **letter** alone. The chief point of interest centres in the letter. Does Paul mean that his first letter to the Thessalonians had been misconstrued, or was there some other letter which he had sent of which we know nothing, or is he alleging that a forged letter was being circulated ? He seems to suggest the possibility of forgery in the next verse and in iii. 17. But what would be the point of such a forgery and who would be guilty of it ? The apostle is still alive and easily able to contradict any forged epistle. Further, the Jews—who were his only real opponents—would gain nothing by pretending that the apostle had said that the Day of the Lord was upon them. Paul would also have handled such an imposture more drastically.

On the other hand, his odd insistence on having his previous letter read to all without exception (1 v. 27) suggests the possibility that it may have been among people who were absenting themselves from the meetings that the rumours had gained most currency. If in fact his first letter had not been read to them, they might easily have heard only garbled versions of what it contained—especially of 1 v. 1–11. But in this case why should he say a ' letter purporting to come from me ' ? Everybody knew that in fact 1 Thessalonians was from him. If anything, the balance would come down in favour of the view that Paul had reason to think that someone, not by forging his signature but with the intention of interpreting his ideas, had written to the Thessalonians saying that, according to Paul, the Day had arrived. From what he says here it is impossible to tell, and in view of this it is most likely that he himself had no definite information. All he knew from rumour was that it was being said in Thessalonica that Paul had said that **the Day of the Lord is already here.**

Paul had certainly said that the Day would break in their lifetime (1 iv. 17). What he had not said at any time was that anyone could say with certainty that to-day or to-morrow was the appointed time. The Lord Himself had made that clear to His disciples (Matt. xxiv. 26–7 ; Luke xvii. 23–4). Paul's real concern had been with the need for spiritual readiness on the part of those upon whom the end of the Old Age and the beginning of the New had come. He now has to face the consequences of treating the Day of the Lord as an imminent spiritual reality in the case of men who could only see its material implications (see note on 1 i. 10). The sense in which the Day of the Lord is **already here** is, of course, not that the Son of Man has appeared, but that the period of time signified by the word ' Day ' has begun and that now at any moment the crisis may be upon them. The word for **is already here** (*enestēke*) is used in the papyri with reference to the current year. The excitement would, in this case, be based on the rumour that ' the world is to come to an end this year ! Paul has said so ! ' This is the dangerous *canard* that Paul has now to scotch. He does so by specifying the conditions that must obtain before any talk of the end of the world becomes relevant. And he does so reproachfully, as if to say, ' You know all this already. You ought to have more sense.'

Let nobody delude you into this belief, whatever he may say, 3 i.e. whether I am quoted as the authority or not. Our Lord had already said in the same connexion : ' Take care that no one misleads you ' (Matt. xxiv. 4). **It will not come till the Rebellion takes place first of all.** No explanation is given of what is meant by the Rebellion. The idea is, apparently, familiar to the readers from Paul's previous teaching. Unfortunately, it is far from familiar to us. It is safe, at any rate, not to look in the classics for the meaning of the word *apostasia*. There it is used of political rebellion. But here it is something wider than a revolt against the lordship of Rome which Paul envisages as a prelude to the End. The parallels for the word are to be sought in the Old Testament and Apocrypha, where it means 'rebellion against God' (Josh. xxii. 22 ; 1 Macc. ii. 15), and in the New Testament itself, where either *apostasia* (Acts xxi. 21), or its verb-form (Heb. iii. 12 ; 1 Tim. iv. 1) has a definitely religious—as opposed to political—connotation.

Clearly Paul uses it as a technical term—part of the apocalyptic vocabulary which this passage presupposes among the readers—and we must be content to accept it with limited understanding. It is to be one of the unnatural portents and manifestations that precede the end of the world (cf. 2 Esdras v. 1 ff. ; Matt. xxiv. 10 ff.). It will take the form of a widespread and violent defiance of the authority of God. And at the time of writing it has not yet taken place. It is therefore in this context not to be identified with Jewish rejection of Christ—for that has already happened ; nor with Christian apostasy—for Paul assumes that election almost certainly eventually guarantees salvation (see note on i. 11) ; nor with the co-existence in the world of the Wheat and the Tares as forecast in our Lord's parable (Matt. xiii. 24–30). The Rebellion is to be a definite event, an apocalyptic happening ; it may conceivably be an earthly parallel to the revolt in heaven (Rev. xii. 7 ff.). Such a prophecy as the assault on Jerusalem by the barbarians under Gog of Magog is a possible basis for the idea (Ezek. xxxviii. and xxxix. ; cf. Rev. xx. 7–10). More than this it is difficult to say precisely.

Associated with the Rebellion—either at the same time or as its climax—will come **the revealing of the Lawless One.** This carries us a stage farther into the apocalyptic imagery of the passage. The Lawless One is, literally translated : the Man of Lawlessness (*ho anthrōpos tēs anomias*). The MSS. authorities are divided between this and the Man of Sin (*ho anthrōpos tēs hamartias*). Both mean the same, for according to 1 John iii. 4, sin is lawlessness. In either case the expression is Hebraic, and means the Man whose nature is either Lawlessness or Sin, whose character is the essence of evil. On the face of it this cannot mean Satan, since Satan is spoken of in verse 9 as the Lawless One's master, and the use of the word ' Man' indicates a human being. Clearly what is meant is an apparently human being with the characteristics of the Devil.

The clue lies in the word **revealed**. The same word has been used recently (i. 7) of the coming Advent of the Lord Jesus. The Lord is at the moment hidden from men's sight : soon He will appear. So the Lawless One is now hidden and will likewise soon be made manifest. Where he is concealed—whether in heaven or hell—Paul does not say ; he will at all events appear as part of the prelude to the Coming of the Lord. From the following verses it is obvious that there is a close relationship between the Advent of the Lawless One and the Advent of Christ. It is the contrast between the true and the false Messiah—between Christ and Antichrist. Paul does not use here the word which later became current in the Church. It is first used in the Johannine epistles (1 John ii. 18, 22, iv. 3 ; 2 John 7). By that time the expectation was that Antichrist—a specific figure—was yet to come, but that his spirit was at work in the world, since many minor antichrists had already appeared. Paul's thought is essentially the same. Both writers draw on a common tradition.

Paul's Lawless One will be the incarnation of evil as Jesus was the incarnation of goodness. His father will be Satan as Jesus's Father was God. He will be able to do mighty works and men will flock to him. He will claim the rights of God Himself. But when Christ returns at the Judgment, He will utterly destroy the Lawless One and those who have followed him. Such is the picture which Paul presents in verses 3–12. We must examine it first more closely before asking what relevance—if any—it has for our own day.

It seems fairly certain that one element which went to make up the picture of Antichrist here is the Jewish-apocalyptic figure of Belial or Beliar. This difficult word, which probably originally meant ' worthlessness ' in the Old Testament, became in time progressively personified as a Satanic spirit. Paul uses it as the equivalent of Satan (2 Cor. vi. 15). Conversely, the Septuagint translates the Hebrew word in 2 Sam. xxii. 5 = Ps. xviii. 4 (xvii. 4) as *anomia*. There is therefore no reason to suppose that the word was unknown to pagan adherents of the Synagogue. The words ' Man of Lawlessness ' might well suggest to them this connexion with Beliar— a supernatural Satanic figure. At all events there is a strong possibility that the picture of Beliar given in the Jewish *Sibylline Oracles* is pre-Christian (and not a Christian interpolation) and therefore possibly in Paul's mind as he wrote. There Beliar will come and do many signs among men, and deceive many even of the faithful Chosen People the Jews, before being finally destroyed. Obviously, however, Antichrist is not simply to be equated with Beliar. It is apparent from what follows that other elements are involved.

The Lawless One is called also **the doomed One** (literally, the son of destruction). This, like the Man of Lawlessness, is a Hebraism comparable to ' Sons of Light ' (see note on 1 v. 5) or ' Son of Death ' (1 Sam. xx. 31 : A.V. ' For he shall surely die '). A ' Son of Destruction ' is one whose nature and destiny it is to be doomed. The words are used of Judas in John xvii. 12 and of Israel (' children of destruction ') in Isa. lvii. 4, and should be understood here in the same sense as ' eternal destruction ' in i. 9, i.e. destined to eternal separation from God, which is the opposite of salvation, eternal fellowship with God.

4 Now follows a description of the Lawless One in action. He is **the adversary** *who vaunts himself above and against every* **so-called** *god* **or object of worship, actually** *seating himself in the* **temple** *of God* **with the proclamation that he himself is God.** The thought of this passage is obviously based upon the apocalyptic passages in Dan. vii. 25, viii. 25, and especially xi. 36 ff., where, after foretelling a rebellion against God (vers. 30 and 32 ; cf. ver. 3 here), the prophecy describes a wicked king who ' shall exalt himself and magnify himself above every god ' (vers. 36–7) and ' profane the sanctuary '

(ver. 31). The climax of these events will be the destruction of the wicked king (xi. 45) and the deliverance of God's people (xii. 1). The prototype there is Antiochus Ephiphanes, whose misguided attempt to introduce the Greek spirit into Jewish life included setting up an altar of Zeus in the Temple at Jerusalem, which to the Jews was desecration and idolatry and led to the Maccabean revolt of 167 B.C. A similar Old Testament reference to a human being who aspires to be God is to be found in Ezek. xxviii. 2, where the prophet foretells the doom of the king of Tyre, regarded as embodying the sinfulness of all his people, because he said : ' I am a god. I sit in the seat of God.' The king of Babylon likewise (Isa. xiv. 13–14), in a magnificent taunt-song, is, on his arrival in Sheol, greeted by his fellow kings as one who had determined to usurp the place of God.

All of these prophecies found their place in association with the Day of the Lord which was to mark the complete downfall of all evil and oppression of the Jews and usher in the Golden Age. In part the prophecies were historically fulfilled, but the main burden—namely, the advent of the Golden Age for the Jews—remained only a hope for the future. Therefore in the later apocalyptic literature generally—which grew out of unfulfilled prophecy—this element of rebellion against God and of a human figure who incarnates defiance of God's laws was perpetuated as a feature of eschatological expectations, as part of the prelude to the final catastrophe and eventual deliverance. In Christian apocalyptic, which drew largely on its Jewish precursors, this figure reappears as Antichrist and as a prelude to the Second Coming of the Lord. From time to time historical events and personages led to the identification of the various oppressors of the Church as Antichrist. The demand of the Roman Emperors to have divine honours paid to them gave rise to such identification, and the persecutions of the Christians consequent on their refusal gave colour to the conviction that the End was at hand. Ten years before this epistle was written, in A.D. 40, the Emperor Caligula had caused riots in Jerusalem by attempting to have his statue set up in the Temple. Some commentators have found in this the explanation of Paul's words here. Certainly the parallel with the attempt of Antiochus Epiphanes is close, but the **adversary** in Paul's mind is very much alive, whereas Caligula had died during the upheaval.

The question arises, can the figure in this verse be identified with an historical personage at all ? The language of verse 4, though clearly dependent on the Old Testament, has been slightly altered. Paul introduces the word **so-called** to make plain the monotheistic claim of Christianity (though ' everyone called God ' is a better translation than ' every so-called God ' which excludes the true God : Paul means ' the Christian God and every other so-called god ') ; and **object of worship** (cf. Acts xvii. 23) is added to the Danielic text to include everything religious. It may be that the particular **object of worship** is in fact the Temple at Jerusalem. There is no doubt that a literal violation of the Temple building is involved in Daniel's view of Antichrist ; the association of ideas would certainly be encouraged by Caligula's recent affront. But unlike both the account of Antiochus in Daniel and the historical actions of Caligula, the **adversary** here does not cause his statue to be exhibited in the Temple like Caligula, or profane it by setting up an altar to Zeus, as did Antiochus. He actually takes his seat himself in the Temple, i.e. puts himself in the place of God, usurps His authority and status. Emperor-worship at this early stage offers no real historical parallel for this.

It is indeed not likely that the actual Temple at Jerusalem is in Paul's mind at all, but that he is thinking rather in the sense of Ps. xi. 4 (LXX x. 5) of the Temple of God in heaven— ' The Lord is in His Holy Temple : the Lord's Throne is in Heaven ' (cf. Rev. xi. 19). Whatever be the local background of the thought, the Temple here is surely more than local. It is a storming of the Citadel of Heaven by the Man of Sin. Paul uses the words ' Temple of God ' in a metaphorical sense in 1 Cor. iii. 16 ; 2 Cor. vi. 16. Older commentators wrongly equated the Temple of God with the Church—which provided them with a glorious opportunity for anti-Papal propaganda. The connexion of this passage with the Little Apocalypse in

Mark xiii. is obscure. There, at verse 14, 'the appalling Horror' (A.V.: abomination of desolation) 'standing where he has no right to stand,' i.e. in the Temple, is clearly a personification as Antichrist of the 'appalling Horror,' viz. the altar of Zeus in Dan. xii. 11. This is to be a sign of the End, probably the destruction of Jerusalem. Whether Paul knew of this prophecy or not—assuming that Mark xiii. or part of it is of independent origin earlier than the gospel—it is unlikely that in this passage he is thinking of Jerusalem at all. At all events, it is quite clear that there was no obscurity in the mind of the apostle, and that he rather impatiently reminded his readers that there ought to be no difficulty in their minds either. **Do you not remember I used to tell you this when I 5 was with you ?**

But for us obscurity deepens as the apostle goes on to say: 6 **Well, you can recall now what it is that restrains him from being revealed before his appointed time.** Why should they suddenly recall now—since Paul has told them nothing new— and without further explanation, what **restrains him** ? If we take the word **now,** not as opposed to the time of the mission at Thessalonica, but in contrast with **his appointed time,** a more intelligible translation would be : ' And you know what restrains him now from being revealed before his appointed time.' That is, nothing new has happened since the mission which makes any difference to the situation. What the apostle had said then was that the Lawless One was not being permitted to show himself because he was held in check. It is quite clear, incidentally, that ' him ' refers to the Lawless One and not to Christ. It is the revelation of Antichrist that is in question. **His appointed time** is one of the eschatological ' times and seasons ' referred to in 1 v. 1.

The next words complete the problem. **For the secret force 7 of lawlessness is at work already ; only, it cannot be revealed till he who at present restrains it is removed.** There is no great difficulty in the thought of the first part of this sentence. The lawlessness or rebellion against God which will be finally incarnated in the Lawless One is already present in the world ; the power of evil is already active, though not yet fully revealed (cf. 1 John ii. 18, iv. 3). The difficulty arises in the introduction of the idea of **restraint**. In verse 6 the power that up till now has prevented the Lawless One from appearing is spoken of as a thing (*to katechon*—neut.), in verse 7 as a person (*ho katechōn*—masc.). It is this restraining fact or person which prevents the advent of the Man of Lawlessness **before his appointed time**. Who or what is this restraining power and how is the restraint exercised ?

Much of the interpretation turns upon the meaning of the word *katechō*, here translated, ' restrain.' (1) It is the word used in 1 v. 21 for ' retain (or hold fast) what is good.' (2) Another possible meaning is to ' hold sway.' This suggests an explanation along the line that the Lawless One cannot be revealed until he who at present ' holds sway ' is removed. This would, of course, suggest Satan, ruler of the earth and the air, and would make sense of the passage except for the closing words of verse 7. Satan's earthly downfall would hardly be the prelude to the appearance of his chief instrument, and ' remove ' in verse 7 cannot mean anything but ' be taken out of the way.' (3) But as well as meaning to ' hold sway,' the word frequently means to ' detain, hold back, put under arrest.' And such is the sense here. Understanding the word in this way, one possibility can be disposed of at once. (*a*) The ' restraining power ' cannot be God or the Holy Spirit because of the closing words of verse 7. Paul does not envisage the removal of either. (*b*) It might, on the other hand, be Satan, if Paul thought of the Rebellion (ver. 3) on earth as parallel with the war in heaven of Revelation (xii. 7). In this case Satan's defeat would end his power in heaven but not necessarily on earth. His final throw might be the letting loose of the Lawless One upon the world. This possibility is weakened because there is nothing to show that Paul was thinking of war in heaven. There remain two main interpretations, one historical, the other mythological—if one discounts such eccentric solutions as that the restraining power is Paul himself.

(*c*) The traditional explanation of the restraining power—and therefore indeed of the whole passage—finds the clue in the historical fact of the Roman Empire. This was Tertullian's solution, it has been the general view of commentators, and it has much to commend it. Paul was notably well disposed to Rome, he was proud to be a *Civis Romanus* (Acts xvi. 37–9). The Empire's determination to maintain law and order in the provinces had saved him more than once from the ill-will of the Jews, and it was in fact at the time of writing this letter treating him singularly kindly (Acts xviii. 12–17). In a notable passage he warmly commends the State and its servants for justice and integrity (Rom. xiii. 1–6). What, then, is more apt than that he should regard the power of Rome—personified by Claudius the reigning Emperor—as the deterrent factor determining the non-appearance of the Lawless One. This would, in the first place, account for the neuter and masculine uses of ' restrain,' viz. the Empire and the Emperor. It would also provide a characteristic word-play, since Claudius connects with *claudo*, the Latin word for ' close,' ' stop,' ' restrain.' Further, it would explain the puzzling conclusion of verse 7, since Paul obviously expected the downfall of the Empire as part of the final catastrophe, but had to conceal his hopes in such a cryptic allusion.

But if this explanation is adopted, the Lawless One almost inevitably becomes an historical personage, and we are led into the same kind of profitless speculation as in later days, when Antichrist was identified with Popes and dictators according to the circumstances of the time. On this historical view the most likely explanation of the Lawless One would be that the Emperor Caligula had by his actions shown that the **secret force of lawlessness** was already at work. Claudius, one might argue, by his tolerance, exercised a **restraining** hand, while what was already known of the private life of his successor Nero could have led Paul to the belief that his accession would be marked by such an outburst of violence against the young Church that it would be the Rebellion against God so long prophesied, and that Nero himself would be Antichrist. The practical difficulty of this solution is that Nero was born in A.D. 37. If the Thessalonian epistles were written in A.D. 50, Nero was a boy of thirteen at the time, and could hardly

have given much reason for Paul—or Christians generally—
to expect that he would emerge on his accession four years
later as the Man of Sin. A possible escape from this would,
of course, be to date the epistle—or this part of it—considerably later than A.D. 50 (and therefore non-Pauline), when Nero
had had time to show his true character. Neither of these
solutions is, however, borne out by any other evidence. If we
admit the genuineness of the letter, and that this passage is
an integral part of it, the real difficulty of adopting a solution
along historical lines is the general character of apocalyptic
writing.

Prediction of this kind was invariably wise after the event.
This is clear in the case of the two Biblical specimens of
apocalyptic writing. The book of Daniel was written to meet
a perilous situation. Antiochus had already shown his hand.
His affront to God, and his oppression of His people, were
facts that needed only to be alluded to to be understood.
Similarly, Nero Redivivus is in fact in the book of Revelation
to be equated with Antichrist, because by this time the persecution of A.D. 64 was past history (Rev. xvii. 5–7), and the
more widespread persecution under Domitian lent colour to
the legend that Nero was not dead, but had remained in hiding
among the Parthians, and was about to return at the head of
a barbarian army to harry the Empire. In Domitian the
scourge of the saints seemed to be reincarnated. Antichrist
had come. The End was at hand. If Paul is embarking
upon prophecy here regarding historical events in the future,
he is giving apocalyptic writing a character which is foreign
to its nature. Nor are those explanations satisfying which
identify the Lawless One with Jewish opposition. True, Paul
had suffered his only real set-backs from that quarter, and the
restraining power had certainly been Rome. Further, if the
Temple at Jerusalem is indicated by the allusion in verse 4,
the Jews may be said to assume exclusive divine authority
for their beliefs. But Paul clearly refers to a definite and
specific figure, not a nation or a priesthood, and the difficulty
remains of accounting for the ' miracles and portents ' of verse
9 If this difficulty is side-stepped by saying that the Lawless

One is a Jewish pseudo-Messiah, and that the opposition of the Jews is the **secret force of lawlessness**, the objection is that their opposition was by no means secret. It is also hard to imagine Paul, a Jew, crediting his countrymen, whose fundamental opposition to the new religion was that it made Christ equal with God, with falling under the spell of some pseudo-Messiah whose claims and actions would be even more unambiguous. To seek some other more adequate explanation is not to deny any historical allusions in the passage, but to say that a merely historical interpretation is insufficient to account for all the facets of the apostle's thought in these verses. It is worth noting that if a beneficent Rome is the restraining power, this is an idea quite foreign to Jewish apocalyptic thought, which it is difficult to exclude from this passage, and that such a political reference is quite unlike anything else in Paul's eschatology.

(*d*) Accordingly, there is much to be said in favour of looking for the clue to the **restraining** power, not in history, but in some kind of theological or even mythological speculation. To do this seems truer, both to the mind of Paul generally, and to the passage itself. It differs from the passages in Daniel and Revelation alike, in that it does not invest the fact of a present or past oppressor—whether Antiochus, Nero, or Domitian—with the attributes of an Antichrist still to come. In Paul's case the emphasis is religious. His concern is with the Parousia in the first instance, and only with the Lawless One as the necessary prelude. Clearly he has not yet appeared, though he might at any time be expected. He is not known either to Paul or his readers, and while he is referred to as a human figure, there is much in these verses that cannot be reduced to merely human terms. One who sets himself up as a rival to the Messiah, who usurps the authority of God, and who is in a special way to be revealed, is already a supernatural being. Accordingly, we are probably right to see in the whole passage a blend of Old Testament reminiscences and mythological speculation rather than historical allusion.

The problem becomes soluble—so far as it can be solved by us—if we look for the clue to the ' restraining power ' in Rev.

xx. There, as part of the eschatological happenings, the dragon, who is also called the old serpent, the Devil, and Satan, is bound in chains by an angel and left in the bottomless pit for a thousand years while Christ reigns supreme. At the end of that time he must be released to fulfil his appointed task of wreaking havoc upon the world for a space before being finally destroyed. There, then, is a conception in Christian apocalyptic of the power of evil being restrained or held in check by some angelic power until the final outburst of lawlessness before Christ's ultimate victory. Some such idea probably lies behind the apostle's statement here. There is a striking correspondence with a scene from the Acts of Pilate, where Christ, in committing Satan to Hades, says : ' Take him and hold him securely until my Second Coming '—using this very word *katechein*. The ' restraining power ' is therefore probably supernatural. The Lawless One is held in check meantime by some angelic power appointed by God. When the time comes, the restraint will be removed and the Lawless One will be revealed. Thus it is in a setting of traditional mythology that the most likely explanation of this obscure thought is to be found. If that is so, however, is it not likely that the same kind of background should be sought for the whole passage, and that the Lawless One himself has his roots in mythological speculation ?

In Babylonian and Persian mythology, a feature of the Creation stories is a battle between the Creator and His archenemy, a monster, in which the Creator is victorious. On the principle that the world will end as it began, this battle was to be repeated at the close of history. In Jewish apocalyptic literature, the monsters, Behemoth and Leviathan, are expected to rise out of the sea as a prelude to their final destruction, and a similar belief was part of Persian eschatology. Meantime, the arch-enemy is held in bondage until the appointed time. Such a situation is suggested by Job. vii. 12 : ' Am I a sea or a dragon that thou hast put a guard over me ? ' So may be explained also the various Old Testament references to monsters, e.g. Amos ix. 3 ; Job. xli. 1 ff. All this is of the same stuff as the almost universal motif in folk-lore of monsters and giants, hounds of hell and such-like, who are only kept from laying waste the earth by the strength of their chains and the remoteness of their prison—the bottomless pit as in Rev. xx. 3, the heart of a mountain, or the depths of the sea. Thus there is a general correspondence among the myths arising in different civilizations, pointing to a widespread belief that the elemental power of evil—incarnate in some monster—is not destroyed, but is in bondage, or somehow kept in check, until the Last Days when it will be freed, and after a short spell of liberty, in which it will do its best to destroy the Good, it will be finally defeated and destroyed. This, then, is very probably an ingredient in the origins of the Christian conception of Antichrist as of Paul's figure of the Lawless One. It is in this context that verse 4 can best be understood. The dragon of the old myths had made war on heaven and fought to expel the gods from their rightful place. So it will be at the end of time. This is the apocalyptic presupposition of the Lawless One's assault on the Temple of God. He will try to usurp God's place—perhaps even by a literal storming of heaven—before he meets his end, destroyed by the breath of the lips of the Lord.

Paul's conception is, however, not of the arch-enemy in the shape of a fabulous monster—nor of Satan, nor of Death (cf. 1 Cor. xv. 26)—but of a human being who is the arch-fiend's emissary and is evil incarnate. What we have is, therefore, a blend of history and mythology. In Jewish life, against the background of the conviction that at the end of time a mighty conflict between good and evil must take place, sprang up the certainty from time to time that that Day was at hand. The stronger grew the certainty, the more likely was it that evidence should be sought of the power of evil in the world. Human personages whose acts epitomized the works of darkness were naturally brought into this framework. Conversely, of course, the more diabolical the nature of the oppressor seemed the nearer must be the End. Thus Antiochus in Daniel's day, like Caligula and Nero in later days—all of them violators of the sanctities of the Jewish or Christian religions—were fitted into this mythological background. They ceased to be merely human monsters and became themselves in popular thought manifestations of the arch-enemy of God himself.

As the belief in the (Second) Coming of the Messiah developed, so these historical and mythological expectations came to centre in the conception of a rival Messiah, an Antichrist. This is the supernatural type of being whom Paul describes in verse 4—one who like Satan tries to usurp the place of God and who like the monster of mythology can still trouble the earth. Paul does not, like the old mythologists, detail the ways in which the power of evil, though bound and restrained, can still torment the earth. In the Sagas the striving of the monster to break free was the cause of earthquakes, and Amos's fettered serpent can still bite (ix. 3). Paul contents himself with saying that the evil power is at work secretly already (ver. 7). Most probably he means nothing definite at all. The fact that Jesus has died and risen is the token that the End is at hand ; therefore the power of evil must inevitably be at work somewhere secretly or openly until the day when it is fully revealed.

In view of these considerations it would seem to be the most satisfactory solution of the problem—not, however, an explanation of all the presuppositions—to see little, if any, relation to historical events in the apostle's words. He introduces a feature of current eschatological expectation—namely, the appearance of the Lawless One, the Man of Sin, Antichrist—not with any intention of veiling an allusion to a reigning or a future emperor, to the Empire itself, or to the Jews. This mysterious figure, this vice-regent of the Evil One, is a personification of traditional mythology. Paul's rôle is not that of a soothsayer, clouding his oracles in dark words ; his motive, as always, is practical. Here are these people in Thessalonica, fretting and fluttering : the Last Day has come. Do they not know that more serious things must happen ere then ; that the whole power of evil must yet break loose on the world, that there must be war and tumult and suffering, not brought on by some mere Roman princeling, but by the demoniac forces of darkness? The power of evil is now held

in check by the Will of God, perhaps by Michael, perhaps by
Elijah (Matt. xvii. 11 ; Rev. xi. 3)—more probably by someone or something somehow !—else would it rend the world this
very moment. But it is not dead. The old serpent still
lives, though bound in chains. Do not, then, be deceived.
This is the calm before the storm. At any time evil may be
upon us. Be assured that the power of darkness is secretly
at work even now. Soon in all its horror it will be revealed
in rebellion against God, and the coming of Satan's rod to do
violence against His Saints. These things will be only too
plain for us all, and they cannot be far off now because we are
living in the Last Days. But lift up your hearts. Victory is
not to Antichrist, but to our Lord and Saviour. Thus the
passage ends on a note of triumph (vers. 8–12). Once more
the apostle's message is that men in Christ are more than
conquerors through Him that loved us.

Then shall the Lawless One be revealed, i.e. when it pleases 8
God to let him loose—**whom the Lord Jesus** *will destroy with
the breath of his lips* **and quell by his appearing and arrival.**
Here the Old Testament atmosphere of verse 4 is resumed.
The background is again the book of Daniel (vii. 10, 11).
In Isa. xi. 4 it is foretold of the Messiah that ' with the breath
of his lips shall he slay the wicked ' ; and in 2 Esdras xiii.
1–11 there is a vivid description of how at his Coming the
Messiah (the Man who comes out of the sea) destroys the multi-
tude of the wicked who make war against him with fire and
flame from his mouth. In the Targum of Isa. xi. 4, the
curious marginal addition (according to Dalman in a different
hand) of '*urmilos*, after the words ' shall slay the wicked,'
seems to have been the origin of a legendary Jewish figure
Armillus, who came to be regarded as the embodiment of evil
and the Jewish equivalent of Antichrist. The explanation,
however, would appear to be that '*urmilos* = Romulus =
Rome, and was the comment of some scribe on the implications of Isaiah's words. So the Lord will, at His Coming,
quell the Lawless One, literally, ' by the manifestation of His
Parousia.' The expression is tautological—both words mean
the revelation of the Divine presence (see note on 1 ii. 19),

and here emphasize the decisive intervention of God in the coming crisis.

9   Further description of Antichrist follows : **that One whose arrival is due to Satan's activity, with the full power, the miracles and portents, of falsehood.** This disposes of any suggestion that Antichrist will be the Devil himself. The Lawless One will be a combination of what in Revelation is represented by two figures—the Beast and the False Prophet. What Paul has in mind, however, is one who is in every respect a caricature of the Messiah. He will have the indwelling spirit (**activity**) of Satan as Christ has that of God. By the power of Satan's spirit he will be enabled to do mighty acts and wonders like the Messiah, but their aim will be not good but evil. It is the climax foretold in Matt. xxiv. 24 : ' False Christs and false prophets will rise and bring forward great signs and wonders so as to mislead the very elect—if that were possible.' His coming will be the full manifestation of Satan as Christ's will be that of God. The picture of the revelation of Antichrist in apocalyptic literature, both Jewish and Christian, stresses generally his miraculous powers. He will work signs and wonders (*Didache*, xvi. 4), he will bring the dead to life (*Sibylline Oracles*, iii. 66), he will walk on the sea and on the rivers as if on dry land, he will make the deaf hear, the dumb speak, and the blind see ; he will turn stones into bread, and water into wine. When Christian thought came to identify Antichrist with a Jewish pretender, there grew up such an assimilation as the following passage from Hippolytus (third century), *De Antichristo*, describes :—' For in every respect the Deceiver wishes to be like the Son of God. As Christ is a Lion, so is Antichrist ; Christ is King, so Antichrist is an earthly king: the Saviour was revealed as a Lamb, so he likewise will appear to be a lamb though inwardly a wolf. The Saviour came of the circumcized race into the world, so he will come too. The Lord sent apostles into all the nations, so he will send false apostles. The Saviour gathered the scattered sheep together, so he will gather together the scattered people of the Jews.' Sometimes Antichrist's power of working wonders is described in language that recalls Old

Testament prophecy of the Day of the Lord, as in the Apocalypse of Elijah, where Joel ii. 31 is clearly the background : ' He will say to the sun fall, and it will fall : He will summon forth the lightning and bring on the darkness ' (see Dibelius, ad loc.). The point to note is that it is not by virtue of working wonders that Christ is Messiah, but by the moral quality of His mighty works.

Not only will Antichrist come with specious miraculous 10 powers, but **with the full deceitfulness of evil for those who are doomed to perish, since they refuse to love the Truth that would save them.** It is progressively made clear that Paul has in mind no historical person as Antichrist. Roman Emperors— or other oppressors—though they may work wonders (Rev. xiii. 13 f.) do not achieve their ends by deceit. Clearly there is no allusion to imperial persecution of the Christians—this was something that did not arise till later. Thus, while Revelation can speak of the Emperor as the Beast, and the Empire as the Mystery of Iniquity (xiii. and xvii.) from bitter experience of oppression and persecution, here Antichrist works by guile instead of by violence. He will deceive men, not bludgeon them, into his service—his words will be false but honeyed. Those who listen to him are doomed men. Not because they have been damned from eternity—there is no predestination here—but because they turn their backs upon the truth. Literally, Paul's words are : ' They did not receive the love of the truth that would save them.' Truth, like the Word of God, is a living force (1 i. 8, etc.). What he means is that they not only reject the Gospel when they hear it, but stifle also the inward promptings of the Spirit which God has imparted to them, enabling them to know the true from the false. They have been given every chance and have rejected it, therefore they have brought their inevitable doom upon themselves. The thought is the same as in i. 9. Those who are thus the victims of their own obduracy are certainly not only the Jews, but Jews and Gentiles alike who refuse the Gospel. Those who are saved are from all nations, likewise those who are damned.

Therefore God visits them with an active delusion, till they 11 put faith in falsehood, so that all may be doomed who refuse faith in the Truth but delight in evil. Therefore, that is, at the coming of the Lawless One, **God visits them with an active delusion.** Significantly, now, God is introduced as the author of the whole process—the moving power behind the two Parousias. Antichrist is the servant of the Devil, the incarnation of evil—but both he and his master Satan are under the hand of God. It is, in the ultimate sense, God who will send him, and in the same sense it is **God** and not Satan who **will visit them with an active delusion,** that is, take from them the ability to distinguish between true and false, just as it is God who puts a lying spirit into the mouths of the prophets (1 Kings xxii. 22 ; Ezek. xiv. 9). Once more Paul's strongly theistic interpretation of the universe—which is the Hebrew one—leads him to attribute to God's direct agency what we should rather call the inevitability of the moral law. And of course Paul and the Old Testament are right. The moral law is not self-existent. It operates because it is the Will of God, and Paul's religious insight grasps that truth. Men start by rejecting the Gospel voluntarily ; they then reach the stage when they are unable to tell what is gospel and what is fallacy. This is the powerful **delusion** which Paul rightly regards as an Act of God. It is the state of mind which **puts faith in falsehood.**

12   The end result is equally inevitable—moral and spiritual death. **So that all may be doomed**—literally, ' judged,' that is, irrevocably separated from God (i. 9)—**who refuse faith in the Truth but delight in evil.** This is evil pursued, not through folly or ignorance, but from the sheer love of it. It is Satan's apostrophe : ' Farewell remorse, all good to me is lost : Evil, be thou my good ! ' Paul will have no intellectualization of the Gospel. **Faith in the Truth** is not academic assent to theoretical propositions. It is the opposite of **to delight in evil.** Here—as in Rom. i. 18–32, which is the best commentary on these verses—the inexorability of God's judgment on those who flout His Word is coupled with an equally clear assertion that His Word demands ethical obedience. The thought of verses 11, 12 is of course focused on the Lawless One. He is

the incarnation of **Falsehood**. Men will turn to him in the Coming Time because they have turned their backs upon the Gospel while they were still able to distinguish between true and false. Now that possibility is no longer open to them. They fall under his evil spell because they can do no other. They have forfeited their chance of salvation.

This whole passage (vers. 1-12), unique alike in its content and in its obscurity, has been the happy hunting-ground, not only of serious commentators, but of crackpot theorists. Antichrist has been identified, not only with almost every known opponent of Christianity, but with the enemies of the particular brand of Christianity that the writer happened to favour. Protestants have found him in the Lateran and the Vatican, Romanists in the Reformers, and at least one Anglican commentator in the General Assembly of the Church of Scotland. Outside the Church, secular tyrants and modern dictators from Nero to Stalin have been drawn into this fruitless quest for an historical counterpart of Paul's prophecy. The volumes that have been written on the subject of Antichrist, and the variety of interpretations of Paul's words, should send us back the more sympathetically to Augustine's honest confession of ignorance. Denney scoffs at the ' cheap reputation for humility ' of those who agree with Augustine— and then proceeds to apply the passage to the Papacy! Having said firmly that no historical reference is intended, it is surely true to say, further, with Augustine, that we have no real means of knowing what the apostle meant, or of doing any more than approximating to an idea of the various features of this passage which assumes so much and leaves so much to the imagination.

The most we can say is that in a mixture of concepts drawn originally from the Old Testament, Jewish apocalyptic, and mythology, Paul expresses an apparently general conviction among the early Christians that a mysterious supernatural figure, the incarnation of evil, a fantastic blend of Beliar, the Dragon, Antiochus, and pseudo-Messiah, must shortly appear as a prelude to the Second Advent. It is an historical fact that Paul was wrong. The Second Advent did not happen in his lifetime, neither, therefore, did the Lawless One appear. But in religious insight in both respects Paul was right (see note on 1 i. 10), and here, as in the Second Advent expectation, we must distinguish between the imagery and the reality, between the prophetic imagination and the underlying truth. The relevance and value of this passage for to-day is to be found, not in trying to find its historical fulfilment, but in the religious message that it contains. (1) The world will not grow better and better every day. There will be conflict and tension between good and evil till the end of time. The parable of the Wheat and the Tares is in fact a true analysis of history. As the field of potential goodness widens, so also does that of evil. Both grow and intensify together until the final crisis (ver. 3), when the Judgment of God falls upon the Church and the world. (2) The conditions of the Second Advent and the Judgment are present here and now. The secret force of lawlessness (ver. 7) is in fact at work in the world, and we stand continually under the Judgment of God as we respond to His Word or to the specious voices that bid us spurn it. (3) Whatever forms evil may take in the world, the root of it all is the pride that seeks to make man equal with God and rejects His proper status as a worshipping creature (ver. 4).

The two traditional aspects of Antichrist—the demonic and the human—remind us both that Evil, alas, like God's mercy, new every morning, yet the same in principle throughout the ages, is a force of darkness calling men to its service and binding them fast in its chains, and also that Evil as an abstraction means nothing, but that it must always be incarnated in human personalities. Evil as we know it—the evil that defies God, that scourges men, is the evil in human life, in all of us. Without involving ourselves in dualism, it would seem (as H. H. Rowley suggests in *The Relevance of Apocalyptic*, p. 150) that we can best understand this perennial power of evil—the reality behind Antichrist—by falling back upon the Old Testament view of ' corporate personality.' The Man of Sin who, according to Paul, fights stoutly to the end of time, is Man in the Hebrew sense—Man as the inheritor of the past, the sharer of the present, and partaker of the

future.   Each one of us represents Man—each one of us manifests in his own dealings, in his own thoughts, something of
the great mass of human iniquity of which the race has been
guilty down the ages.   We are caught up into the stream of
evil, our sins are the common guilt of humanity, and humanity's
guilt is ours.   We bear each other's burdens in this sense too,
and we add our quota to the power of evil.   In this sense
Antichrist—Satan's henchman—is always being incarnated
afresh.   We do not need to look far afield for Napoleons,
Hitlers, and Stalins, but to search our own hearts for the
self-same sins.   Only when the evil in men is overcome, when
Antichrist is vanquished by Christ, will the Kingly Rule of
God be complete.   Whether it comes quickly and suddenly
as the early Church believed, or whether slowly by the spread
of the Gospel, it is still, as Paul would tell us, an Act of God
and of God alone.

IV. THE ETERNAL PURPOSE OF GOD
(ii. 13-17)

Now we are bound always to thank God for you, brothers 13
beloved by the Lord, because God has chosen you as the
first to be reaped for salvation, by the consecration of
your spirit and by faith in the Truth ; it was for this that 14
he called you by our gospel, to gain the glory of our Lord
Jesus Christ. Well, then, brothers, stand firm and hold 15
to the rules which you have learned from us orally or by
letter. And may our Lord Jesus Christ himself and God 16
our Father, who has loved us and given us eternal encouragement and good hope, graciously encourage your 17
hearts and strengthen them for all good in deed and word.

Following hard on the mysterious description and forbidding
fate of Antichrist and his dupes, the apostle strikes a strongly
contrasting note of joyfulness.   He turns his eyes from the
gloomy deeds of the wicked to the happy state of those who
have committed their lives to God.   This he sums up in a few
words, which are indeed, as Denney says, ' a system of theology in miniature ' (vers. 13-14).   He sees the little flock at

Thessalonica, despondent, discouraged, and self-diffident as they are, *sub specie aeternitatis*; shows them the timeless nature of their place in God's plan, the origin of their conversion in the eternal purpose of the Creator, and its climax in life with Christ in glory. Paul's aim is, as ever, practical. Neither speculative philosophizing on free will and predestination prompts him, nor concern with the metaphysical aspects of election, but a real pastoral desire to comfort his flock in their perplexity, by reassuring them that, as God's people, they have nothing to fear.

13   With a slight rearrangement the opening words of this new subject repeat those of i. 3 (see note), and are to be understood in the same sense. **Now we are bound always to thank God for you.** The ' we ' is very emphatic in the Greek—including presumably Silvanus and Timothy as well—and the point is as in i. 3 that, despite the self-depreciation of the Thessalonians expressed in word or letter, the apostles cannot but regard them as witnesses to the glory of God. But there is obviously now the added point that Paul is contrasting them in his mind with those who reject the Gospel and therefore are doomed to perish (ver. 10). He is resuming the line on which he started the letter with greater emphasis now that he has further disposed of another cause of their anxiety, namely, their concern that the Last Day was upon them. Further, the picture which has just flashed through his mind of the fate of those who turn their backs upon the truth confirms his thankfulness to God for the Thessalonians who so warmly received it. He calls them now **brothers** *beloved by the Lord* (Deut. xxxiii. 12 ; see note on 1 i. 4) as an introduction to what he has to say about God's call to them which ought to banish every doubt or uneasiness from their minds. You are beloved, he says, **because God has chosen you** (see note on 1 i. 4) **as the first to be reaped for salvation.** The words are cumulative. Christ loves you and God has chosen you for salvation. This is your starting-point : that God loves you, therefore He chose you to be His own. The words are reminiscent of Deut. vii. 6, 8 : ' The Lord thy God hath chosen thee to be a special people unto himself . . . because the Lord loveth you.' There is an

interesting variant reading here. A.V. reads : because God hath ' from the beginning ' chosen you, whereas Moffatt translates : ' as the first to be reaped.'

The difference is between *ap' archēs* and *aparchēn*. Both are well attested in the MSS. The former means ' from the beginning,' while the latter means ' as first-fruits.' If we accept Moffatt's choice of *aparchēn*, it would mean simply that God had chosen the Thessalonians to be among the first converts to the new faith, whether in Macedonia or the world generally. A more significant translation would be to associate ' first-fruits ' with ' beloved ' and ' chosen.' Both the latter are used in the Old Testament with reference to God's call of His people Israel. The word ' *aparchēn* ' is also used in the same connexion as a term of distinction or honour with regard to Israel by Philo : ' Israel was set apart as a kind of first-fruits to the Creator.' The vocabulary of the status of Israel passed into the Christian Church, and was applied to the New Israel as heirs of the promise. Thus James and the author of the Apocalypse both use the word *aparchē* of redeemed Christians (Jas. i. 18 ; Rev. xiv. 4). This may be the sense in which Paul uses it here. God has honoured the Thessalonians, not only by choosing them, but by choosing them to be first in His new order of Creation, and therefore as an offering to Himself.

But it is surely preferable, despite the unusual nature of the expression, to read *ap' archēs*, and in its deepest sense. Paul is not here indulging in platitudes, as it would be to take ' in the beginning ' as meaning ' in the beginning of the Christian Mission.' He is setting out a theology as profound as that of Rom. viii. 28-30. God has chosen you, not merely in that sense of which you are all most deeply aware—the knowledge you have that He has laid hold on you and that His Spirit lives within you—but in its ultimate sense also. It was His purpose to choose you in the beginning, i.e. from eternity, as in Eph. i. 4. What you now know and experience of His love and grace had its roots in the mind and intention of God from before the world was made. This was His real purpose of Creation, that you and such as you should hear His voice and respond to His Word, and that thereby you should be saved. Your **salvation** (see notes on 1 ii. 16, v. 9), the deliverance of your whole selves from sin, death, and damnation, is not a thing of to-day and to-morrow, it is grounded in the timeless Will of God.

Now the breadth of the apostle's thought is added to its depth—this eternal purpose of God to save men, this manifestation of His love in choosing men to be His, is no esoteric mystery. Paul has no place in his theology for an inscrutable despot who ' sends ane to heaven an' ten to hell a' for his glory.' God's choice of men is not deterministic—however much some interpretations of Paul suggest that it is ; it is by the interplay of Spirit upon spirit, **by the consecration** (see 1 iv. 3, iv. 7) **of your spirit and by faith in the Truth.** Moffatt is surely wrong in translating this ' *your* spirit.' The A.V. once more is equally faithful to the Greek and more profound in interpretation when it recognizes the ' spirit,' not as man's, but God's. Your salvation is made possible by the consecrating or sanctifying power of *His* Spirit and by *your* faith in the Truth. This last is clearly contrasted with those who do not believe in the Truth (ver. 12). The phrase reappears in 1 Pet. i. 2 with clear reference to the Holy Spirit, and was probably part of the common missionary terminology.

It is the work of the Holy Spirit of God in men's hearts, recreating sinful humanity into the likeness of Christ, that brings salvation ; but it is also only by men's faith in the truth of the Gospel—not philosophical truth in general—that the Spirit can sanctify them. To accept the Gospel as true, and to trust in God, ensures that His Spirit makes us new creatures, though indeed it is in the last resort the work of the Spirit that increases our faith in the power of the Spirit. But the operation is mutual. God is the author, but man must make his response. This does not in any way deny either that the prime mover in the whole work of salvation is God, or that some are slower to respond than others and some do not respond at all. What it does say is that the twin marks of the Christian life are God's indwelling power in man and man's committal of himself to God.

It was for this, that is, to obtain salvation through the power 14 of the Spirit and the response of faith, **that he called you** (1 ii. 12–13, iv. 7, v. 24) **by our gospel.** Having laid the foundations of salvation in God's eternal purpose, Paul now goes on to incorporate it in time. ' On God's side your salvation began before the world was made, on your side it was when you heard and answered His call when I preached His Gospel to you.' Paul has no false modesty about the status of the preacher when he properly mediates God's Word. It was by the mouth of the apostles as God's ministers that He achieved in time what He had planned in eternity. **Our gospel** is, needless to say, not the private perquisite of the apostles, but ' the gospel which we believe and preach '—the Good News of salvation (1 i. 5). Finally, the apostle points forward to the culmination of God's favour. It is that you should **gain the glory of our Lord Jesus Christ** (see note on 1 ii. 12). That His people should enjoy life with Christ in God's presence and share His glory is the end of His eternal plan, and the climax of **salvation** (see note on 1 v. 9). Christ's **glory** was in a sense won on earth (John xiii. 31) and imparted to His followers (John xvii. 5, 22). But its full perfection lies yet ahead, as Paul has just said (i. 10), at His Coming, when those who are in Him will be partners with Him in the splendour that is to be. God's Will has been from eternity to make men His children, to call them into the service of His Kingdom, that coming to Him through the preaching of the Good News, and growing in grace through the power of His spirit, they might reach the full stature of sonship in life eternal as joint-heirs with Christ.

This *multum in parvo* not only contains implicitly Paul's whole theology of salvation, it contains also unconsciously the elements which eventually issued in Trinitarian dogma. God is the loving Father, Christ is Lord, and the Holy Spirit is Sanctifier. It is a token of the religious motive of the apostle that his theological sketch leaves many questions unanswered and many facets of Christian truth unexpressed. Nothing, for example, is said of what happens to those who are not chosen, and the place of the Cross and Resurrection in salvation is glossed over. But as a message of encouragement to meet the perplexities of simple men whose faith is wavering it is superb. They know they have been called—for that they have the witness of their own experience. They have felt the power of God within them. They know what they were like before the coming of Christ into their lives, and however they have faltered and stumbled since, something of that new-found power and assurance remains. What, then, could more hearten this handful of timid working folk, surrounded by everything that militated against their faith, than to show them behind their tiny glimpses of the Kingdom the majesty of God's purpose for their redemption. The Christian Gospel, says Paul, in effect, lifts us out of our weakness and insignificance, and sets us within the framework of God's universal goodwill towards men. His love is behind and around and before us, and underneath are the everlasting arms.

15   Then, magnificently, comes the reminder of the Christian's obligations, the implications of God's call. ' This is how God loves you, therefore stand fast in the faith and do your duty as Christian men.' What God has done for us and still does is by no means a substitute for what we must do ourselves. It is because God does so much that our human efforts are called forth and have their only hope of success. **Well then, brothers, stand firm** (cf. 1 iii. 8) **and hold to the rules which you have learned from us orally or by letter.** Paul's use of the word **brothers** invariably means something. It is real affection, not formal address. **Stand firm** refers to the doubts and fears which occasioned the writing of the letter. They are not to allow themselves to be carried away by rumours that the End is here. The best defence against all such anxiety is to plant their feet firmly on what they know of the Gospel. On all matters they are to be guided by what the apostles have told them or written to them. **Orally** must mean the mission at Thessalonica and the **letter** is clearly 1 Thessalonians as opposed to any other (cf. ver. 2) purporting to come from Paul, and with special reference no doubt to chapters iv. and v.

The **rules** suggest the *kērygma* and *didachē* which Christian

missionaries in general were charged to pass on to the con-
gregations (cf. 2 iii. 6 ; 1 Cor. xi. 2, 23). From the frequent
references to what appears to have been a fixed tradition, and
the use of the same technical vocabulary in describing its
transmission (1 Cor. xv. 1-11 ; Rom. vi. 17, xvi. 17 ; Phil. iv.
9), it would seem that from the very earliest days of the Christian mission there was a common corpus of instruction and
information, comprising credal or catechetical formulæ and
moral precepts. The word translated here ' rules ' (*para-
doseis*—A.V. 'traditions') is found in inscriptions of the time
with reference to inventories and treasure lists, the various
items being ' passed on ' (cf. 1 Cor. xi. 23) ' from one set of
officers to their successors ' (Milligan, ad loc.). Then, since to
stand firm in the faith and hold fast to the teaching they had
received was an impossibility for the Thessalonians without
help from beyond themselves, Paul rounds off this little paragraph with a prayer.

And may our Lord Jesus Christ himself and God our Father, 16
who has loved us and given us eternal encouragement and
good hope, graciously encourage your hearts and strengthen 17
them for all good in deed and word. The opening words are
practically the same as 1 iii. 11 with this difference, that the
name of Christ comes before that of God, as it does in the
Benediction formula of 2 Cor. xiii. 14. Generally, the order
in Paul's letters is God first and then Christ. Here, possibly
because his thoughts have just culminated in the glory of the
Lord Jesus Christ (ver. 14), Christ's name comes before God's.
The only theological significance to be attached to the variations in order is that there is complete equality in the apostle's
mind between the Father and the Son. It is only through his
knowledge of Christ that he has come really to know God.
For him they are One. The next words, however, seem grammatically to apply to God alone—**who has loved us,** that is,
in sending His Son into the world, and—thereby—**given us**
eternal encouragement and good hope. Encouragement
(*paraklēsis*) is the word generally translated in the A.V.
' consolation ' or ' comfort ' (cf. the Holy Spirit as ' Paraclete ').
But it includes more than ministration in suffering. Paul has

already used it in its other sense of ' appeal ' (A.V. ' exhortation ') (1 ii. 3). It has always the idea of benefit bestowed.
Here it is doubtless with reference both to the depressing effect
of persecution on the Thessalonians (i. 4) and uncertainty about
the End (vers. 2–3) and their need for God's help It may be
that in using the word translated **eternal** (*aiōnian*) Paul is
thinking of its secondary sense as ' agelong,' i.e. lasting for
this present period (see note on i. 9). The suggestion would
be that, until the end of this present age, we need encouragement, while for the Age to Come we have the Christian hope.
On the other hand, it seems more probable that he means
encouragement, which, unlike any that the world might give,
is everlasting, **and good,** i.e. joyful **hope** (see note on 1 i. 3).
No matter what happens here, the Christian has a present
assurance and future glory which are equally imperishable.
These gifts from God have been lavished upon us freely and
undeservedly (literally, ' in grace ')—**graciously.** So Paul
concludes, may Father and Son **encourage your hearts and
strengthen them**—he has used these same two verbs in 1 iii. 2
—**for all good in deed and word**—that is, to do good in everything you do or say.   Once again it is not enough to take heart
in the knowledge that they are God's own children ; Paul reminds them that as God's children they must do God's Will.

V. A REQUEST FOR INTERCESSIONS—
(iii. 1–2)

1 **Finally, brothers, pray for us, that the word of the Lord may**
2 **speed on and triumph, as in your own case, and that we**
 may be delivered from perverse and evil men—for the faith
 is not held by all.

1   The opening words of this chapter introduce a new line of
thought which is disclosed in verse 6. What precedes this,
the second main theme of the letter, is a characteristic Pauline
introduction to an awkward topic (cf. 1 iv. 1, 10, v. 11). The
apostle draws attention to his own perilous circumstances,
and invites the prayers of the Thessalonians (vers. 1–2). He

then assures them of his confidence in their Christian witness (vers. 3–5) before going on to utter some stern words about the misdemeanours of the work-shy section of the community whose behaviour was still causing grave concern (vers. 6–15). **Finally, brothers**—Paul used these same words in 1 iv. 1 to mark the transition to a topic of practical morality (see note) —and made a similar request to **pray for us** in 1 v. 25 (see note). Paul would subscribe to Luther's words : ' As a shoe-maker makes a shoe and a tailor makes a coat, so must a Christian pray. A Christian's trade is prayer.' Their prayers are asked for here, however, for a specific purpose, **that the word of the Lord may speed on and triumph**—not, it should be noted, prayer for the apostles' own safety primarily, though their difficulties and dangers in Corinth are clearly described, but for the Cause.

The word of the Lord is spoken of as if it were almost an independent spiritual force (cf. notes on 1 i. 8, ii. 13) sweeping through the country under its own impetus, and not relying on the eloquence and physical powers of the missionaries. When Paul speaks of it **speeding on** he may be using one of his many metaphors from the Greek games, or more probably echoing Ps. cxlvii. 15 (LXX 4) : ' His word will run swiftly.' It is a further mark of Paul's conception of the innate, almost independent, Divine power of the Gospel, that he speaks of its **triumph**, since the Greek word is ' that it may be glorified ' (*doxazētai*), which is normally an expression used only of the honour due to God or Christ. Paul means that when the Gospel is allowed to spread freely and is properly received, the results speak for themselves, as had happened at Thessalonica. There indeed the Gospel was ' glorified.' The point of the intercession for which Paul asks the Thessalonians is that his mission should be as successful in Corinth as it had been in Macedonia. ' May the Gospel be allowed to exercise its own saving power in this difficult situation as it was **in your own case**' (cf. 1 i. 5).

But this is not being permitted. The missionaries are be- 2 ing thwarted, and so the prayers of the Thessalonians are to have a concrete reference, as is essential with all good prayer, namely, that we may be delivered from perverse and evil men. The allusion is to Paul's old enemies the Jews, who, according to Acts xviii. 6, 12–17, were at this time making his work in Corinth as difficult as possible and of whose activities among themselves the Thessalonians had first-hand knowledge (Acts xvii. 5 ; 1 ii. 14 ff.). The prayer is still for the free propagation of the Gospel, not for personal safety—Tertullian's observation seems to have been true from the start : ' *synagogas Judaeorum, fontes persecutionum* '—and it was promptly answered (Acts xviii. 9 ff.). The word translated ' perverse ' (*atopos*) means literally ' out of place,' from which the derived ethical sense of ' improper ' easily follows. Among the papyri a public notice by a young man's parents disclaims all liability for the wayward youth, including his debts and any other misdemeanour (*atopon*) he might commit (Milligan, ad. loc.). This is generally the sense of the word in LXX and New Testament, and not as in A.V. and R.V. ' unreasonable.' Then, as if in a rueful undertone, Paul adds for the faith is not held by all. From the following verse it would seem as if the A.V. was right in omitting the article : ' For all men have not faith.' There is no real difference in meaning here between ' faith ' as the subjective attitude which receives the Gospel, and ' the faith,' namely, the Gospel itself. But the former leads more naturally into verse 3. The words are an almost certain reference to that stubborn refusal of the Jews to accept the Gospel, which was an acute problem to the early Church.

—AND A WORD OF ENCOURAGEMENT
(iii. 3–5)

3 However, the Lord is faithful ; he will be sure to strengthen
4   you and protect you from the Evil one. Now, we rely on
    you in the Lord, confident that you do and will do what
5   we enjoin. May the Lord direct your hearts towards
    God's love and towards Christ's patience !

3   The last word of the previous sentence was *pistis*—' faith.'
The first word of this sentence is *pistos*—' faithful.' Unless

this is a play on words, it is difficult to see the connexion between the two verses. However, although the transition is abrupt, the line of thought is still apt enough as an attempt to awaken a sympathetic attitude on the part of the readers in preparation for the injunctions that follow in verses 6–15. Though it is not everybody who has faith, Paul goes on, **however, the Lord is faithful** (*pistis* can mean both ' faith ' and ' faithfulness ' : *pistos* may mean ' believing ' and also ' faithful '). The lack of faith in the Jews throws into relief the faithfulness of Christ which shows itself in His concern for His people. **He will be sure to strengthen you and protect you from the Evil one.** The Greek (*apo tou ponērou*) may mean either ' from evil ' (neuter) or ' from the evil one ' (masculine). The same alternative exists in the Greek text of the Lord's Prayer (Matt. vi. 13) and in Jesus's words in John xvii. 15. However, in places where there is no such ambiguity (e.g. Matt. xiii. 19 ; 1 John ii. 13, etc.), the masculine is used, and this is in keeping with the general New Testament view of evil, not as an impersonal power, but as the direct result of the machinations of Satan (cf. note on 1 ii. 18, iii. 5 ; 2 ii. 9). It does not, however, follow that Paul's words here are an echo of the Lord's Prayer. What particular temptation of the Devil the Lord was to protect the Thessalonians against is not clear. Paul's words about his own persecution in Corinth may suggest a reference to the Thessalonian Christians' danger of weakening in their loyalty under strain of opposition. Or he may be referring to some difficulty of which the Thessalonians had informed the apostles, or to a specific excuse proffered by the idlers, to which problem Paul is now turning, or simply to the general temptations of the ordinary Christian life. At all events Paul, as Calvin said, at this point ' was more anxious for them than for himself.' His thoughts have turned from his own plight and continue to rest on the Thessalonians.

Now we rely on you in the Lord, confident that you do and 4 **will do what we enjoin.** Paul's confidence that his readers will carry out the instructions he is about to give is based on their common allegiance to Christ and His Spirit within them.

This thought, coupled with the tactful acknowledgment that they are already fulfilling his instructions, as a prelude to asking for further loyalty, is paralleled in 1 iv. 1. Before the injunctions, however, comes a spontaneous and beautiful little prayer.

5 **May the Lord direct your hearts towards God's love and towards Christ's patience !** Paul is about to issue his orders and expects them to be obeyed. But there is a higher Authority than his under whom both he and his converts stand. Without His sanction any human authority is vain. It is He who must incline their hearts to keep His laws, which the apostle as His minister enjoins upon them. Further, they will only keep His laws if first they have a deep sense of **God's love**—for their love to God springs from His love for them. Similarly, it is only Christ Himself who can produce in them that same quality of **patience** and endurance which He possessed under the suffering which was His lot and which is the inevitable result of witnessing for Him (see note on 1 i. 3). If this refers to a concrete situation, it may be taken with the allusion to the temptations of the Evil One (ver. 4) as indicating the local opposition in Thessalonica which tested the fidelity of the Church (i. 4). Paul's reference here to the **patience** of Christ is one of several in the epistles which indicate a very deep knowledge and understanding of the earthly ministry and character of Jesus. One cannot think that allusions to the grace (2 Cor. viii. 9), gentleness (2 Cor. x. 1), obedience (Phil. ii. 8), and consideration (2 Cor. x. 1) of Jesus are casual. Paul's theology may have centred on the Risen Christ, but surely no one has understood the Man Jesus so profoundly as Paul. Despite the general character of verses 1–5 as a fitting prelude to the admonitions of verses 6–15, their disjointed nature is sufficiently obvious to merit the suggestion that Paul's remarks may at this point have been prompted by various items unknown to us in a letter from Thessalonica which he had in his hand as he dictated.

VI. 'WORK OR WANT'
(iii. 6–15)

Brothers, we charge you in the name of the Lord Jesus Christ 6
to shun any brother who is loafing, instead of following
the rule you got from us. For you know quite well how 7
to copy us ; we did not loaf in your midst, we did not 8
take free meals from anyone ; no, toiling hard at our
trade, we worked night and day, so as not to be a burden
to any of you. Not that we have no right to such support ; 9
it was simply to give you a pattern to copy. We used to 10
charge you, even when we were with you, ' If a man will
not work, he shall not eat.' But we are informed that 11
some of your number are loafing, busybodies instead of
busy. Now in the Lord Jesus Christ we charge and exhort 12
such persons to keep quiet, to do their work and earn their
own living. As for yourselves, brothers, never grow tired 13
of doing what is right. Only, if anyone will not obey our 14
orders in this letter, mark that man, do not associate with
him—that will make him feel ashamed ! You are not to 15
treat him as an enemy, but to put him under discipline
as a brother.

The amount of space devoted to the question of the ' Thessalonian loafers ' in this short letter is an indication of the importance which the apostle attached to it. It forms indeed
the second, if subsidiary, topic after the primary question of
the Advent date. And indeed the one depends upon the
other. Whatever may have been the result of a depressed
class being confronted with the concept of Christian freedom—
and no doubt the foreign mission field to-day again provides
the best clue to the situation in the early Church as a whole,
in the tension which results from the impact of Christianity
upon economic conditions which resemble slavery—it was the
expectation of the impending end of the world that gave rise
to the particular Thessalonian problem. Paul had already
had occasion in his first letter (see note on iv. 11–12) to caution
the converts gently about the danger of allowing Advent
expectations to unsettle them, make them reluctant to carry

on with their ordinary work, and keep them in a state of profit-less fluttering and overwrought nerves. By the time the second letter was written both symptoms had become aggra-vated. The Last Day was felt to be upon them, and in con-sequence the excitement of some of the members had com-pletely unbalanced them and made them quite unfit to carry out their daily duties.

Paul now feels that he must take a strong line in the matter : it is neither healthy for the members concerned, fair to the remainder, nor an advertisement for the Church. It would appear from what he says here that the offending members were not only unwilling to work themselves but were quite prepared to live off the work of others, and not content with that to meddle in their affairs at the same time. Now that the apostle has removed the theoretical grounds for any such conduct by reassuring them that the End is not yet (ii. 1–12), he deals with the practical issue. His method of handling the situation is threefold : (1) he cites his own example of independence and self-support ; (2) he makes a further appeal to the loafers to go back to their jobs ; (3) if these fail, he in-structs that the offending members are to be ' sent to Coven-try ' until they come to their senses—not, however, to be ex-communicated from the fellowship (as in 1 Cor. v. 11, where the prohibition to eat with the offenders, i.e. at the common meal, is tantamount to expulsion).

6 **Brothers, we charge you in the name of the Lord Jesus Christ**—not ' in ' the Lord Jesus Christ, but with emphasis on the authority behind the command, which constitutes as solemn an adjuration as words can make it—**to shun any brother who is loafing, instead of following the rule you got from us.** There may be a faded metaphor here in that the word for **shun** meant originally to shorten sail. The picture is of a ship taking in sail to avoid some danger. We should say ' steer clear ' of him or ' give him a wide berth '—a suit-able word in writing to a seaport. Although he may be a drone in the community, exploiting the generosity of the workers, the loafer is still a **brother.** He is to be punished by ostracism, not by expulsion. The word for **loafing** (literally,

who is living in idleness) is *ataktōs*, the adverbial form of the word found in 1 v. 14 (see note). In the first letter the Church as a whole is told to ' keep a check on them ' (1 v. 14), i.e. the loafers. Here it is to go a stage farther. **The rule** (see note on ii. 15) which they had received, given orally during the mission and reinforced in the previous letter, namely, that no man should be dependent on the charity of others, but should keep himself by his own efforts (1 iv. 11–12), is quoted in principle at any rate in verse 10.

Paul now cites the example of the missionaries when they 7 were in Thessalonica. **For you know quite well**—one of Paul's many appeals to the previous knowledge of his readers—**how** (you ought) **to copy us.** Moffatt for some reason omits ' you ought,' which is in the Greek text. The Christian life is, in its first stages in a pagan community, imitation of the missionary as it is to-day in the field (see note on 1 i. 6). Goethe's dictum is apt : ' The finest metempsychosis is when we see ourselves reappearing in others.'

We did not loaf in your midst, we did not take free meals 8 (literally, eat bread for nothing) **from anyone ; no, toiling hard at our trade, we worked night and day, so as not to be a burden to any of you.** Paul has said all this before—largely in the same words—in 1 ii. 9 (see note). His main purpose then was to clear himself of the charge of making money out of his missionary campaigns, whereas the point of mentioning his exhausting programme at Thessalonica here is to remind his readers of the kind of example he set the whole community, an example of hard work and a refusal to live on other people's charity. Jason (Acts xvii) was no doubt willing and in a position to support Paul, but the apostle was shrewd enough to foresee the consequences.

He hastens to add that for a missionary of the Gospel to 9 receive the voluntary support of the Church members was no more than his due (cf. Matt. x. 9–10) : **not that we have no right** (not ' power ' as in A.V.) **to such support.** Paul exercised this right in accepting help on several occasions from the Philippian Church (Phil. iv. 16). But in Thessalonica his labours had a definite aim : **it was simply to give you a pattern to copy.**

10   Paul further reminds his readers, as he did in 1 iv. 11, that his example had been supported by precept. **We used to charge you, even when we were with you, ' If a man will not work, he shall not eat.'** There is no known origin for this saying, though the substance of it is common enough. As it stands, it is not specifically Christian and might quite well be of Jewish or Greek origin. In view of the Jewish conception of the dignity of work—apart from the authority of Gen. iii. 19 —it is perhaps more likely to be a rabbinical saw than a Greek maxim. Some commentators trace it back to an unrecorded saying of Jesus ; it might, however, equally well come from the morality of the workshop. It belongs to the universal realm of common sense. Whatever its origin, Paul gives it here the sanction of a Christian principle. The emphasis is not on ability to work, but on willingness to work. The Christian as well as the Communist must say that voluntary idleness, whether among rich or poor, is an offence against society, and ought to be attended with the same penalty in both cases. The Christian, however, would add that it is also an offence against God.

11   Now follows the actual occasion for Paul's concern. **But we are informed**—by letter or hearsay—**that some of your number are loafing, busybodies instead of busy.** Moffatt reproduces the word-play—*ergazomenous* and *periergazomenous*. One of the older commentators has a delightful phrase about the idle handful in the community who ' do nothing but fetch frisks and vagaries.' They seem, however, to have done more than frisking, and to have caused considerable trouble. An Eastern proverb has it that ' the devil tempts other men, but idle men tempt the devil.' What the nature of their interference was we can only speculate. In the circumstances the most natural interpretation is that their anxiety about the end of the world led them to stop work and then to try to persuade their more level-headed brethren to do likewise. It is probably not meddlesomeness in their neighbours' domestic affairs that is meant so much as a misguided interference in their spiritual affairs, and entreaties to prepare for the Great Day.

For them the apostle has some trenchant words. **Now in 12 the Lord Jesus Christ we charge and exhort such persons to keep quiet, to do their work and earn their own living.** ' Stop fussing, stop idling, and stop sponging.' Paul is speaking the truth in love !

He then turns to the community as a whole and adds : **As 13 for yourselves, brothers, never grow tired of doing what is right.** From this it sounds as if the brothers *had* grown tired a bit, which is not to be wondered at. Exasperated with the excited and possibly hysterical minority, tired of their demands on their generosity, the leaders of the community and the members generally had perhaps not been as patient and tactful as they might have been. Paul gives them a gentle caution on this point, and also probably ensures that, despite his summary prescription for loafers, it should not be forgotten that they are still ' brothers ' and must be treated as such. On the other hand, the point of the remark may be simply a contrast between the idleness of the few and the desirability of continued active Christian service by the main body of the Church. ' They may neglect their duty, but you must not neglect yours.'

However, if tactful exhortation and the apostle's direct 14 injunction have no effect, there must be strong action. **Only, if anyone will not obey our orders in this letter, mark that man, do not associate with him—that will make him feel ashamed !** This seems to imply a public reading of the letter at a service of worship (see note on 1 v. 27), and in members' homes in special cases—whether of illness or recalcitrance. If, in spite of this, there is still trouble with the work-shy, they are to be **marked.** What this means is not clear. It may simply mean privately ' noted,' or it may mean publicly ' named.' Whichever is intended, it is as a prelude to a period of social ostracism, the aim of which is reformative rather than punitive. Paul assumes that a Christian will repond to Christian treatment, and that shame will bring him to his senses. Carlyle has called shame of this kind ' the soul of all virtues, of all good manners, and good morals.'

To make the position quite clear, Paul adds : **You are not 15** to treat him as an enemy, but to put him under discipline as a brother. The ultimate aim of discipline is to bring back the offender into the fellowship, not to alienate him. Paul had already denounced idleness while in Thessalonica ; he had referred to it in his first letter and again in this passage. He had therefore done all that our Lord enjoined in the conciliation of defaulting brothers. He is now carrying out the further evangelical command to treat them, failing response and amendment, as 'pagans and tax-gatherers' (Matt. xviii. 15–17). .He is, however, more concerned about the stage beyond that, when the repentant pagan and tax-gatherer are received into the Kingdom (e.g. Mark vii. 26 ff., ii. 14).

The interest of this passage lies in (*a*) Paul's view of discipline in the Church, and (*b*) his attitude to work. (*a*) On the positive side it is plain that he regarded the social relationships of individual members as a matter of concern for the whole Church. A man no longer lives for himself once he has entered the fellowship : he is responsible to God and to his brothers in Christ. Society judges the Church on the public actions of those who profess the Christian Faith. For the good name of Christ and the inner health of His Body it is therefore essential that all should feel themselves equally obliged to maintain both. But the negative side necessarily follows. Should anyone in the fellowship break faith and dishonour the Christian name, then it is the concern of all to redeem it and him. Things must not be allowed to slide, out of a mistaken sense of brotherly love, and certainly not through indifference. Moral courage is a Christian virtue and the offence must be dealt with.

Paul's method of social ostracism in dealing with offending members is not at present always effective. In a divided Church unity of action cannot be relied on. Further, there is always the danger of fastening on the obvious sins of drunkenness and sexual immorality, and condoning commercial malpractice, exploitation of workers by employers and of employers by workers. There is, however, a pointer here to the desirability of local Christian Councils, which represent the united Christian opinion of the town or parish, taking action by publicly condemning, and, if necessary, enjoining ostracism, in cases where flagrant disservice is being done to the Church by anti-social behaviour on the part of Church members. The threat of publicity would, in these days, in many cases be sufficient. It should be noted, however, that expulsion from the fellowship or excommunication is not the first step in discipline, but the last resort. An erring Christian is still a brother, and it is only when it brings him to himself and back to God that discipline can be said to be effective.

(*b*) The main value which the apostle attaches to work here is that it makes a man independent. He neither regards it in the spirit of Gen. iii. 19 as an unfortunate necessity brought about by the Fall, nor in the modern Christian sense, as something to be done to the glory of God. He dissociates himself from the general Greek view which regarded manual labour as the vocation of slaves and not of gentlemen, and supports the Jewish rabbinical insistence on the dignity of hard work. His own training as a rabbi had necessarily included an apprenticeship to a trade—despite his father's probable affluence—and this no doubt coloured his outlook. The Talmud teaching was crystal clear that service of the community in the most menial task was honourable, though the Wisdom scribes had inclined to the Greek view. Here, however, Paul is offering no general theory. Other facets of his attitude to work appear in other references—as a means of helping the needy (Eph. iv. 28), or to keep people out of mischief (1 iv. 11). In this case all he is concerned to stress is that it is a right and proper thing for a Christian man to be self-supporting and not to live off the community. He assumes that employment is available, and takes no account of such a phenomenon as enforced idleness in an industrial society. It would be interesting to hear Paul's views on independence and social security (see note by Bicknell, pp. 95–7).

VII. CLOSING WORDS
(iii. 16–18)

16 May the Lord of peace himself grant you peace continually,
17   whatever comes. The Lord be with you all. The saluta-
    tion is in my own hand, Paul's ; that is a mark in every
18   letter of mine. This is how I write. ' The grace of our
    Lord Jesus Christ be with you all.'

16   The final prayer with which Paul ends the letter is not merely
a recapitulation of verse 5 as if verses 6–15 had been a casual
interpolation. As we have seen, verses 1–5 prepare the
readers' minds for the important topic of verses 6–15, and the
earlier prayer of verse 5 is directed towards that end. So the
prayer which now follows has a direct association with what
has just been said. There is little outward peace for the unfortunate Thessalonians ; they are subject to persecution
(i. 4), they are plagued by excited speculation about the imminence of the end of the world (ii. 1 ff.), and they have in
their midst a problem of no mean order in the vagaries of the
idle vagabonds just mentioned. It is with special reference
to the real difficulties which beset the little Church that Paul
now invokes on their behalf the inward peace of God which
alone can give confidence and courage. **May the Lord of
peace himself grant you peace continually, whatever comes.**
Not all the apostle's reassurances and sobering practical sense
can bring tranquillity to disordered minds, but only Christ
the **Lord of peace** both by what He had done and was still
doing (see notes on 1 i. 1 and 1 v. 23). It is on this note of
Christ's peace that must rule in men's hearts (Col. iii. 15) that
Paul begins and ends the letter (cf. i. 2). Then with marked
emphasis he adds : **the Lord be with you all**—with the mourners
(1 iv. 13), with the distraught (2 ii. 2), with the victims of
persecution (2 i. 4), even with the loafers, or rather most of
all with them who need Him most.

17   Next comes what might seem to be a curious irrelevance.
**The salutation is in my own hand, Paul's ; that is a mark in
every letter of mine. This is how I write.** The import is
clear enough that at this point the apostle, who has been

dictating to a scribe, takes up the pen and, beginning probably with the word **Paul's** adds these and perhaps the following words. That this was his practice is seen from the concluding words of other epistles (1 Cor. xvi. 21 ; Col. iv. 18), as also from the greeting of Tertius the amanuensis in Rom. xvi. 22. Paul's writing was distinctive, if Gal. vi. 11 is to be taken at its face value, and he seems here to be drawing special attention to it in order to authenticate this and other letters. It is not quite clear why. So far as we know, this is only at the most the third letter of Paul to his converts (after 1 Thessalonians and possibly Galatians), a personal signature **in every letter** must therefore refer to the future. The fact that he does not always specifically draw attention to this autographic conclusion (except in Colossians and 1 Corinthians) does not mean that it is not there. The letter of Mystarion of A.D. 50 (reproduced by Deissmann, *Light from the Ancient East*, p. 157) ends with a salutation and date in a hand—presumably Mystarion's—different from that of the rest of the letter, indicating that at the time when the Thessalonian letters were being written, a sender might add his contribution to the scribe's without mentioning it expressly.

Some commentators regard these words as clear proof that 2 Thessalonians is not a genuine Pauline letter. The forger ' doth protest too much.' But this verse alone would be insufficient to establish the fact. Others see in the words a safeguard against forgery. But (see note on ii. 2) forgery in Paul's lifetime is hardly credible. The point is surely simply to provide a convincing authentication, in view of the fact that some people in Thessalonica were attributing statements to the apostle which he had not made. He has now given an authoritative pronouncement on the question of the Lord's return (ii. 1-12). There must be no further dubiety. There is the added possible consideration that any recalcitrant loafer could be confronted with the unambiguous denunciation of iii. 6-15 as unquestionably the mind of the apostle. It seems unnecessary to adopt the idea already referred to (see Introduction, p. xiv. f.) that this second letter was intended for (*a*) a special group in the community, or for (*b*) liturgical purposes, in which case the apostle's words here would be intended to satisfy those (*a*) who formed the majority, or (*b*) who merely heard the letter read aloud in church.

18   Last of all comes a blessing identical with that in 1 v. 28, save for the magnanimous and significant **all**—an inclusion as in verse 16 of the troublesome few: **the grace of our Lord Jesus Christ be with you all.**

INDEX

INDEX

INDEX

204